Sovereignty in China's Perspective

SCHRIFTEN
zum internationalen und zum öffentlichen
RECHT

Herausgegeben von Gilbert Gornig

Band 118

Zu Qualitätssicherung und Peer Review der vorliegenden Publikation

Die Qualität der in dieser Reihe erscheinenden Arbeiten wird vor der Publikation durch den Herausgeber der Reihe geprüft.

Notes on the quality assurance and peer review of this publication

Prior to publication, the quality of the work published in this series is reviewed by the editor of the series.

Yonghong Yang

Sovereignty in China's Perspective

PL ACADEMIC RESEARCH

Bibliographic Information published by the Deutsche Nationalbibliothek
The Deutsche Nationalbibliotheklists this publication in
the Deutsche Nationalbibliografie; detailed bibliographic
data is available in the internet at http://dnb.d-nb.de.

Zugl.: Marburg, Univ., Diss., 2016

Library of Congress Cataloging-in-Publication Data
Names: Yang, Yonghong, author.
Title: Sovereignty in China's perspective / Yonghong Yang.
Description: Frankfurt am Main : Peter Lang GmbH, [2017] | Series: Schriften zum internationalen und zum offentlichen recht / vol. 118
Identifiers: LCCN 2017001541 | ISBN 9783631719282
Subjects: LCSH: China--International status. | Internationallaw--China. | Sovereignty. | China--Foreign relations. | China--History.
Classification: LCC KZ4376 .Y36 2017 | DDC 341.26--dc23 LC record available at https://lccn.loc.gov/2017001541

D 4
ISSN 0943-173X
ISBN 978-3-631-71928-2 (Print)
E-ISBN 978-3-631-71933-6 (E-PDF)
E-ISBN 978-3-631-71934-3 (EPUB)
E-ISBN 978-3-631-71935-0 (MOBI)
DOI 10.3726/b11052

Peter Lang GmbH
Internationaler Verlag der Wissenschaften
Frankfurt am Main 2017

PL Academic Research is an Imprint of Peter Lang GmbH.

Peter Lang – Frankfurt am Main · Bern · Bruxelles · New York · Oxford · Warszawa · Wien

This publication has been peer reviewed.

www.peterlang.com

Table of Contents

Introduction

This thesis is about the concept of sovereignty in China's perspective. The concept of sovereignty is universal, however, the understanding of it is varies in states and its people due to cultural backgrounds, the position of strength of states, the history, composition of ethnic groups, the strategy of developing, etc.[1] In order to comprehend China's current perspective on sovereignty, I try to connect Chinese historical ideas into the current international society. Hence, I analyze a part of China's imperial history concerning sovereignty and foreign policies and try to dig deep within the cultural, political, administrative and legal roots of the ancient empires because of the great influence that China's antique political systems and culture has had on its current political arrangements. The comprehension of political systems of ancient China should help to better understand the current perception China has on sovereignty. The thesis focuses on sovereignty in ancient China, modern China, and current China. Furthermore, this thesis will draw a comparison between European states' perceptions and China's perception on sovereignty. Whilst the focus is on sovereignty, the close relationship between sovereignty and human rights in China cannot be left unexamined and a comparison of the divergence between the European and Chinese understanding on human rights is also a part of the thesis.

The structure of the thesis is outlined as follows:

Firstly, Chapter 1 analyzes the concept of sovereignty in general. After the traditional Westphalian concept of sovereignty is described in the beginning of this chapter, the thesis also introduces the current concepts of sovereignty. The fact that the sovereign state plays a major role in today's world means that the Westphalian idea has not been abandoned but has changed. Sovereignty is progressively limited by more and more international constraints, particularly by the overarching demand of universal human rights.

The second chapter attempts to examine the political system of the Chinese empire in different dynasties. It concludes that the Chinese empire since the Qin-Han dynasties was a unitary state with a centralized administrative system ruled by emperors who had absolute power within the territory. The chapter tries to clarify the different meanings of the Tianxia in a bid to comprehend ancient China from the political and geographic definition to the cultural definition. Moreover, it describes a special period of China, so-called the period of Spring-Autumn and Warring states, in which the empire was similar to Europe in the Westphalia period. Furthermore, it gives a focus to the Chinese tributary system, which was a logical consequence of the "Tianxia" view. It attempts to reveal the nature of the Chinese tributary system

1 Wang Yizhou, 'Guoji Cuanxi Yanjiu Ruogan Wenti' ('several issues in the study of international relations'), Ouzhou Yanzhou [European Research] no. 3, (2006), p. 131.

as a pragmatically and flexible foreign policy to seek a peaceful surrounding and also offers a comparison between the tributary system and colonialism.

The third chapter concentrates on the period when the concept of modern sovereignty was introduced into China. The experience of losing sovereignty in that period has had an unimaginable impact on Chinese perceptions of sovereignty, human rights and other relatable political and social issues. That period's transformation is decisive for current China's identity and China's position on sovereignty. It is also attributed as the birth of modern nationalism which is rather disparate from China's traditional nationalism in the sense of 'the Great Unification'. Both of them are the focus of the fourth chapter. A number of scholars, particularly, Western scholars hold that no nationalism existed in ancient China and nationalism only emerged after China was attacked by Britain during the Opium Wars because ancient China's Tianxia view impeded Chinese from identifying them as a nation. This chapter reveals that romantic nationalism had emerged in ancient China and developed as the view of 'the Great Unification', which is still a part of today's Chinese identification. Admittedly, China's perspective on sovereignty is heavily influenced by nationalism. It drives the Chinese government to cautiously take a hard position on sovereignty today, particularly, when the domestic society is unstable with multiple conflicts.

Chapter 5 discusses the controversial issue of Chinese human rights. It elaborates on China's human rights policy and the reasons behind China's human rights problem. It is an attempt to reduce the misunderstanding between the two sides by comparing China's human rights policy to Europeans. Additionally, through addressing China's practice in humanitarian crises, it provides an outline of the transformation of China's policy on humanitarian intervention.

The sixth chapter describes the change of interpretation on sovereignty from the early stage of the People's Republic of China to today. It explores the connection between China's present policy and Chinese ancient thoughts. After concluding China's major thoughts on sovereignty, the chapter elaborates on the comparison between Chinese and European understandings of sovereignty. Interestingly, the idea that sovereignty has changed but is not dead is accepted by both sides. Both differences and mutual understandings between the two are elaborated on in the last part of my thesis.

The whole thesis is intended to provide a grasp on the Chinese traditional system and thoughts for the purpose of understanding current China's perception of sovereignty. Meanwhile, it also attempts to explain why China is so different from European states with regards to the perception of sovereignty. Understandably, the two sides are both influential in the international community. A mutual understanding of the two sides is definitely important not only for both of them but also for the whole world. I hope that this thesis may provide a little help.

Chapter 1. The Concept of Sovereignty

Introduction

It is always rather practical or convenient to trace the origin of a theme when exploring a dynamic concept in contemporary academic discourse. It is typically believed that the Westphalian Peace Treaties are the first step to understanding the notion of sovereignty. In the Middle Ages, Europeans believed that all humans lived under the same laws and morals. They existed under the combined spiritual and temporal guidance of both the Pope and the Emperor. Meanwhile, the Chinese were convinced that the emperors had the Mandate of Heaven to rule the world. Under the theory of the Christian Commonwealth, power was organized in terms of overlapping, concentric circles. While Westphalia ended the old epoch in Europe, at the same time, it replaced the Christian Commonwealth and opened a new epoch. During this new epoch sovereign states were deemed equal and became major subjects of the new, so-called international community. About two hundred years later, Westphalia sovereignty spread to China through guns and cannons. It crashed down on the China-central world as China struggled to regain its sovereignty. This chapter focuses on the introduction of general ideas of sovereignty and the non-intervention principle for the purpose of elaborating upon China's evolving understanding of sovereignty.

Section 1. The Westphalian Sovereignty

Westphalia has achieved hallmark recognition for the inauguration of the interstate system in modern academic discourse even though some questioned its historical benchmark because of the absence of the word "sovereignty" in the peace treaties.[2] However, it did not accidently adopt the concept of 'sovereignty', which was definitely constructed purposefully on the base of a number of academic achievements.

1. The Academic Idea of Sovereignty during Westphalia Time

As sovereignty is mentioned, one may think about Niccolo Machiavelli, Jean Bodin, Hugo Grotius, Thomas Hobbes, John Locke, J. J. Rousseau, Emer de Vattel, Friedrich Hegel and others. Generally speaking, Jean Bodin is considered as the one who in 1583 presented the first systematic introduction of the idea.[3] Bodin asserted that sovereignty was a state's absolute supreme authority within its territory which

2 Gross, The Peace of Westphalia, 1648–1948, in: American Journal of International Law, 42, 1948, p. 26.

3 Jean Bodin, Les six livres de la Republique ("Six Books Concerning Public Affairs"), Paris: Fayerd, 1986, p. 74.

was only limited by natural and divine law. His theory of sovereignty represented a conceptual breakthrough in the history of political thought and shaped the fundamental principles of international relations.[4] The later works of the English philosopher Thomas Hobbes introduced the idea of "contractual sovereignty". This meant that the people established sovereign authority through a contract in which they transferred all of their rights to 'the Leviathan', which represented the abstract notion of the State. The will of 'the Leviathan' reigned supreme and represented the will of all those who had alienated their rights to it. Similar to Bodin's sovereign, Hobbes' 'Leviathan' was above the law, a mortal God unbound by any constitution or contractual obligations with external parties. Hobbes also thought the sovereign to be accountable to God and to the natural law. Law was the command of the sovereign ruler, emanating from his will, and the obligation to obey it absolutely.[5] Rousseau, differed from Bodin or Hobbes, in that he saw the collective people within a State as the sovereign. They ruled through their general will. In a constitutional government, it is the people ruling through a body of law that have sovereignty. Rousseau's version of sovereignty is the one that is most commonly regarded as legitimate in the current world. Although new notions of the holders of sovereignty have evolved and more and more restraints are imposed on sovereignty, Bodin and Hobbes' concept of sovereignty as supreme authority continues to prevail as the presumption of political rule in states throughout the globe today.[6] In reality, the Westphalian Peace takes credit for the birth of sovereignty by imposing itself as a determining reality of the way in which the state entity is structured and interacts, both internally, with its subjects—citizens of the state–, and externally, within interstate relations. Its dimensions and validity remain in direct relationship to the power of state entities to which it is associated.

2. Westphalian Model Sovereignty

2.1. The Peace of Westphalia as the Beginning of Sovereignty

First of all, the Peace of Westphalia curtailed the power of the Pope and Emperor. It moved to an alternative foundation of authority based on exclusive jurisdictions of equal and independent entities. These entities were superior within territorial borders, so-called sovereignty. Moreover, the significance of Westphalia was the building of an archetype which functioned as the territorial anchor and fostered the concomitant distinction between domestic and international, inside and outside. This archetype retrospectively indicates the transition from medieval to modern

4 Jean Bodin, On Sovereignty, Cambridge: Cambridge University Press, 1992, p. 78.
5 Thomas Hobbes, Leviathan: Or the Matter, Forme, and Power of a Common-Wealth Ecclesiastical and Civil (ed. by Ian Shapiro), London: Yale University Press, 2010, pp. 103–107.
6 Sovereignty, Stanford Encyclopedia of Philosophy, available at: http://plato.stanford.edu/entries/sovereignty/.

society.[7] Thus, the Peace of Westphalia which settled the bloody Thirty Year war is widely accepted as the birth of equal, sovereign states and a foundational moment of international law and international relations.[8]

2.2. The Westphalian Pattern of Sovereignty

The perception of Westphalian sovereignty can briefly be presented as follows: The world consists of and is divided into sovereign territorial states that recognize no superior authority over states. The sovereignty connotes an absolute, invisible feature, which purports a legal status with internal and external dimensions based on mutually recognized territorial definition. It combines domestic hierarchy with international anarchy by identifying states as supreme authorities. The sovereign states are all equal and independent from each other.[9] They are both the international law makers and law enforcers. Everything, including illegal issues, that occurs within state borders are internal affairs and concerns only the involved states.[10] Under the Westphalia system, international law is mainly constituted by customary law and bilateral treaties. Treaties represent a surrogate for the absent central lawmaking authority and the sovereign states are the actual international law making and enforcement authorities.[11] The sovereign right of states to freely go to war is the holy doctrine of the jungle. This results in a scenario of big fish eating small fish and powerful states end up with all the rights and benefits.

2.3. Westphalian Sovereignty Accepted as the Base of International Society

Generally, the Westphalia regime covers the period of international law and regulation from 1648 to the early twentieth century although some major rules still have application today.[12] Indeed, the regime did not receive its fullest articulation until the late eighteenth and early nineteenth centuries, when territorial sovereignty, the

---

7 John Gerard Ruggie, Continuity and Transformation in the World Polity: Towards a Neorealist Synthesis, World Politics, Vol. 35, Iss. 2, 1983, pp. 261–285; John Gerard Ruggie, 'Territoriality and Beyond: Problematizing Modernity in International Relations', in: International Organization, Vol. 47, Iss. 1, 1993, pp. 139–174; Rob Walker, Inside/Outside: International Relations as Political Theory, Cambridge, Cambridge University Press, 1992, pp. 152–178.

8 Gross L., 1948, pp. 20–41.

9 Tanja Aalberts, Constructing Sovereignty Between Political and Law, New York: Routledge, 2012, p. 20.

10 Simona Ţuţuianu, Towards Global Justice: Sovereignty in an Interdependent World, The Hague: Asser Press, 2013, p. 4.

11 Francis Harry Hinsley, Sovereignty, London: Penguin, 1986, pp. 203, 213.

12 David Held, The Changing Structure of International Law: Sovereignty Transformed? The Global Transformations Reader: an Introduction to the Globalization Debate (ed. by David Held and Anthony McGrew), Cambridge: Polity Press, 2003, p. 162.

formal equality of states, non-intervention in the domestic affairs of other recognized states, and state consent as the basis of international legal obligation became the core principles of the international society.[13] That means that territories were consolidated, unified, and centralized under sovereign governments. Meanwhile, the population of the territories now owed allegiance to the sovereign and they had a duty to obey the laws of the land. All territories in Europe and, eventually, all territories around the world were partitioned by sovereign governments and placed under their independent authorities.[14]

Westphalia has been identified as the first modern, institutionalized practice of multilateral diplomacy on the basis of mutual agreement of participating state parties, and codification through treaty-making.[15] Moreover, whilst the peace conference where the state parties participated can be conceived as early examples of multilateral diplomacy, it should be noted that the concluding treaties were still in the form of bilateral agreements and were signed on the personal title of the Emperor and other royal participants.[16] The state as an international legal personality, capable of bearing rights and obligations under international law, only developed towards the end of the seventeenth century.[17] The significance is that sovereign statehood was established on convention, rather than having its base in power capacities. Also, states formed a society in the sense that they conceived themselves to be bound by a common set of rules in their relations with one another.[18]

It is necessary to emphasize that the international community was confined to Europe since for a long time European states did not recognize other countries as sovereign states except those that were Christian or European.[19] The socio-political changes and technological breakthroughs enabled the European states to expand through colonialism and to spread the notion of sovereignty around the world by treating the non-Christian states as inferior savages. Most of these non-Christian states were not deemed as sovereign and were colonized. China was one of the many states which were colonized. The Europeans profited the most from wars since they won tributes and colonies through wars. In other words, the international world became largely Euro-centric. Ironically, as the European states waged wars

---

13 James Crawford and Susan Marks, The Global Democracy Deficit: An Essay on International Law and Its Limits. In D. Archibugi et al. (eds.), Re-Imagining Political Community: Studies in Cosmopolitan Democracy, Cambridge: Polity Press, 1998, pp. 137–156.

14 Robert Jackson, Sovereignty in World Politics: a Glance at the Conceptual and Historical Landscape, Political Studies, Volume 47, Issue 3, 1999, p. 440.

15 Kalevi Holsti, Taming the Sovereigns: Institutional Change in International Politics, Cambridge: Cambridge University Press, 2004, p. 53.

16 W. G. Grewe, The Epoch of International Law, Berlin: de Gruyter, 2000, p. 196.

17 Ibid., p. 361.

18 H. Bull, The Anarchical Society: A Study of Order in World Politics', 2nd ed., London: Macmillan, [1977] 1995, p. 40.

19 Tanja E. Aalberts 2012, p. 17.

around the world, the concept of sovereignty was introduced to and accepted by the world. The 'colonies', 'protectorates', 'condominiums', 'mandates', 'trust territories', 'concessions' conquered by European states are terms for referring to the non-Christian world. They represent non-sovereign entities which have no supreme internal autonomy and no external independence. Clearly, at that period, an international order based on sovereignty only existed in a relatively small group of technologically advanced and militarily powerful sovereign states with various kinds of formal dependencies and semi-dependencies in their rear. Since the status of those entities might have been considerably different in terms of their internal systems and relations with European states, their sovereignty was manifestly denied. They lacked independence and international legal personalities as far as international law was concerned.[20] Up until the end of Second World War, the Westphalian model of sovereignty was not the dominant system of international relations between European states and the other states. Indeed, China regained its sovereignty and became a member of the international community as late as the 1940's.[21]

Nonetheless, Westphalia only offers a blueprint for international society of sovereign states, developments on sovereignty have been constantly evolving. The concept of sovereignty is changing; however, Westphalia is not certified false or void. Rather, its legacy as a model confirms its enduring centrality amid challenges.[22] The Westphalia model still continues to function as the base of current concepts of sovereignty in today's international law and international society.

Section 2. Sovereignty in the Post-Second World War Era

The United Nations charter, the constituted treaty of the United Nations (UN), stipulates the principles of equal sovereignty and non-intervention as the basis of the UN, which is the most influential international organization in the world. The fact that these two principles are generally admitted as the base of international society is reconfirmed by numerous documents and treaties. The sovereign equality of states has received its most concrete affirmation after the Second World War, particularly in the era of decolonization by the newly independent states.[23] Manifestly, sovereignty becomes the most important concept of the international society.

---

20 Gerard Kreijen, The Transformation of Sovereignty an African Independence: No Shortcut to Statehood, in "State, Sovereignty, and International Governance"(ed. By Gerard Kreijen), Oxford: Oxford University Press, 2002, p. 56.

21 Extraterritorial jurisdiction was fully abrogated in China till the end of 1940s, in: Pär Kristoffer Cassel, Grounds of Judgment: Extraterritoriality and Imperial Power in Nineteenth-Century China and Japan New York: Oxford University Press, 2012, p. 179.

22 Tanja Aalberts, 2012, p. 162.

23 The Report of ICISS, the Responsibility to Protect, 2001, para. 2.8.

1. The Concepts of Sovereignty

Indisputably, sovereignty is completely derived from politics.[24] It is a central concept in international relations, international law, political theory, political philosophy and modern history.[25] Moreover, it is a dynamic institution flourishing within a legal framework precisely through the daily routine of political practices. Noticeably, the term "sovereignty" permeates the language of law and politics.[26] There are plenty of definitions of sovereignty from both sides. The Max Weber's famous definition from political perspective emphasizes: a corporate group that has compulsory jurisdiction, exercises continuous organization, and claims a monopoly of force over a territory and its population, including "all action taking place in the area of its jurisdiction."[27] Jackson defines: sovereignty, strictly speaking, as a legal institution that authenticates a political order based on independent states whose governments are the principal authorities both domestically and internationally.[28] According to Jack Levy, an international system is composed of "states characterized by the centralization of political power within a given territory, independent from any higher secular authority and interacting in an interdependent system of security relations."[29] Morris asserts that sovereignty is that of an ultimate source of political power or authority in a realm.[30] The historian Francis Hinsley gives a similar definition, "at the beginning, the idea of sovereignty was the idea that there is a final and absolute political authority in the political community and no final and absolute authority exists elsewhere"[31]. He particularly emphasizes 'the exclusively jurisdiction' which is the implication of final and absolute authority. It is exactly the same as what Steinberger says of sovereignty: "Exclusivity of jurisdiction of states over their respective territories is a central attribute of sovereignty."[32] British publicist Martin

24 David J. Betz, Tim Stevens, Cyberal and the States, London: Rought, June 2014, p. 56.
25 Trudy Jacobsen, Charles Sampford and Ramesh Thakur, Introduction in "Re-Envisioning Sovereignty, The End of Westphalia?"(ed. by Trudy Jacobsen, Charles Sampford and Ramesh Thakur), Vermont: Ashgate Publishing Limited Company, 2008, p. 1.
26 Winston Nagan, Craig Hammer, The Hanging Character of Sovereignty in International Law and International Relations, Columbia Journal of Transnational Law, Vol. 43, 2004, p. 141.
27 Weber, The Theory of Social and Economic Organization, ed. by Talcott Parsons, New York: Free Press, 1964, pp. 1, 56.
28 Robert Jackson, 1999, p. 432.
29 Jack Levy, War in the Modern Great Power System, 1495–1975, Lexington: University Press of Kentucky, 1983, p. 21.
30 Christopher W. Morris, The Very Idea of Popular Sovereignty: "We the People Reconsideration", Social Philosophy and Policy, Vol. 17, Part 1, 2000, pp. 1–26.
31 F. H. Hinsley, 1986, pp. 25–26.
32 Steinberger, Helmut, Sovereignty, in: Encyclopedia of Public International Law (ed. by Bernhardt, R.), Vol. IV, Amsterdam: Elsvier, 2000, p. 516.

Loughlin defines sovereignty with the states' four critics[33] as follows: Sovereignty is profoundly political in nature, and 'comes into existence through a process in which a group of people within a defined territory is molded into an orderly cohesion through the establishment of a governing authority that can be differentiated from society and which is able to exercise an absolute political power'.[34]

Law and politics have similarities and differences. They are similar in that they are broadly concerned with the problem of power. "Law is politics, not because law is subject to political value choice, but rather because law is a form that power sometimes takes".[35] Political concepts may more emphasize the empirical rather than the juridical, the *de facto* rather than the *de jure,* attributes of statehood, the internal supremacy rather than independence from outside. Legal concepts may focus more on legal status, rights and duties. Certainly, sovereignty embodies power and authority; it is a politico-legal concept.[36] No matter how one defines sovereignty, whether from a legal angle or a political one, the core meaning of sovereignty is the same: "the supreme authority within a territory". These simple words contain the most complicated and controversial connotation. At first, the holders of sovereignty are various, represented by diverse authorities, which mean kings, dictators, peoples ruling through constitutions, and the like; how the holders of sovereignty are chosen is relegated to 'domestic matters'. Therefore, the form of government that exercises sovereign powers could legitimately be a monarchy, an aristocracy or a democracy. Regardless of the type of government, the sovereignty of the people is widely accepted in the current world.

Secondly, territoriality is also a key ingredient of sovereignty. Within geographic borders, people who belong to a state fall under the authority of its governor. Internally, sovereignty connotes supreme authority over a population inhabiting a territory. Externally, sovereign states are all equal and independent from each other. The independence in international relations does not just indicate freedom to enter into the international society but also implies a non-hierarchical society.

It is essential to distinguish between 'internal sovereignty' and 'external sovereignty'. When sovereignty is at stake, it must be clear as to which plane sovereignty is running.[37] The fact there is a lack of overarching authority structures in international relations reflects the opposite of internal sovereignty. Certainly, there is a huge difference between what a government does within its own territory and what

---

33 Article 1 of the Montevideo Convention on Rights and Duties of States of 1933, which provides: "The State as a person of international law should possess the following qualifications:
(a) a permanent population; (b) a defined territory; (c) government; and (d) capacity to enter into relations with other States".

34 Martin Loughlin, Ten Tenets of Sovereignty, in: Sovereignty in Transition (ed. by Walker, Neil), Oxford: Hart Publishing, 2003, p. 56.

35 Schlag, 1991, p. 448.

36 Tanja Aalberts, 2012, p. 155.

37 Elihu Lauterpacht, Sovereignty-Myth or Reality, Int'l. Aff., Vol. 73, 1997, p. 137.

it does in its relations with other governments. While internal sovereignty is based on supremacy that signifies hierarchy in domestic politics, external sovereignty is based on equality and implies anarchy in international politics. Nonetheless, the two aspects of sovereignty connect closely. International capacity is dependent upon the existence and reality of the government's internal sovereignty. It is the internal sovereignty of the government to carry out international commitments. Likewise, without 'external' sovereignty, no 'internal' sovereignty exists.[38] Therefore, external and internal sovereignty are mutually complementary. Internal sovereignty is a premise to external sovereignty: "[A]s seen from inside a state, sovereignty is paramount authority, and as seen from outside it is self-governing authority"[39]. They are the inward and outward expressions, the obverse and reverse sides of the same idea, which implies that there is a final and absolute political authority in the domestic community and no final and absolute authority exist elsewhere.[40] It is also rectified by the failing states of sub-Saharan, which cannot enjoy exclusive sovereignty because of the lack of internal sovereignty.

Some also use Westphalia sovereignty to indicate the exclusion of external actors from authority inside instead of internal sovereignty, and international legal sovereignty to signal mutual recognition of territorial entities instead of external sovereignty.[41] The external and internal sovereignty were connected within positive and negative sovereignty by van Kleffens as the following statement: "Sovereignty has two faces. One looks outward, towards the outside world, being concerned with foreign relations.... It defines a free nation as 'not being subject to another nation's power'. But in addition to this negative side there is yet another, a positive face, a face with looks inward, and refers to a nation's power to regulate its own affairs; call it autonomy if you like, these aspects are what is currently known as external and internal sovereignty."[42]

The very distinction between internal and external sovereignty serves to reconcile freedom inside with constraints outside as dual sides of the sovereignty coin.[43] Thus, sovereignty is what connects the international arena to the domestic system, as well as being the link among a population, territory and government.

---

38 Jens Bartelson, A Genealogy of Sovereignty, Cambridge: Cambridge University Press, 1995, pp. 4.7.

39 Jackson, 1999, p. 431.

40 Francis Hinsley, 1986, pp. 26, 158.

41 Tanja Aalberts, 2012, p. 37.

42 Eeolco van Kleffens, Sovereignty in International Law, in: 82 Recueil des Cours (1953-I), p. 1.

43 Martti Koskeniemi, From Apology to Utopic: The Structure of International Legal Argument, Cambridge: Cambridge University Press, 2005, p. 240.

2. Sovereign Rights and Duties

As early as the 20th century, Judge Huber pointed out the duties accompanying sovereignty.

> "This right has as corollary a duty: the obligation to protect within the territory the rights of other states, in particular their right to integrity and inviolability in peace and in war, together with the rights which each state may claim for its nationals in foreign territory."[44]

Moreover, the scope of these obligations has widened extensively in the course of the twentieth century and even more rapidly increased since the 21st century. The UN Charter bans the use of force except in self-defense and collective force authorized by the UN Security Council. Peace became the principal goal of the international community at large.[45] More new rules and principles were proclaimed and acted upon and new international organizations were established with the purpose of placing ever-increasing restraints on sovereigns.[46] Such trends have exacerbated since globalization began. They impose more circumscription on external sovereignty but not on domestic affairs, therefore, states have no strong opposition against such developments. Such a paradox is similar to the situation in which individuals within domestic legal system find themselves. Individuals constantly employ their rights and independence by entering into contracts, establishing a family, getting themselves appointments, and other activities which make them bear more legal responsibilities and sacrifice valuable liberties and privilege.[47] The conflicts do not affect the independent status of individuals. The same logic is also applied to sovereign states as long as it remains a sovereign state. While a state enters into a treaty, the treaty does not only create binding obligations for it, but also confers rights for it and modifies correspondingly the rights and duties of the other states parties to the treaty.

2.1. Sovereignty as Rights to Exclude Jurisdiction of Other States

No doubt, sovereignty as an ultimate authority has a right to rule over a delimited territory and the population resided within it.[48] Certainly, the exclusivity of

---

44 Island of Palmas Case (the Netherlands v. United State), Permanent Court of Arbitration, 2 RIAA 829, 1928, p. 839.

45 Antonio Casseses, International Law, Oxford: Oxford University Press, 2005, p. 39.

46 Ibid.

47 Robert Jennings, Sovereignty and International Law, in State, Sovereignty, and International Governance (ed. by Gerard Kreijen), Oxford: Oxford University Press, 2002, p. 36.

48 Janice Thomson, State Sovereignty in International Relations: Bridging the Gap between Theory and Empirical Research, in: International Studies Quarterly, Vol. 39, No. 2, June 1995 pp. 213–33.

jurisdiction denotes the basic international legal status of a state that is not subject, within its territorial jurisdiction, to the governmental, executive, legislative, or judicial jurisdiction of a foreign state or to foreign law other than public international law.[49] Judge Huber confirmed it in the Island of Palmas case:

> "Sovereignty in the relations between states signifies independence. Independence in regard to a portion of the globe is the right to exercise therein, the exclusion of any other State, the functions of a state."[50]

Hence, a sovereign state is empowered in international law to exercise exclusive and total jurisdiction within its territorial borders. Other states have the corresponding duty not to intervene in the internal affairs of a sovereign state. If that duty is violated, the victim state has the further right to defend its territorial integrity and political independence. This basic right has been clarified as fundamental by the UN Charter.[51] Furthermore, the 1970 Declaration on Principles of International Law emphasizes that each state enjoys the rights inherent in full sovereignty and inviolable territorial integrity and political independence, and has the right to freely choose and develop its political, social, economic and cultural systems.[52]

2.2. Sovereignty as Equal Rights and Duties

Sovereignty inherently implies equality which provides order, stability and predictability in international relations since sovereign states are regarded as equal, regardless of comparative size or wealth. It is affirmed as the base of the UN, and the friendly declaration stresses that all states have equal rights and duties and are equal members of the international community, notwithstanding differences of an economic, social, political or other nature. However, states are by their nature certainly not equal in regards to power, territory and the like. But as members of the community of nations they are, in principle, equal despite differences between them that may otherwise exist.[53]

---

49 Steinberger, Helmut, Sovereignty, in: Bernhardt, R. (ed.), Encyclopedia of Public International Law, Vol. IV (Amsterdam, etc.: Elsvier, 2000), p. 511; Torres Bernádez, Santiago, Territorial Sovereignty, in: Bernhardt, op. cit., note 1, at 826, where the author says: "Sovereignty is traditionally understood to represent the summa potestas or supreme power of command inherent in the concept of the State."

50 Island of Palmas Case (the Netherlands v. United State), Permanent Court of Arbitration, in: 2 RIAA 829, 1928, p. 838.

51 Article 2.7 of UN Charter provides: Neither other states nor international organizations including the UN have any right to intervene in matter which are within the domestic jurisdiction of a state.

52 Declaration on Principles of International Law Concerning Friendly Relations and Cooperation among States in Accordance with the Charter of the United Nations, GA Resolution 2625 (XXV), October 24, 1970.

53 Robert Jenning and Arthur Watts (eds.), Oppenheim's International Law, Vol. 1, London: Oxford University Press, 9th ed., 2008, p. 339.

Indeed, the idea of equality was another powerful force contributing to colonialism's decline. The demand for equality undermined the concept of the sacred trust of civilization as the basic justification for colonialism. Colonization of a territory began to be perceived as the confirmation of its inferiority – an outright humiliation.[54] It is unsurprising that the developing countries with colonial experiences appreciate equal sovereignty because they had struggled without it and fought for it for a rather long time. The fact that equal sovereignty had been gained after a century's fighting attributes to China's sensitive position on equality of sovereignty.

2.3. *Sovereignty as Responsibility*

Indeed, there is an increasing international involvement in the protection of human rights. The obligations also incorporate domestic duties, with the development of the human rights regime as the most remarkable instance. Crucially, as a corollary of the notion that rights stem from the international society, domestic duties can count as international obligations. In the domestic sphere, sovereignty rules work to foster individual sovereign freedom and autonomy, and to mold that freedom into a particular direction and turn it into various goals.[55] Now nobody can deny that the internal sovereign rights reverses as a responsibility to ensure individual well-being. Such a responsibility is elaborated in the report of International Commission on Intervention and state Sovereignty through the concept of sovereignty responsibility in 2001. It points out that sovereign rights imply responsibility, which is owned by the state both to its people and to the international community. The concept of sovereignty as responsibility focuses on the responsibilities of governments towards their own population and maintained that effective and legitimate states were the best way to protect vulnerable populations. A 'residual' or 'fallback' responsibility to protect on the part of the international society can be activated where the state does not have the power, the capacity or the will to meet its responsibility to protect.[56]

The reinterpretation of sovereignty as responsibility for the first time puts sovereignty and human rights into an interdependent situation where human rights depend on sovereignty to protect while sovereignty depends on its protective function well to avoid intervention beyond the border. In the Outcome Document of 2005 World Summit, the idea of responsibility to protect is interpreted as such: "Each individual state has the responsibility to protect its populations from genocide, war crimes, ethnic cleansing and crimes against humanity". The international community has the responsibility to use appropriate diplomatic, humanitarian and other

54 Henri Grimal, Decolonization: The British, French, Dutch and Belgian Empires 1919–1963, Colorado: Westview Press, 1978, pp. 36–37.

55 Samantha Besson, Sovereignty, International Law and Democracy, European Journal of International Law, Vol. 22, No. 2, 2011, pp. 373–387.

56 The Report of ICISS, the Responsibility to Protect, p. 17.

peaceful means to help to protect populations from the aforementioned atrocities, and also permit collective coercive actions in exceptional situations.[57]

3. Sovereignty as both Absolute and Relative

So far, a government or institution that has power over the sovereign states in the sense of a supra-national style of decision-making aimed at upgrading the common interest still only exists in utopia. It means that sovereignty remains the last authority. Notwithstanding, the state has no other authority other than international law.[58] How can international law have any authority beyond the political wills of individual sovereign states if sovereignty entails *suprema potestas*? Indeed, sovereignty can be both supreme and indivisible, or not be.[59]

According to the Permanent Court's famous statement, treaty making- and hence restricting sovereign power is not a forsaking of sovereignty, but rather an exerciser of sovereignty.

> "No doubt any convention creating an obligation of this kind places a restriction upon the exercise of the sovereign rights of the state, in the sense that it requires them to be exercised in a certain way. But the right of entering into international engagements is an attribute of state sovereignty."[60]

Klabber pointed out the same perception, "One can usurp all attributes of sovereignty yet remain fully sovereign."[61]

This dual dimension of sovereignty as an abstract status and its practical exercise runs parallel to the aforementioned distinction between the status and rights. On the one hand, sovereignty is used to indicate the legal status of a state or rather, to present a particular entity as a sovereign state. It means that sovereignty has come to signify the legal identity of a state in international law. On the other hand, it works to bestow political entities with particular rights, power, and duties.[62] International legal personality as a particular entity with the rights, powers, duties and responsibilities connotes a status within the institutional framework of international

57 The Outcome Documents, para. 138, 139.

58 Separate Opinion of Judge Anzilotti in the Austro-German Custom Union case (Austria v. Germany), Advisory Opinion, in: PCIJ Series A/B, No. 41, 1931.

59 Steven Lee, A Puzzle of Sovereignty: Sovereignty either is or is not?, in: California Western International Law Journal, 1997, Vol. 27, No. 2, pp. 241–63; Tanja E. Aalberts, 2012, pp. 59–60.

60 S.S. Wimbledon Case (France, Italy, Japan, United Kingdom v. Germany), in: PCIJ Series A, No. 1, 1923, p. 25.

61 Jan Klabbers, Clinching the Concept of Sovereignty: Wimbledon Redux, in: 3 Austrian Review of International and European Law (1998), p. 362.

62 Martti Koskenniemi, The Future of Statehood, in: Harvard International Law Journal, Vol. 32, 1991, pp. 397–410; Wouter Werner, From Justus Hostis to Rogue State, in: International Journal for the Semiotics of Law, Vol. 3, 2004, pp. 74–92.

relations to exercise its rights and fulfill its duties. It does not specify which capacities this includes exactly. Therefore, sovereignty is absolute as a legal status, but can act as a 'relative notion, variable in the course of times, adaptable to new situations and exigencies, a discretionary freedom within, and not from, international law.[63]

Moreover, internal sovereignty is also exercised within domestic legal order and thus limited by domestic law. Sovereignty signifies the capacity to make authoritative decisions with regard to the people and resources within the territory of the state. The authorities of a state are constrained and regulated internally by constitutional power sharing arrangements.

Consequently, sovereignty is absolute because it represents the final and supreme authority where it enjoys exclusive jurisdiction within a certain territory and independence from other outside powers. On the other hand, it is non-absolute on the ground that sovereignty is limited by both international law and internal law. Therefore, the sovereign must abide by the law in order to legitimize itself politically but he paradoxically limits his absolute sovereignty in this way.[64]

4. Divergent Stages of Sovereignty

As Rosalyn Higgins comments, "Sovereignty is a relative concept in international affairs that changes through time, and it has become common-place to say that there has been tremendous erosion in the concept of sovereignty, relating particularly to the areas of human rights."[65] The renowned scholar Hekin also argues, "It is time to bring sovereignty down to earth; to examine, analyze, reconceive the concept, cut it down to size, break out its normative content, repackage it, perhaps even rename it."[66] Nowadays, Westphalian sovereignty – internal authority and external independence – are being challenged and disrupted by globalization, integration and the development of human rights law. On the one hand, the member states of the European Union (EU) volunteer and legally limit their sovereignty by transferring some of sovereign rights to the EU institution, which has collected partial sovereign rights. The development of the 'ever closer Union' in Europe has raised a debate about the progress towards postmodern statehood in multilevel governance structure. It is reasonable to assume

63 Luzius Wildhaber, Sovereignty and International Law, in R. S. J. Macdonald and D. M. Johnston (eds.) Structure and Process of International Law: Essays in Legal Philosophy Doctrine and Theory, The Hague: Martinus Nijhoff, 1983, p. 441.

64 Tomislav Zelic, The Paradox of Sovereignty in Modern German History Plays, Columbia University, 2009, p. 15, available at: http://media.proquest.com/media/pq/classic/doc/1694328941/fmt/ai/rep/SPDF?_s=EWwNSmF12%2F2rLDm38GBTPqUFWRE%3D.

65 1994 American Society of International Law (ASIL) Proceeding, Theme of Panel IV, 88 the Annual Meeting, at 73.

66 Louis Henkin, The Mythology of Sovereignty, in: ASIL Newsletter, March–May 1993, pp. 1–2, available at: http://www.asil.org/pres.htm.

that European demands led to the cutting down of sovereignty, which has lasted more than 300 years, because of the huge change in the international community.

On the other hand, the difficulties of hardly survivable states or quasi-state in Sub-Saharan Africa which were subject to overnight decolonization have instigated analyses of state failure. It is not something new, but happened continuously over time, while the states fell into civil wars, or seceded. In the Westphalia period, many of the German principalities begot sovereign rights in 1648 not by their own powers, but due to multilateral agreements and the emerging structure on the basis of 'sovereignty'.[67] Similarly, the current failing states obviously lack the capacity for effective and civil government, there is positive sovereignty but with formal negative sovereignty.

Comparing the EU as an evolved organization pooling with sovereign rights, the failing states in Sub-Sahara are still struggling to establish a sound government with the capacity to exercise sovereignty. Although such quasi-statehood is attributed to colonial history which confers rights to self-determination, the situation of quasi-statehood does not differ so fundamentally from the former German principalities in 1648.[68] A strong sovereign authority is seemly the right way for them. On the other hand, European states request underplaying sovereignty. Strikingly, in today's world, various states are not on the same page at all, the difference between the European states and failed states in Sub-Sahara is too remote to permit the sharing of a similar interpretation of sovereignty. Additionally, the reality that intervening states are generally powerful states convinces weaker states that the non-intervention principle is still a necessity for them. Consequently, it is difficult for the international community as a whole to reach consensus on how to interpret sovereignty. Arguably, the traditional interpretation of sovereignty must remain until a new consensus can be reached.

Section 3. The Principle of Non-intervention

1. Non-intervention as Inalienable Rights and Duties

Non-intervention and external sovereignty are basically two sides of the same coin. It is defined as an 'inalienable' right for one state to 'conduct its affairs without interference'[69] and a fundamental duty for other states not to intervene in matters within the domestic jurisdiction of any state. Clearly, non-intervention principle provides a shield for weak states, and moderates existing inequalities of power between states,[70]

67 Tanja E. Aalberts, 2012, p. 33.

68 Ibid.

69 Military and Paramilitary Activities in and against Nicaragua (Nicaragua v. United States of America), Merits, Judgment of 27 June 1986, [1986] ICJ Rep. 14, at 106, para. 202.

70 Mohammed Ayoob, Humanitarian Intervention and State Sovereignty, in: The International Journal of Human Rights, 2002, Vol. 6, No. 1, pp. 81–102.

therefore it is widely supported by developing states but normally challenged by powerful states. It is logical that it has always been the most controversial principle. Generally, the current interpretation of the non-intervention principle reflects the majority's voice which are mainly from developing states. According to the interpretation of the Friendly Relations Declaration, the non-intervention principle banned various interventions: military or non-military, direct or indirect interference, economic or political or any other form interference towards the internal or external affairs of any other state are not allowed.[71] The internal or external affairs have been listed as affairs with political, economic and cultural elements, rights to choose its political, economic, social and cultural systems. Anything regarding overthrowing of the regime of another state, or interfering in civil strife is labeled under the category of illegal intervention.

Moreover, under the Charter, even the UN has no right to intervene in matters which are essentially within the domestic jurisdiction of any state with only one important exception. Only if there is any threat to the peace, breach of the peace, or act of aggression, the Security Council can decide to take measures to maintain or restore international peace and security, regardless of whether the measures would amount to intervention in a state's internal affairs or not. This exception provides a legal basis for the UN to intervene in states' internal affairs. The interpretation of non-intervention in the Friendly Declaration was reaffirmed in the relevant interpretation of the 1986 *Nicaragua* judgment:

> "The principle forbids all states or groups of states to intervene directly or indirectly in internal or external affairs of other states. A prohibited intervention must accordingly

---

71 See the 1970 Declaration on Principles of International Law concerning Friendly Relations and Cooperation among states in accordance with the Charter of the United Nations: "No State or group of States has the right to intervene, directly or indirectly, for any reason whatever, in the internal or external affairs of any other State. Consequently, armed intervention and all other forms of interference or attempted threats against the personality of the State or against its political, economic and cultural elements, are in violation of international law.
No State may use or encourage the use of economic political or any other type of measures to coerce another State in order to obtain from it the subordination of the exercise of its sovereign rights and to secure from it advantages of any kind. Also, no State shall organize, assist, foment, finance, incite or tolerate subversive, terrorist or armed activities directed towards the violent overthrow of the regime of another State, or interfere in civil strife in another State.
The use of force to deprive peoples of their national identity constitutes a violation of their inalienable rights and of the principle of non-intervention.
Every State has an inalienable right to choose its political, economic, social and cultural systems, without interference in any form by another State.
Nothing in the foregoing paragraphs shall be construed as reflecting the relevant provisions of the Charter relating to the maintenance of international peace and security."

be one bearing on matters in which each state is permitted, by the principle of state sovereignty, to decide freely. One of these is the choice of a political, economic, social and cultural system, and the formulation of foreign policy. Intervention is wrongful when it uses methods of coercion in regard to such choices, which must remain free ones. The element of coercion, which defines, and indeed forms the very essence of, prohibited intervention, is particularly obvious in the case of an intervention which uses force, either in the direct form of military action, or in the indirect form of support for subversive or terrorist armed activities within another state."[72]

2. The New Challenges to Non-intervention Principle

Even though loud voices call for making a change and for a new phase of the international community, it is difficult to deny that the principle is still a fundamental part of international law. Certainly, states are free to make their decisions in an independent way on matters especially falling within the realm of their national concern.[73]

2.1. The Exception of Non-intervention Principle

Whether the humanitarian intervention shall be the second exception has been debated for decades. Ensuing development of human rights protection, the principle of human rights protection requests more compromise with the principle of non-intervention. However, the system of the UN charter based on sovereignty and humanitarian intervention has not been recognized as a new exception. So far, it has not generated any substantial change in the non-intervention principle. However, an expansion has been made on the issues under the umbrella of "any threat to the peace, breach of the peace, or act of aggression" which is recognized by the UN Security Council. It constituted that humanitarian crises within a state reaching a certain degree can be identified as a threat to international peace or breach of the peace.

2.2. Breach of Non-intervention Principle

Indeed, the notion of sovereignty and its effect of non-intervention in the domestic affairs of states act as a 'no trespassing' sign to protect the exclusive territorial domain of states.[8] Unfortunately, this sign has not prevented all external intervention into the affairs of states because signs by themselves are never able to keep away all trespassers. For instance, military invaders frequently disturb the development of the Balkan states, which means they may never have the chance to develop a well-functioning

---

72 Military and Paramilitary Activities in and against Nicaragua (Nicaragua v. United States of America), Merits, Judgment of 27 June 1986, [1986] ICJ Rep. 14, p. 108, para. 205.

73 Marcelo Kohen, The Principle of Non-Intervention 25 Years after the Nicaragua Judgment, Leiden Journal of International Law, 2012, Vol. 25, p. 160.

governmental system.[74] As Krasner highlights, "principles [of noninterference] have been enduring but violated. Rulers in more powerful states have justified violations of Westphalian principles by invoking alternative norms such as the illegitimacy of revolutionary regimes (the Holy Alliance), the provision of national security (the Platt Amendment imposed on Cuba by the United States), problems of drug running (the 1989 U.S. invasion of Panama) or the protection of the Soviet commonwealth (the Brezhnev doctrine)."[75] Strong states have routinely intervened, even forcibly, in the affairs of weaker ones. However, those violations have not amounted to invalidating sovereignty and the non-intervention principle. After all, during the past 50 years, following the emergence of post-colonial states in large numbers, the notion of sovereignty and non-intervention have forced the strong to make at least mildly credible cases for intervention into the affairs of the weak. Sovereignty had thus acted as a restraint on the former's interventionist instincts.[76] On the inside of states, "domestic sovereignty" is clearly a reality. On the outside, "external sovereignty" can also been seen. States do treat other states, vast or mini, as juridical equals; they accept others' right to representation in the United Nations and other international organizations; their authority to sign contracts and conventions are recognized. Indeed, sovereignty remains true whilst the non-intervention principle is a fundamental rule which is both obeyed and challenged in reality.

Conclusion

Westphalia has been identified as the birth of sovereignty and the first block in the foundation of modern international law. The Westphalia's sovereignty connotes an absolute, invisible feature, which has minimum restrictions. The fact that the sovereign state plays a major role in today's world means that the classical Westphalian sovereignty has not been abandoned but has evolved. It can be both absolute and relative; it can be both rights and duties. Sovereignty is progressively limited by more and more international constraints, particularly by the overarching demand of universal human rights. However, the sovereignty equality principle with the non-intervention principle work alongside each other, mirroring and supporting, and remain the basis of present international relations.

---

74 Herry Schermers, Different Aspects of Sovereignty, in: State, Sovereignty, and International Governance (ed. by Gerard Kreijen), London: Oxford University Press, p. 186.

75 Stephen Krasner, Sovereignty: Organized Hypocrisy, Princeton: Princeton University Press, 1999, p. 69.

76 M. Ayoob, 2002, p. 83.

Chapter 2. Sovereignty in Ancient China

Introduction

It is widely accepted that sovereignty originated from modern Europe through the development of a system of sovereign states, culminating at the Peace of Westphalia in 1648. Thus, sovereignty did not exist in ancient time in either the West or the East. It is also dominant in both western and Chinese academes that ancient China did not have the conditions to create the idea of sovereignty. However, a number of scholars have argued that the ancient Chinese system in the period of the Spring and Autumn and Warring States shows the emergence of territorial sovereignty and the formation of inter-state anarchy which was similar to the early modern European system.[77] That being said, except for this period, it is generally admitted that sovereignty, as either a political or legal concept, did not exist before China's colonial period.

In this chapter, the first focus will be about the earliest period of China and the development of Chinese statecraft, and mainly on the polity in ancient China as a final and absolute political authority over a certain territory and no final and absolute authority exist elsewhere[78]. Secondly, the emerging of sovereignty in Spring and Autumn and Warring States periods is discussed. Finally, an analysis of the typical Chinese foreign policy for the understanding of characteristics of imperial China and the foreign policies of contemporary China is presented.

Section 1. Ancient China as a State with 'Sovereignty'

The formation of China can be traced back to about 3000 years ago, to the dynasty of Xia, Shang and Zhou (Chow). During that period, ancient China was hardly a state, at best, a city state. However, it plays a crucial role in Confucianism which lauds the early time as the glory exemplar for all later dynasties.

1. The Earliest Period of China: Xia, Shang, and Western Zhou

At the end of the third millennium BC, the first central government of Xia rose in North China. In the second millennium BC, the Shang dynasty succeeded the Xia dynasty to rule in the Yellow River valley. By practicing a religious cult of the

77 Victoria Tin-bor Hui, Toward a Dynamic Theory of International Politics: Insights from Comparing Ancient China and Early Modern Europe, International Organization, Vol. 58, Winter 2004, pp. 175–205; William Alexander Parsons Martin, Traces of International Law in Ancient China, in: International Review (New York, N.Y.: 1874), pp. 63–77.

78 Francis Harry Hinsley, 1986, p. 26.

ancestors, the rulers of Xia and Shang dynasties legitimized their authority. After the conquest of the Shang dynasty, Zhou had established its power on a new basis of legitimacy by espousing the theory of Tianxia (Heaven), which continued for thousands of years to legitimize the highest power. The Zhou dynasty is the crucial dynasty which substantially influenced later dynasties in politics and culture. For the first time, it broke the balance of the king and dukes, who had to accept the highest power of the King of Zhou as the son of Heaven.[79] In the Zhou dynasty, the house of Zhou asserted the central superiority over the surrounding people by labelling them as "barbarians" who did not acknowledge the central government's supremacy. The most important point is that the Zhou invented the idea of the Tianxia which has been inherited by all later dynasties. Moreover, the core ideas of the Western Zhou created the origin of the Confucianism. Western Zhou constantly promoted a steady cultural assimilation based on the efficacy of the Chinese way of life and government; *Yi, Man, Rong,* and *Di* were the generic names for "barbarian" from four wards of 'Middle of China', all outsiders of Chinese culture. For the purpose of expanding and maintaining its supremacy, the kings made use of ritual and art, warfare, writing, and family connections. This model was praised as a perfect system by Confucius and became the ideal to deal with aliens. Meanwhile, like Xia, the Zhou continued to use kinship as a main element of political organization. The founding king of the Zhou dynasty bonded dukes and princes with the same surname by the patriarchal clan system, and bonded alliances with other surnames by marriage. He conferred each of the dukes and princes of small kingdoms with specific duties and responsibilities, and stipulated different positions of nobilities from within five ranks. The king owned the right to call up troops of the kingdoms.[80] Indeed, the central kingdom in the Zhou dynasty was not perceived at the time to be the polity of the sovereign in a purely vertical arrangement; rather it was seen to be one part of a much greater entity. "Union of plural kingdoms" is a more suitable term for it.[81] Such a decentralized political system was incapable of assuring the final authority of the royal power. Lack of clear boundaries and absolute power meant the kings in the Zhou dynasty hardly qualified as a sovereign. However, Zhou's system was repeatedly extolled in Confucian works; it was worshiped and tried to be revived by Confucians as the perfect political system. Unsurprisingly, it was exaggerated and misunderstood as a system throughout Chinese history by a number of sinologists who emphasized a China bonded by ritual or culture.

---

79 Fang Qing (方卿), Autarchy and Order (专制与秩序), Doctor Thesis of Fudan University, pp. 26–28.

80 In the early period of the Zhou dynasty, the feudalism system applied. The major feuds were from Ji's family, 53 feuds of all 71 feuds. See Xunzi: Ru xiao Pian (荀子・儒效篇); Guo Feifei, The Evolution of the Central Plain Civilization in China, in: China & The World Cultural Exchange, Vol. 11, 2012, pp. 30–33.

81 Martin Stuart-Fox, China and Southeast Asia: Tribute, Trade and Influence, Crows Nest: Allen & Unwin, 2003, pp. 75–78.

2. The Tianxia View in the Chinese Political System

2.1. The Origin of the Tianxia View

The Tianxia view was initiated by the Zhou dynasty, as discussed above, and it has remained the fundamental principle for other later dynasties and further developed. Tianxia literally means all under heaven. Theoretically, it was regarded as an abstract force, which people simply had to obey. The theory of Tianxia asserted the ruler's power from an impersonal deity (Tian) and his accountability to a supreme moral force that guides the human community. The core point is that the whole universe is dominated by an impersonal but omnipotent Heaven. A man needs to have the Mandate of Heaven, which entrusts the ruler in the name of Heaven's son with responsibilities for 'all under heaven' (Tianxia), one country as a whole.[82] It is not surprising that Westerners often translated 'Tianxia'to mean 'empire'.[83] The theory was distinct from the doctrine of the divine right which rested on birth alone. The Tianxia's mandate (天命) set up moral criteria for power-holders who might be conferred to by being morally worthy of the responsibility.[84] The emperors or kings held the central power in Chinese society. Exemplary behavior, rites, morality and indoctrination have always been considered in China as means of government.[85] Like one sun in the sky, Confucians claimed that China was the only one empire and true civilization in the world. It appeared in the Classic of Poetry, the oldest existing collection of Chinese poetry dating from the 11th to 7th centuries BC. "Under the wide heaven, all is the king's land. Within the sea-boundaries of the land, all are the king's servants."[86] Eventually, the Tianxia idea starting from Western Zhou developed in Eastern Zhou and increased in importance after the Han dynasty and continued as the legitimization of the ruler's power for the following dynasties till the end of Qing dynasty. Chinese central spheres of influence echoed and radiated from the tributary system; influence was greater closer to its core and lesser on its periphery. Theoretically, Chinese international relations were conducted as an extension of Chinese domestic policy under the theory of Tianxia.

Moreover, the basic framework of the Zhou worldview was a reformulated system of 'five zones' (五服) which was, at the same time, both centrifugal and centripetal. In political-geographic terms, these zones (invented, in legend, in the Tributaries of Yu the Great [Yu Gong] of Xia) referred to the five levels of the Zhou's

---

82 Charles Hucker, China's Imperial Past: An Introduction to Chinese History and Culture, Stanford: Stanford University Press, 1975, p. 55.

83 Marcel Granet, Chinese Civilization, New York: Knopf, 1930.

84 John King Fairbank, China a New History, Harvard: The Belknap Press of Harvard University Press, 1992, p. 40.

85 Keith Knapp, The Confucian Tradition in China, in: Companion to Chinese Religions (edited by Randall Nadeau), New Jersey: The Wiley Blackwell, 2012, p. 149.

86 Section II Minor odes of the Kingdom (小雅), Chapter 6 Decade of Bei Shan (北山之什), Shijing II. 6., p. 205.

mapping of their own world but as an imaginary cosmography, the five zones comprised a worldwide order.[87] The founding king of Zhou established these different zones (fu), whereby the inner domain of the capital was defined as dianfu (甸服) and the outer domain of the princes as houfu (侯服). Surrounding the princely domains and protecting them, was the zone of pacification (binfu, 宾服), which was in turn surrounded by the allied groups of the Yi and the Man who formed a semi-cultured zone (yaofu,要服), and by the Rong and the Di who formed a deserted zone (huangfu, 荒服) of savagery.[88] Overall, in the center was the king's capital and region of its direct control, which was surrounded by a circle of provinces ruled by princes or governors appointed by the king, and these again were surrounded by more or less independent 'tributary polities'. The five zones could be said to comprise a world system of outspreading levels of culture that were at the same time the extensions of civilization radiating from the center and the degrees of closeness were oriented toward civilization in a centripetal manner and finally the Harmony world.[89] However, such concentricity was only one side of two mutually complementary aspects of one system.[90] For the Zhou rulers, the five zones constituted a complex system of relationships, a catalog of people, and a structure of hierarchy deployed to institute, to describe, and to manage Tianxia. They marked out the cultural boundaries between the son of heaven and the lords of principalities, and between the principalities and semi-cultured others.[91]

For the other side, the five zones system was totally a different story. The Zhou order thinly held together by means of rites broke down in the East-Zhou dynasty, but the concept of Tianxia continued to serve to the following dynasties in their legitimacy. The Tianxia view was inherited by all later dynasties but the five zones system was replaced in the Qin dynasty by centralized governance which controlled territory far wider. While the realistic geography was limited by the territorial

87 Joseph Needham The shorter science and civilization in China, Vol. 2. Abridged by Colin Ronan. Cambridge: Cambridge University Press, 1981, pp. 238–239; Wang Mingming, All under Heaven (tianxia): Cosmological Perspectives and Political Ontologies in Pre-modern China, in: Hau-Journal of Ethnographic Theory, Vol. 2, Iss. 1, 2012, pp. 337–383.

88 Jian Buozan, The History of Pre-Qin (先秦史:), BeijingBeijing University Press, 1999, p. 322.

89 Fairbank 1973; Smith 1996.

90 Wang Mingming, 2012, pp. 337–383.

91 On the one hand, the concentric squares constituted a unity comprising diversity, a system of – rites and styles – defined in terms of hierarchy. In such a hierarchy, different from that of Shang, the institution of gong (or tribute-paying), essential to the later tributary mode of production, was merely applied to describe the interrelationship between the barbarians and princes. The other sorts of relationships were instead described as various levels of ceremony: the great sacrifice (ji), worship (si), and offerings (xian). Thus, on the other hand, the concentric squares were also positions within which the son of heaven was required to pay tributes, not only in the form of sacrifice – to heaven, earth, and other divinities – but also to his underlings.

margins that the emperors' reach was confined to, the imaginary geography, 'all under heaven', remained in the theory.[92]

2.2. *The Emperor as Son of the Heaven at the Center of the Chinese Political System*

At the center of the ancient Chinese political system in the Zhou dynasty was the king's capital and region of direct control, which was surrounded by a circle of provinces ruled by princes or governors appointed by the king, and these again were surrounded by more or less independent tributary 'polities.'[93] Heaven was the ultimate power and judge of morality and civilization.[94] The king as the son of heaven represented heaven and held the supreme power which was the pinnacle of the Chinese order. It was a figure with no parallels in Western society, which combined both the spiritual as well as the secular claims of the social order. He was perceived as mankind's supreme sovereign at the top of a world political hierarchy. The act of ketou (Kowtow), meaning prostration, was the rite showing that people recognized his over-lordship. Meanwhile, his role as the 'son of heaven' imposed upon him a moral obligation which requested him to take care of the people around the world through humane governance. If the king strayed from the path of virtue, the world would fall into chaos. It was the utmost duty of a ruler to serve his people, and whenever the people moaned or rebelled, it was time to change politics. Rebellions would break out, and a new dynasty with the 'Mandate of Heaven' would restore the order of harmony of the universe.[95]

The utopia world which Confucius described in the Yao and Shun time (about 2400 BC–2100 BC), the Dao (Tao) prevailed in the land: the right path was taken, men were upright and amiable and rich, things went the way things ought to go. Confucius held that there was no necessity to innovate but ought to recover the Zhou's rites to achieve a harmonious world. His thoughts had no substantial influential during his lifetime. Until the emperor Wudi of Han dynasty, Confucianism became the national thought and since then the Tianxia theory became fundamental for the Chinese ancient political system. After the Great Expansion of Qin and Han, the city-centered states transferred into a territory-centered state where the system of prefectures and counties substituted Zhou's orthodox zones of relationship which were maintained by merely ceremonies. Therefore, as the territory radically expanded, the former international relations transformed into domestic affairs. The Tianxia view partially came true since such a transformation made the emperor the real last authority within the giant empire. The foreign policies mainly concerned

92 Wang Mingming, 2012, p. 343.
93 Tambiah, 1976, p. 112.
94 Wang Mingming, 2012, p. 364.
95 Benjamin I. Schwartz, The Chinese Perception of the World Order, in: The Chinese World Order (ed. by Fairbank), Harvard: Harvard University Press, 1968, pp. 276–288.

a defense stratagem to pursue peace frontiers. However, the fact that Confucians always sang praise for the ancient time of Zhou may confuse a number of scholars who misunderstand Zhou's model as the major model of the Chinese empire. It also caused furious debates about whether ancient China was a real state or just a civilization which enthusiastically promoted culture.

2.3. From the Idealism to Realism: Multiple Concepts of Tianxia

Firstly, the 'Tianxia' is a 'holistic' concept, literally means: "Heaven covers all and Earth supports all. We will nurture all those who seek us."[96] There were no boundaries, no sovereign powers divisions, only sovereign commission with hierarchy.[97] Meanwhile, Confucians believed that the universe was divided into two separate worlds: a civilized center of Chinese surrounded by an uncivilized world of barbarians. Barbarians who were attracted to Chinese civilization and wished to reside in the Chinese world and adopt Chinese customs were permitted to do so, and it was believed that they would eventually be assimilated to Chinese cultural norms. Those who refused to be absorbed by the civilized center were to be expelled.[98] Thus, the Tianxia is a vast political system. In such a system, China is at the center, surrounded by barbarians from four directions. However, no empire could really fulfill the dream of equalizing its own territory with the concentric squares of Tianxia. The idea that expansion through culture makes 'all under heaven' is a manifestation of the imagination. The Yi (barbarian)-Xia (Chinese) distinction (also called Sino-barbarian dichotomy) was the reality. The distinction between Yi and Xia was based on the culture or civilization but after the Qin dynasty the territorial boundary was the major element of distinction. The two paradoxical ideas were two crucial pillars of the Tianxia theory. The contradiction between those two ideas is inherent in their meaning and thus inevitable. On the one hand, the Tianxia theory justified the expansion of the Chinese empire; on the other hand, the Chinese had to protect themselves and their land from foreign attacks. Chinese history intertwined with expansion and struggles with outsiders perfectly reflects the distinction between Yi and Xia.

In the Zhou dynasty, the king's power mainly relied on decentralized blood relations between the Zhou kings and the regional powers. Its mandate of heaven was more concerning cultural assimilating. However, the unification of Qin is the breaking point which marked an extraordinary change from cultural conquest into territorial expansion. It also brought a transformation of the Tianxia view. The unification of Qin marked the end of city-centered states in which lords or dukes exercised real powers and the king as son of 'heaven' became more symbolic and

---

96 J. K. Fairbank and S. Y. Teng, On the Ch`ing Tributary System, in: Harvard Journal of Asiatic Studies. Vol. 6, No. 2, June, 1941, pp. 137, 139.

97 Xu zhuoyun, Everlasting Land, the Breakthrough and Development of Chinese Historic Culture (万古江河：中国历史文化的转折与开展), Shanghai: Shanghai Arts Press, 2006, p. 76.

98 Gongyang zhuan, in Chunqiu (春秋), fifteenth year of Cheng-ung.

ritual; it indicated the start of a centralized political system by which the emperors were the final power in China. The governance was transformed from mainly culture into focusing on political, military, economic issues.[99] Since then, all officials directly pledged loyalty to the emperor, not to lords or dukes whose power and titles were diminished in this unitary centralized system.[100] The view that people and territory were to be valued equally or even by territory more so, replaced the idea where people were more important than land. The relations between Xia and Yi changed from 'distinction of inside and outside' to 'Zhongguo (the ancient name of China) and foreign'.[101] In this new phase, population mobility, inter-ethnic alliances, economic development, and military competitions gave rise to the extension of the territory of Zhongguo and increased Huaxia's (the ancient name of Chinese people) knowledge about other kingdoms and peoples.[102]

Japanese historian Abe Takeo argues that the Tianxia was first used by Jiuzhou (another name of ancient China) after the warring states period. While the first emperor of Qin unified Jiuzhou, the idea that China or Jiuzhou was equal to Tianxia was clear. Moreover, such a Tianxia view was inherited by later dynasties.[103] Abe Takeo criticized the view that China was a civilization not a state because China saw the world as one state and pointed out that China was a state ruled by a strong centralized power within a defined administrative region, which was so-called Tianxia.[104] He asserted that there were two concepts of "Tianxia", one in a broad sense indicated the Universe – 'all under heaven', but in a narrow sense it was the Jiuzhou which the emperor had ruled effectively. Actually, Tianxia in a narrow meaning is often connected with the word, Zhongguo (literally meaning 'central kingdom').[105] Such a division could explain the contradiction between all under one heaven and the Xia-Yi distinction. It implies that there were two systems in ancient China. One applied within the territory which the Chinese government or the emperor could

---

99 Luo Zhitian, The Pre-modern System of 'Wu Fu' and Ancient Chinese 'Tianxia' View (先秦的五服制与占代的天下中国观), in: Nationalism and Modern Chinese Thoughts (Luo Zhitian ed.), Taibei: Dongda Book Publishing Company, 1998, p. 30.

100 Cheng Qiyun, Feud and Unification – on the Theories and History of Chinese Traditional Politic System (封建与大一统之间——关于中国传统政体的理论和史实), in: Academic Monthly, 2007, Vol. 2, pp. 125–128.

101 Luo Zhitian, 1998, pp. 31–32.

102 Lin Huixiang, Zhongguo Minzu Shi (History of ethnic nationalities in China), 2 vols., Beijing: Shangwu Yinshuguan, [1939] 1993, pp. 26–27.

103 Abe Takeo (Japan), Chinese 'Tianxia' View: Analysis of Political Thoughts (中国人之天下观念一政治思想的试论), in: Research on History of Yuan Dynasty (元代史之研究), Tokyo: Chuangweng Press (1972), p. 508, as cited in Shinichiro Watanabe: Kingship of Ancient China and Tianxia Order (Translated by Xuchong), Beijing: Zhonghua Book Company, 2008, pp. 10–11.

104 Ibid.

105 Therefore, for the purpose of clarity, in this thesis, Zhongguo has the same meaning as Tianxia in the narrow sense.

control, another one was enforced outside of Zhongguo, where the Chinese tried to play a dominate role in its peripheral area. In the former one, namely Zhongguo, emperors were sovereigns who exercised the absolute authority within the territory. The latter one applied in the outside world, today's 'international plane', in which China at that time attempted to make other states nominally subordinate to him through the tributary system consistent with the theory of 'all under heaven'. The dichotomy of Tianxia of Abe Takeo is widely accepted in Asia.[106]

However, in Chinese history, three concepts of Tianxia actually developed and were applied in different contexts. The first one is the Tianxia in the narrow sense, Zhongguo, where the central dynasties directly controlled post-Qin dynasty. The second one is the one in a geographical and security sense, including Zhongguo and its peripheral areas, where Zhongguo attempted to defend itself from foreign attacks through the tributary system, cultural converting, or punitive expeditions. The third one, we might say is in the broadest sense of Tianxia, which generally refers to the all under heaven, including Zhongguo, peripheral countries, and the outside world which ancient Chinese could not reach or was beyond its limit. Logically, the last one is rather theoretical. The emperors with their officials generally had no intention to deal with places unreachable or beyond its limit. For example, ancient China was aware of the Roman empire ('Da Qin' in ancient Chinese) for a long time[107], but never considered to bring Rome under Chinese Tianxia order although Rome should be under its reign according to the Tianxia theory. All three norms of Tianxia functioned for various purposes.

Although the Chinese were aware of the possibilities of the Tianxia theory, the idea of 'all under heaven' generally applied for the justification of superior authority of the emperors. The other two concepts of Tianxia co-played in Chinese history in different spheres, the narrow sense of Tianxia, namely Zhongguo, indicated the domestic sphere, and the second one represented the international community where Zhongguo was involved. However, those three meanings of Tianxia are found in ancient literature, and frequently intertwined so that opinions regarding China's

106 Zhang Qixian, Analysis on the Concepts of Zhongguo and Tianxia (「中国」与「天下」概念探源), The Soochow Journal of Political Science, Vol. 27, 2009, pp. 169–256.

107 As early as 97 CE, a Chinese envoy named Gan Ying, sent by the general Ban Chao, intended to sail to the Roman Empire, however, it made his way from the Tarim Basin to Parthia and reached the Persian Gulf but failed to arrive at Rome. In 166 the first Roman envoy was sent by Roman emperor Marcus Aurelius, from the Persian Gulf and successfully arrived in China. See John E. Hill, Through the Jade Gate to Rome: A Study of the Silk Routes during the Later Han Dynasty, First to Second Centuries CE, North Charleston: BookSurge, 2009, pp. 5, 27, 481–483.

state status are rather inconsistent.[108] The complex is as Ge comments, "ancient China was a real limited state where the infinite 'Tianxia' remained imagination."[109]

3. The Sovereignty in the Sense of Supreme Authority since the Qin-Han Dynasties

As analyzed in chapter one, the core idea of sovereignty is that of an ultimate source of political power or authority in a realm. Bearing this in mind, the next part analyzes whether China is an actual state with sovereignty or a civilization with the cover of a state.

3.1. Centralized Administrative System

As discussed, the Zhou dynasty ruling heavily relied upon and utilized cultural means. From the period of the Spring and Autumn Warring States to the Qin dynasty, the monarchs' power in these kingdoms gradually shifted down to bureaucrats. The Qin dynasty marked the establishment of a complete centralized political system, which lasted for two thousand years in China. The emperor and his family relied on a professional bureaucratic system to rule the country. They enjoyed absolute dominance over their subjects. There were no codified or legal restraints on the emperor. He was the legislator, the chief executive, the head of military force and the supreme judge of the empire. He ruled the empire through his officials and both the central and local governments within an unprecedented size territory as the supreme sovereign.[110]

3.1.1. The Qin Bureaucratic System

The Qin dynasty established a highly centralized bureaucratic government, which was administered by a hierarchy of officials, all serving the Emperor. The Qin premier minister, Shang Yang, introduced new laws and practices that obliterated feudalism in China, replacing it with an administrative hierarchy of prefectures, counties, townships, and villages. All imperial governments resembled a pyramid, with the emperor at the peak and groups of agencies in central, regional and local apparatuses under the emperor, and each level of the pyramid had three faces - administration, military and censorial surveillance.[111] Under the Emperor, the top ministerial dignitaries were comprised of a chief counselor (cheng xiang), a grand marshal (tai wei), and the censor-in-chief. The chief counselor functioned as the

108 Zhang Qixian, 2009, pp. 169–256.
109 Ge Zhaoguang, As Scholars 'Dwelling in China: on Reconstruction of Relative Chinese History, Beijing: Zhonghua Book Company, 2011, pp. 28–29.
110 Jack L. Dull, the Evolution of Government in China, in Heritage of China (ed. by Paul S. Ropp.), 1990, Oakland: University of California Press, p. 62.
111 Charles Hucker, 1975, pp. 150–151.

prime minister for the emperor. He presided over a number of central government agencies, which included the offices of 'the nine chief ministers' (jiu qing). They took charge of imperial rituals, palace maintenance, judiciary, the imperial commissariat, revenue and tax, land tax and manufacture industries, foreign affairs, etc. The Qin government removed the land from the control of the feudal fiefdoms and local clans. Land was viewed abstractly as consisting of quantifiable units by a state which could minutely survey its products, efficiently tax it, and redistribute it for its own ends.[112] It conducted the first population censuses in China using a new household registering system which recorded population by a unit of household. The abstraction of the land and the population and their re-codification by a centralized state apparatus made it possible for the emperor's will to reach the people in the form of a self-policing body of law. Appointments were based on merit instead of hereditary rights. Meanwhile, the Qin dynasty unified China economically by standardizing Chinese writing and Chinese units of measurements such as weights and measures, currency, the length of the axles of carts to facilitate transport on the road system and so it expanded the network of roads and canals. It also unified thoughts by defining legalism[113] as the main philosophy to guide the ruling system and suppressing Confucianism along with all other non-legalistic philosophies.[114]

Regarding the territory demarcation, the Qin built the initial construction of what later became the Great Wall of China in order to fortify the northern border against incursions from the Xiongnu (a nomadic ethnic group). The boundary was as far south as Guangdong, towards the west to Linzao, towards the east to Liaodong, towards southwest to Basu, towards southeast the East sea and Taiwan Strait. This region became traditional territory of China or heartland of China.[115] The emperor definitively established his absolute authority through centralized political and military control over this territory.

---

112 Brian Massumi, First and Last Emperors: The Absolute State and the Body of the Despot, Brooklyn: Autonomedia, December 1992, p. 208.

113 The legalism emphasizes strict obedience to the legal system and valued "law", "shu", "shi". The law code must be clearly written and made public. All people under the ruler were equal before the law. Laws should reward those who obey them and punish accordingly those who dare to break them. Thus it is guaranteed that actions taken are systematically predictable. In addition, the system of law, not the ruler, ran the state, a statement of rule of law. If the law is successfully enforced, even a weak ruler will be strong. Special tactics and 'secrets' are to be employed by the ruler to make sure others don't take over control of the state. Especially important is that no one can fathom the ruler's motivations, and thus no one can know which behavior might help them get ahead, other than following the laws. Thirdly, the critical matter is the position of the power holders, not themselves. Logically, analysis of the trends, the context, and the facts are essential for rulers.

114 Brian Massumi, 1992, p. 27.

115 Michael D. Swaine, Ashley J. Tellis, Interpreting China's Grand Strategy: Past, Present, and Future, Washington, D.C: Rand, 2000, pp. 22–24.

3.1.2. Dynasties after Qin

The Han dynasty, as the successor of the Qin, largely followed the governing system of the Qin but made some changes, which had not amount to a fundamental reform until the Sui dynasty. The three Departments and Six Ministries system (三省六部) was the main central administrative structure adopted in China during its imperial period. It was developed on the basis of the Qin dynasty while its separate departments first took shape during the Han dynasty; it emerged in a more complete form during the Sui dynasty, and has been adopted in some form by all Chinese dynasties since. The Tang dynasty certainly developed a rather mature system to rule China. The Tang central government manifested the traditional tripartite. There were three departments (省), which consisted of a staff of generals who commanded the imperial armies; a Censorate that was somewhat more elaborate than its Han antecedent; and a grand council for general administration. The three departments had prestigious status in the overall administration. The three were the Secretariat (中书省), the Chancellery (门下省), and the Department of State Affairs (尚书省). Under this system, the Department of State Affairs, which controlled the six ministries, was the highest executive institution of the imperial government. The Secretariat was the main policy-formulating agency that was responsible for proposing and drafting all imperial decrees. The main function of the Chancellery was to advise the Emperor and the Secretariat, and to review edicts and commands. The head of the Secretariat or the Department of State Affairs was generally referred to as the Chancellor, next only to the Emperor in rank and power.

In the Yuan dynasty, the Department of State Affairs was the only one which continually governed the Six Ministries, the other two were later abolished. However, the Minhongwu Emperor tore down the Department of State Affairs and directly led the Six Ministries. The Six Ministries took charge of ruling China under the Emperor. The Ministry of Personnel made civil service appointments to those who passed the examination system; the Ministry of Revenue collected taxes; the Ministry of Rites supervised the examination system, state festivals, and government-sponsored schools; the Ministry of War appointed military officers to those who had passed the separate military examination system; the Ministry of Punishment presided over the court system; and the Ministry of Works was in charge of building, irrigation, and "the production of mines and marshes", mostly, salt. The Censorate, the seventh entity, was a uniquely Chinese institution for the purpose of criticizing the other organs of government including the emperor. The censorial officials had a more specifically defined responsibility to ensure that the government functioned as intended in sharing the responsibility of the emperor as the father and mother of the people. They had the sole prescribed function of maintaining surveillance over all governmental operations for the purpose of prosecuting officials who violated laws, administrative regulations, or traditional moral standards. They had the right to submit their prosecution requests directly to the throne and enjoyed considerable independence of action and high prestige. However, they were not immune from punishment if their accusations offended an emperor.

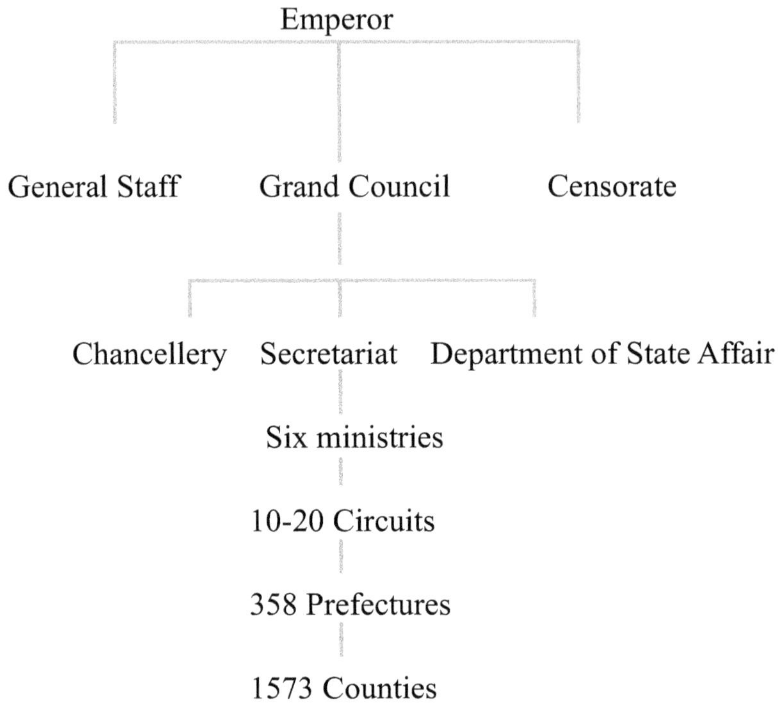

(Basic Governmental Organization in Tang Dynasty)[116]

Unlike European law, Chinese law was always merely an instrument of government; it was not thought to have divine sanction, nor was it considered an inviolable constitution. It was an inseparable part of a routine administration. There were no provisions limiting state authority, and there was no church or independent judiciary before which the state could legally be held accountable. Laws were promulgated for one purpose only – to spell out what kind of behavior the state wanted its subjects to avoid and what it would do to them if they misbehaved. The code was implemented and enforced primarily by county magistrates who were the emperor's all-purpose surrogates in dealing with the people at large. They served as investigators, prosecutors, defenders, juries, and judges all in one.[117]

116 Charles O. Hucker, 1975, p. 155.
117 Charles Hucker, 1975, p. 155.

The unitary centralized bureaucratic system ensured the doctrine of the Mandate of Heaven thorough the whole empire history making Chinese rulers absolutists.[118] Even though some emperors were restrained by the powers of influential ministers, semi-autonomous aristocratic families, and uncontrollable regional generals, the absolute power of emperors cannot be denied. From the unification of the Warring States by the first Emperor Qin Shi Huang in 221 BC to the last Emperor Xiantong of the Qing dynasty (abdicated in 1912 AD), imperial China provides a comforting illusion of continuity and stability, but the collapse of one dynasty and its replacement by the new one generally happened with rebellion or war. Meanwhile, Zhongguo was frequently under military threat from some strong hostile neighboring countries or tribes. When an ambitious adversary threatened the central dynasty, where actual control ended became the boundary. For example, the famous Great Wall was constructed along a major portion of China's northern frontier to protect against nomadic attacks. The Chinese also at times built fortifications and garrisons at various points along China's southern maritime borders, primarily to defend against attacks by pirates.[119] The Tang dynasty established the Junzhen defense (军镇屯戍) system as a major frontier system against foreign forces. "A bigger unit of force to stay and defense frontier is so-called 'Jun', a smaller unit of force to defense frontier is so-called 'Shouzhuo, or Cheng, or Zheng', and all of them are generally called 'Dao'".[120] Different sizes of military forces were regularly stationed at different frontiers for the purpose of defending the territory of Zhongguo. This defense system was further developed in later dynasties. During the Song dynasty, the borders of Zhongguo had to be clarified since it faced stronger adversaries, Liao and Jin, who successfully reformed and developed a similar Tianxia country by introducing Chinese civilization.[121] Noticeably, the existence of a border defense system certifies that from the Qin-Han dynasty to the Qing dynasty the major part of Zhonguo's territory was clear even though the boundaries changed from time to time, based on centralized political and military controlling, not on cultural boundary. In Chinese history, no matter which dynasty ruled, Zhongguo always had its frontiers, frontier defense system, and territorial disputes.

Moreover, the foreign policies that China implemented in the realm of external security all revolved around the defense of the Chinese "cultural, geographic, and socio-political heartland, namely Zhongguo".[122] Even the tributary system was

118 In the Tang dynasty, China was revolutionized in the paraphernalia life of everyday life from earlier dynasties. Chinese burned coal, wrote on paper, saw printing, sat at a table on a chair, drank tea, or rode in a sedan chair - activities that were all commonplace in tenth-century China. Tang life had no equal anywhere in the world. Charles O. Hucker, 1975, p. 192.

119 Michael D. Swaine; Ashley J. Telli, 2000, p. 27.

120 Xing Tang Shu·Bingzhi (新唐书・兵志).

121 Ge Zhaoguang, 2011, p. 48.

122 Michael D. Swaine; Ashley J. Telli, 2000, p. 22.

actually for the purpose of defending the geographic territory of Zhongguo. Therefore, Zhongguo was and is clearly a political and geographic entity.

3.2. Zhongguo and Sino-culture Zone

Many think of China as a country without borders because China saw the world from a central state position in terms of the 'Tianxia' view. Nonetheless, Tianxia in the broad sense is an idea or possibility, that could never come true; therefore, it could not truly apply in the relations between Zhongguo and other foreign entities.[123] As previously discussed, the concept of Tianxia has three dimensions, but Zhongguo is the one with the actual demarcation relying on political and geographic standards. Zhongguo was the land the central dynasty could actually control. People there were registered as its subjects, submitting tax, serving their emperors, regulated by local officials appointed by emperors.

However, there were other types of segregations in imperial China. A rather influential one is based on culture. Mark Mancall stresses that China's centrality in the world order was a function of her civilization and China ruled the world by virtue, particularly the virtue of China's ruler.[124] Thus, the Chinese conquered the world by culture rather than military forces. Fairbank defined China's world order on the basis of acceptance of Chinese culture and then states: "the graded and concentric hierarchy of China's foreign relations included peoples and countries which we may group in three main zones: first, the Sinic Zone, consisting of the most nearby and culturally similar territories, Korea and Vietnam, the Ryūkyū Islands, and, at brief times, Japan; secondly, the Inner Asia Zone, consisting of tributary tribes and states of the nomadic or semi-nomadic peoples of Inner Asia, who were on the fringe of the Chinese culture area; thirdly, the Outer Zone, consisting of the 'Outer barbarians', generally at a farther distance over land or sea"[125]

Indeed, this division was simply based on culture, and had nothing to do with actual territory. On the sphere of the Sinic zone, no direct control existed between the central government of Zhongguo to Korea or Vietnam, and Zhongguo was connected with other states by culture or trade or security interests, etc. If it is concluded that ancient China was not a real state but a civilization with no boundary in terms of assimilation of culture in a certain zone, it is incorrect because it confused the broad sense of Tianxia with the real state-Zhongguo and confused the domestic system with foreign policies. This division just demonstrates how far Chinese culture reaches. For example, today globalization means American culture has influence all around world, but we cannot conclude the world into a USA-central world just due to the influence of the American culture.

---

123 Ge Zhaoguang, 2011, p. 29.

124 Mark Mancall, The Persistence of Tradition in Chinese Foreign Policy, in: Annals of the American Academy of Political and Social Science 349 (1963), pp. 17–19.

125 J. K. Fairbank, 1968, p. 2.

As is well-known, following the advice of Dong Zongsu, Han wudi (156 BC - 87 BC), an emperor of the Han dynasty, for the first time officially abandoned Legalism in China and established Confucianism as the state ideology of the Han. Nonetheless, the Confucianism which Dong Zongsu developed in the Han dynasty is widely understood as a legalism with a cover of Confucianism. Consequently, from the Han period onwards, most Chinese emperors have used mix thoughts of Legalism and Confucianism as their ruling doctrine.[126] However, Confucianism as a national philosophy was extolled in public, thus, Confucius was described as a Saint, his works which celebrated the superiority of Chinese culture and perfection of "Yao and Shun" era and the Zhou dynasty became the major textbooks for students who desired to assume an official position in the government by successfully passing the national exams. Undoubtedly, Confucianism deeply affected Chinese cultural, political, and social aspects. However, it did not or could not replace the legalistic political system. It is absurd to conclude that cultural delineation replaced political and geographic demarcation of Zhongguo by mainly following the works of Confucius and his disciples. This is because it simply ignored the real history that China always had a strong centralized government which exploited culture to legitimize its governance.

The territory of Zhongguo must be distinguished using zones where Chinese culture might reach and where the Chinese emperor might claim control. This connotes that ancient China had not only one Tianxia view but a multiple-Tianxia order. The culture demarcation is just one of them, and after all, the political and geographic delineation is rather more substantial and decisive.

3.3. The Han Chinese as the Major Subjects of Zhongguo

The prehistory of the Han Chinese ethnic group is intertwined with the history of Zhongguo. The Han can be traced from the two tribes led by the Yan and Yellow Emperors, who were considered the source of the Chinese people and the initiators of Chinese culture. These tribes are known as the Huaxia people, who lived along the Huang He or Yellow River in northern China and established the Xia dynasty, the first dynasty of ancient China. Initially, the "Huaxia people" was interpreted to mean "civilized society" that was distinct and stood in contrast to what was perceived as the barbaric people around them. They were normally named after the people of the ruling dynasty. During the Han dynasty, many Chinese began addressing themselves as "Han people".[127] Demographically, Chinese society is composed of 90% percent

---

126 Shen Po, Analysis on Legalized transformation on Confucianism by Dong zhongshu (论董仲舒对儒学的法家化改造), in: Social Science Journal of Southwest University of Nationalities, vol. 11, 2008, pp. 76–81.

127 Li Yujie, The Identity of Nationality and State: The Common Identity of Nationality and State of Huaxia Society (民族认同与国家认同一论华夏社会中民族、国家意识的同一性), in: Journal of Chongqing Normal University (the editions of philosophy and social science), 1999, vol. 2, p. 5.

descendants of the Han or descendants of mixed Han – nomadic or southeast Asian people. The Han did not remain separate from other cultures. Throughout Chinese history, non-Han ethnic groups twice conquered and ruled the entire Zhongguo for a considerably long time.[128] The Han and other peoples have mutually absorbed many of the political and social customs from each other and were heavily influenced by each other. They constitute a highly homogeneous culture from the humanistic and ethical doctrine of Confucianism and other ancient thoughts.[129]

4. Pre-modern Sovereignty in Ancient Zhongguo

With the development of the concept of sovereignty, we have the main elements of what is now called "the state system": independent states and "international relations" (and "international law"). In late medieval and early modern times, powerful monarchs and emerging states in Europe faced a number of rivals: city-republics, leagues of cities, empires, the Church, and various remnants of feudalism. Before, the lack of relatively unambiguous geographical boundaries and lack of rival powers resulted in a large missing of exclusivity of rule (a "closed" system of governance) and territoriality in early forms of political organization.[130]

However, Zhongguo as an ancient state had a unique characteristic differing from others. First of all, we must clarify that the ancient China pre-Qin dynasty did not qualify as a state. China in the Zhou dynasty was just a city-state. The Zhou dynasty tried to control central China through the feudal system tied by blood and rites. In fact, during the long Zhou dynasty, the theoretical powers of kings were curtailed in practice by the prestige and military strength of regional feudal lords. Even though the idea of Tianxia provided the king's superiority, under threats from powerful vassals, the king did not possess the actual superiority by rites or cultural supremacy. Secondly, till the Qin dynasty, Zhongguo was unified as a single state and developed a unitary political system in terms of legalism. Afterwards, such a single centralized political system was developed with Confucianism to maintain harmony-oriented Confucian-legalist order.[131] Meanwhile, Chinese culturalism played an important role in the Chinese foreign policy.[132] Nonetheless, Chinese culture never weakened the rulers' power, on the contrary, either Legalism or Confucianism provided a strong organized government. China was a "highly homogeneous culture and civilization incorporating a common set of political and social beliefs about the organizational and procedural requirements for stability, peace, and prosperity in

128 The Yuan dynasty (1264–1368) was established by the Mongols, the Qing dynasty was established by the Manzu.

129 Michael D. Swaine; Ashley J. Telli, 2000, p. 20.

130 Christopher W. Morris, An Essay on the Modern State, Cambridge: Cambridge University Press, 2002, p. 33.

131 Michael D. Swaine; Ashley J. Telli, 2000, p. 40.

132 Xu Daoyuan, The Great Historical Sketch (历史大脉络), Guiling: The Press of Guangxi Normal University, 2009, p. 35.

an often chaos-prone environment".[133] Consequently, the strong well-organized government had been dominant most of the time in the long history of the Chinese.

Thirdly, unlike the European countries, restraint over the power of Chinese sovereigns did not form a real threat. Theoretically, the emperor represented the heaven which no one could challenge and in practice, the centralized bureaucratic system in the post-Qin dynasty made Chinese emperors' power more effectively able to control the whole territory of Zhongguo. The population within the declared territory had to register as legal subjects of the emperors, thus they were directly loyal to the emperor. As we analyzed above, this centralized bureaucratic system ensured Chinese emperors as sovereign holders. That means sovereignty as an absolute authority had existed within Zhongguo since 221 BC.

That being said, whilst such sovereignty in the sense of absolute authority within Zhongguo was apparent, the respective theories or complete thoughts on sovereignty were absent. There are only sporadic descriptions of sovereignty in ancient works. Mencius considers territory, people, governance (政事) as the treasures of monarchs.[134] Here, the governance implies sovereignty. Guan zi used the exact word of 'sovereignty' as 'king's power'.[135] However, different from modern sovereignty, it is rudimentary, and only in the form of internal sovereignty. Since it originates from the mandate of heaven, the sovereign of Zhongguo did not normally acknowledge other states' superior power within their own land because the Tianxia view saw peripheral states of Zhongguo inferior to the emperor's authority. The hierarchy claim of Chinese rulers and its dominance of its neighborhood regions stunted external sovereignty from happening. The nature of the Tianxia view as all under heaven and its side product – the tributary system – blocked the external sovereignty which is based on equality and independence growing in the circle of China and China's peripheral states. The hierarchical foreign relationship which ancient China claimed could not deliver the birth of modern sovereignty. Therefore, absolute power in ancient China is not in the sense of the modern sovereignty as the fundamental concept of international relations.

Section 2. Sovereignty in the Spring and Autumn and Warring States Periods

When the military and political power of the various dukes' houses grew to such an extent their desire for independence from the universal claims of the Zhou kings, the feudal system of Zhou dynasty clashed. The breakdown of the feudal system decentralized the power of the house of Zhou, and allowed the surrounding barbarian

---

133 Michael D. Swaine; Ashley J. Telli, 2000, p. 40.

134 Menzius, Jing Xin Xia (尽心下).

135 If the national Treasury is empty, the sovereignty would decline. If the law is damaged, the door would open for evils. See Guanzi, seven ministers and seven kings (七臣七主).

tribes to rise as a new independent power who contested the power of the central states, the former dukes or vassals of Zhou also joined in scrambling for power. After a few generations the feudal sub-units emerged as autonomous states. Then came a period when those states allied themselves with others for mutual interests; communications between states were improved; centralized bureaucracy was developed; cultural development was unprecedentedly prosperous. A group of writers asserted that the sovereignty in Westphalia model existed in the Spring-and-Autumn period and Warring States period (from 656 BC to 221 BC) when states engaged in diplomatic-military free-for-all. 'International' relations of ancient China that had been sustained for over five centuries, eventually was ended by the establishment of the first unified Chinese empire by the Qin in 221 BC. During this period, those states were in the classic dilemma of any decentralized international relations, that of anarchy. There was certainly no formal legal expression of sovereignty as a constitutional principle in the ancient Chinese states-system. Actually, it witnessed the prevalence of war, formation of alliances, development of centralized bureaucracy, sent diplomatic representatives to others, emergence of citizenship rights, extraditions, and expansion of international trade. The relations among those states were rather like the situation of Europe in the early modern period.[136]

1. Background

After the definitive end of the political and military dominance of the royal house of Western Zhou dynasty in 771 BC, which exercised some hierarchical authority over feudal units, the formal vassals entered into a truly interdependent system of behavior. They engaged in centralization of authority within independent polities. The earliest rivals gradually expanded their territorial control by building larger armies, promoting agricultural productivity, and enhancing their administrative capacity. According to the research of Hui, various states began to be mutually aware of interdependent secure relations around 659 BC.[137] Chu's repeated attacks on Zheng in 659–653 B.C. and Qi's mobilization of a northern alliance to assist Zheng in 656 B.C. Evidently, this period formally marked the first systemic (rather than bilateral and local) war involving most major powers. In mobilizing an anti-Chu alliance, Qi also pioneered the practices of sending envoys and demarcating borders, thereby laying down the foundations for diplomatic exchanges, coalition formation, and territorial sovereignty.

In the beginning of Zhou, the Tianzi (the Son of Heaven) established the state in which vassals had their own feudal systems. From the Western Zhou until the beginning of Eastern Zhou all the princely states were feudal dependencies of the

136 Victoria Tin-bor Hui, War and State Formation in Ancient China and Early Modern Europe, Cambridge: Cambridge University Press, 2005.

137 Victoria Tin-bor Hui, 2004, pp. 175–205, p. 184; also see Barry Buzan and Richard Little, International Systems in World History: Remaking the Study of International Relations, Oxford: Oxford University Press, 2000, pp. 80–84.

Zhou King and hence belonged to the Zhou royal house and could not be considered as independent states in their own right. However, the Zhou court's overall grasp and authority were constantly weakened so that it no longer had the authority to carry out its role of upholding the political order and system of power from the eighth century B.C. Eventually, the kings of Zhou lost their power as supreme ruler and just kept the king's title after the Spring-and-Autumn period starting from the eighth to the sixth century B.C.[138] There were more than 50 states which were relatively independent from other states and the "Tianzi" as well. The situation was very similar to Europe in the Westphalia period, growing disorders and suffering of war, especially of the Thirty Year War. Westphalia treaties rejected any idea that the Pope or Emperor had any universal authority over all states and removed temporal power from the church which could not hold supreme power over the secular world. Substantially it cut down the Emperors' power over principal states.

In the era of Spring-and-Autumn, several large princely states already had at least two basic features of the modern 'state': sovereignty and territory. The states had rather clear borders and had independent and autonomous sovereignty within its border.[139] By the time of Warring States (from fifth to third century BCE), states had competed with each other for centuries under their own rules, meanwhile, the Zhou royal kingdom sank to the level of a small, weak state. Some compare the way in which the various princely states gave feudal homage to the Zhou king as their common lord to the relationship of the members of today's Commonwealth to Great Britain. Both accept the King or the Queen as head of their community while they have complete independent autonomy in their territory.[140] They created and maintained functioning institutions of collective security, balance of power, diplomacy and (in a rather rudimentary form) international law to serve their common interests. Treaties, summit meetings, diplomatic conventions, court intermarriages and even hostage-taking were legitimate and indispensable institutions.[141]

---

138 Sima Qian, The Records of Historian: Zhoubengji, Beijing: Zhonghua Book Company, 1959, p. 128.

139 Yang Qianru, An Examination of the Research Theory of Pre-qin Interstate Political Philosophy, in: Quarterly Journal of International Politics, 2009, Vol. 19, p. 140.

140 Pei Monong, Introduction, in: Diplomatic Constellations in the Spring and Autumn and Warring States Periods, Chongqing: Chongqing Press Group, 1994, p. 1.

141 Liu Boji, Politics of Diplomatic Conventions and Alliances in the Spring and Autumn Period (春秋会盟政治), Taipei: Zhonghua Congshu, 1962; Yang Kuan, A History of the Warring States Period (战国史), Shanghai: Shanghai Renmin Press; Sun Yurong, A study of international law in ancient China (古代中国国际法研究), Beijing: China Politics and Law University Press, 1999; Xu Jieling, A Study of the Diplomatic Relations in the Spring and Autumn Period (春秋邦交研究), Beijing: China Social Science Press, 2004.

2. Interstate system in the Spring and Autumn and Warring State Periods

Since those vassal states became independent and the Zhou king lost superiority, the states launched wars against enemy states and allied with others for survival and growth. In the beginning of the Spring-and-Autumn period, Chu, a southern state, was the first to emerge hegemonic. As Chu sought expansion into the central plain area in the early to mid-seventh century B.C., it was curbed by a Qi-led alliance in 656 B.C. These events marked the onset of the ancient Chinese interstate system as state alliance against powerful states is generally recognized as an obvious phenomenon of interdependent international society. Qi soon fell as a result of internal power struggles. However, Jin then emerged against Chu in 632 B.C. In the ensuing century, the Jin and Chu camps contested head-to-head and were unable to subjugate each other. The two sides finally reached a peace agreement in 546 B.C. Nevertheless, this Jin-Chu balance did not last long. Wu, Chu's south-eastern neighbor, rose in power and managed to capture Chu's capital in 506 B.C. Wu, in turn, suffered from over-expansion and was even conquered by its own southeastern neighbor, Yue, in 473 B.C. Yue left the great-power competition and focused its attention on neighboring weak states. The great power, Jin, was split by three ruling clans into Han, Wei, and Zhao in 453 B.C. In the ensuing Warring States period, Wei was the first state to emerge hegemonic, and then attempted to subjugate its neighbors. However, Wei's expansion into Zhao in 354–352 B.C. and Han in 344–340 B.C. brought about Qi's interference and decisive defeats. Qi's own attempt at domination, in turn, was thwarted by an anti-Qi alliance in 284 B.C. In short, for more than three centuries, ambitious domination-seekers rose but fell, attempts at domination were made but challenged, attempts at foreign policy were pursued, and balances in the distribution of relative capabilities occurred at various times.[142] Like the world in the period of Westphalia, it was an anarchic society with minimum rules.

Before the unification of Qin, the states were constantly entering into relations with each other, as enemies or friends, no one could stay out of involving themselves in interstate relations; they were always in an alliance with other states. For example, in a bilateral treaty between the state of Qin and the state of Chu in 579 BC, it was stipulated that 'Chu and Chin [Qin] shall not go to war with each other'.[143] In sum, the stronger states allied with other states and fought with others for more

---

142 Victoria Tin-bor Hui, 2004, pp. 175–205.

143 Richard L. Walker, Multi-state system of ancient China, Reprint. Westport, Connecticut: Greenwood Publishing Group, Incorporated, 1971. p. 83. It has also been noted that states in ancient China agreed that a state should not be invaded in the year in which its ruler has died, or in which there has been an insurrection within the state. A number of culturally informed rules amounting to the laws of war were also practiced. For more details, see William A. P. Martin, The Lore of Cathay: The Intellect of China, Woodburn: University Press of the Pacific, April 15, 2004, pp. 443–448.

territory, treasures, powers, but the weaker states allied and fought with others for self-preservation. During this period, all vassal states engaged in the anarchic interstate intercourse, no one could exist alone.

3. The States had their Exclusive Jurisdiction over their People and their Territories

3.1. The Substantial Bases of Internal Sovereignty

Due to the frequent wars, states had to own a regular military force for either survival or expansion. States monopolized the right to declare war against each other. Competition for the throne required strong national strength; therefore, in this period, 'self-strengthening reforms' were dominant for almost every state. Guan zhong, the prime minister of Qi, successfully enforced multiple political and economic reforms in Qi. He established permanent military force, centralized power and divided the state into different villages, each carrying out a specific trade. He created a uniform tax code and introduced state monopolies controlling salt and iron. Eventually, he pushed Qi into shifting administrative responsibility from hereditary aristocrats to professional bureaucrats, which made the kings' ruling direct to its people.[144] Ensuing emergence of permanent bureaucrat institutions meant internal sovereignty could be exercised by the king, who was represented by those professional institutions.

Later, Qin's reforms surpassed others in terms of comprehensiveness and institutionalization. To develop 'clever strategies', Qin strictly applied the principle of meritocracy and completely eradicated the nobility from the administration. By emphasizing rule of law, Qin published and enforced various laws to ensure reforms were fully carried out. Most notably, Qin established an administrative hierarchy of prefectures, counties, townships, and villages that allowed the Qin court to penetrate deep into the society down to individual households. With this unprecedented capacity for direct rule, Qin could then engage in total mobilization for war. To 'increase economic capability,' Qin granted lands to the entire registered male population to encourage productivity, and then taxed almost all wealth above the subsistence level. To 'increase military strength,' Qin developed an elite professional force and introduced universal military conscription. To motivate its soldiers, Qin further introduced lucrative rewards for victories (including lands, honors, and servants) and severe punishments for evasion, desertion, surrendering to enemies and losses in war (including torture and death). Qin had built its state in a more modern way whilst it sought to dominate in various states. During that period, Qin generally had relatively high levels of administrative capacity, thus Qin could incorporate conquered states as prefectures and counties.[145]

---

144 The Legend of Guan Yang, Records of the Grand Historian (史记・管晏列传).

145 Victoria Tin-bor Hui, 2004, pp. 175–205, p. 198.

3.2. *Exercising Exclusive Jurisdiction within its Territory*

According to historical documents, some customs had emerged in respecting the sovereignty of other states. For example, when troops or officials passed through a territory of another state, no matter how small or weak that state was, the permission from the other state must be received.[146] For instance, in the Spring-and-Autumn period, despite Yu being small and weak, Jin as a hegemon at that moment had to get consent from Yu for their troop's passing Yu's territory to attack the Fu state.[147]

However, the weak states would take a risk by dare denying the passing demand of powerful states. In 595 BC, Huayuan, a minister of Song, said to Chu's envoy Seng Zhou, "passing our territory without permission was an insult for us because it treated Song as Chu's county. Treating Song as Chu's county is the same as subjugated state. Killing Chu's envoy, Chu will attack Song, and Song will be destroyed. Whatever Song does, Song will perish." Song killed the envoy to defend its independence.[148]

When the state of Jin tried to interfere in Zheng's internal affairs after the death of a Zheng minister, Zichan from Zheng argued that if Zheng indulged Jin in determining the successor of the deceased minister of Zheng, Zheng would then have lost its sovereignty to Jin. He convinced Jin not to interfere in Zheng's internal politics.[149]

Qingfu, a brother of a duke of Lu (Lu Zhuanggong) killed two dukes of Lu. Then he ran to Lü, which was a smaller state near Lu, Lu xigong as the duke of Lu required Lü to extradite Qingfu and Lü agreed and returned him.

From these practices, it is clear that the custom that the state had jurisdiction over its territory was exclusive and independence had formed and been followed by various states.

4. Meetings and Treaties were Frequently Used in Interstates Relations

States frequently engaged in communications with each other. They promoted cross-border trade and cultural activities, and forged political and military leagues. For example, both the 'Spring and Autumn Annals' and 'Zuozhuan' recorded how the 12 states formed alliances in 562 B.C.

4.1. *Covenant Meeting*

In the period of Spring-and-Autumn, great states employed their allies to contend for hegemony and sought dominance as the position of Lord of the Covenants as was the standard for calling themselves a hegemon. A covenant meeting with participating states could determine the public recognition of the status of a hegemon.

146 'Zuo Zhuan', Cheng Gong 8th year.
147 'Zuo Zhuan', Xi Gong 5th year.
148 Ibid, Xuan Gong 14th year.
149 Ibid, Zao Gong 19th year.

In the 'Spring and Autumn Annals' and 'Zou zhuan' alone there are 246 instances of covenant meetings. After Duke Huan of Qi presided at a covenant in Juan, Qi began to be a hegemon. At the peak of Qi's hegemony, there were 39 covenant meetings, of which the duke personally took part in 21. Thanks to the covenant meeting at Jiantu and Zhequan, Duke Wen of Jin was termed as a hegemonic lord.[150] However, Qin could not be a hegemon because it was not able to call together the states and preside over a covenant meeting even though Qin was rich and strong at that time.[151] From those practices, one may conclude that there was a meeting system among a group of states and the meeting system could decide who was a hegemon. Hegemons might regularly hold meetings for members of its group. Indeed, such a covenant meeting system may be considered as an early form of international meeting which began to appear in the forging process of international organizations in Europe in the 19th century.

4.2. The Vertical Alliance and the Horizontal Link

With the lack of restriction on sovereignty, the phenomena that the bigger fish swallowed smaller ones prevailed during that era. A self-interest driving pattern dominated the intercourse between states in the same way as it would two thousand years later. In the Spring-and-Autumn era, hegemons either annexed small states or made alliances with small or middle sized states by signing treaties. Most of time, middle or small sized states generally obeyed treaties. Sometime, states also breached treaties because of driving self-interest and preservation. The Stratagems of the Warring States records the formation of many alliances, which were designed to help weaker states against a stronger state and for some states to gain hegemony as well. The members of alliances should all support each other through military assistance when one member was attacked by a third state. They exchanged hostages among themselves as a guarantee that each state would fulfill its pledges. The covenants were normally written in a very concrete and practical way to be enforced clearly.

The Six states alliance initiated by Suqin was a perfect example of a treaty. Suqin declared:

> "in my humble opinion there is no better plan for the king than to unite the six states of Han, Wei, Qi, Yan, Chu, and Zhao in a vertical alliance[152] to oppose Qin. Give an order to the generals off all under heaven to meet together above the Huan shui River, exchange hostages, and make a covenant in the blood of a white horse."[153]

---

150 Note on Zou's commentary 5 Duke Xi year 29.

151 Records of the Historian 5 Qin.

152 Vertical alliance means 'uniting the weak vertically against the one strong state'. On the other hand, horizontal link was designed to unite one strong state and one weak state together against weak states in order to destroy the vertical alliance. It was referred to as 'serving one strong state and attacking many weak one'.

153 Stratagems 3 (Zhao 2), p. 1.

The oath will read: "If Qin attacks Chu, Qi and Wei will each send armed troops to assist Chu; Han will cut off [Qin's] supply lines; Zhao will ford the Yellow River and the Zhang; and Yan will defend to the north of Mount Heng ... If Qin attacks Han or Wei, then Chu will cut it off from the rear; Qi will send armed troops to assist Chu; Zhao will ford the Yellow River and the Zhang; and Yan will defend Yunzhong ... If Qin attacks Qi, then Chu will cut it off from the rear; Han will defend Cheng Guo; Wei will block Wu Dao; Zhao will ford the Yellow River and the Zhang as far as Bo Pass and Yan will send armed troops to assist Qi ..."[154]

In order to counter the vertical alliance, Qin set the lianheng (horizontal link), which consisted of the strong state 'Qin' and another weak state. The strategy was so-called divide-and-conquer strategy. It was based on one idea, that the six member states' interests were different and they would have difficulties cooperating because the 'six states cannot be united is as obvious as a flock of chickens cannot sit still in the same direction on the same perch.'[155]

Although there was some initial success in the Vertical Alliance, the defeats were not decisive enough to block Qin's rise to domination and mutual suspicions between allied states led to the breakdown of the alliances. Qin repeatedly exploited the lianheng strategy to defeat the states one by one.

The Horizontal Link and the Vertical Alliance were established for certain purposes through the formation of treaties by states. They could be considered an immature form of international organizations.

5. Theories concerning Interstate Relations

The following era was the most chaotic and violent period but also often referred to as 'the period of philosophers', 'the golden age of Chinese philosophy' and 'the period of intellectual creativity'.[156] In the era of Spring-Autumn and Warring States (also called Pre-Qin), following the decline of the Western Zhou feudal system and the destruction of the previous harmony and balanced order between the king's family and the various states, those states sought to develop and resolve the new relationships among them in order to protect their own safety and pursue the highest goal-unification of the Tianxia. Therefore, this complex political configuration created the space for thinkers to provide strategies, rules, ideas, theories of how to rule a state, how to make a state strong, how to deal with other states, etc. Many thinkers wrote books and advanced theories trying to sell their ideas on those questions to the rulers. Moreover, they played major roles in promoting their advice for becoming either a humane ruler or a hegemon. Thoughts flourished more at that

154 Ibid.
155 Ibid, Qin 1, p. 3.
156 Fung Yu-lan, A History of Chinese Philosophy, vol. 1: The period of the philosophers, p. 7; Liang Qichao, History of Chinese Political Thought during the early Tsin [sic] Period, trans. L. T. Chen, London: Routledge, 2001, p. 28; Hsiao Kung-chuan, A History of Chinese political thought, vol. 1, p. 28.

time than ever before. This period is the so-called Hundred Schools of Thought period. The writings of half a dozen of the major schools survived. Some of them have had profound effect on the past and even present China and Asia. Here it introduces three great thinkers' major ideas regarding internal governance and interstate relations.

5.1. Xunzi's Theory of International Relations between States

Xunzi (ca 313 BC-238 BC) was a famous Confucian thinker from the Warring State Period. His thought was close to the Legalists, and two of his disciples, Hanfei and Lisi, were prominent Legalist scholars and politicians. Xunzi's writing had a big impact on Chinese history and a profound influence on Chinese politics and culture. In fact, his writing largely concerned three themes: Humane Governance, Humane Authority and Hegemony, which serve to the nature of state. In the Xunzi theory, being a sage king (wang) means to lead the world; being a hegemon (ba) means to dominate the world, and being a tyrant (qiang) means to be stronger than other states. These three words can be used as norms to refer to states or their leaders. Xunzi discusses the characters of the state, the type of ruler, and the nature of policy as three aspects of the same issue, which is more or less like today's definition of sovereignty.

He discusses how to implement a stable international order from the viewpoint of the policy of a powerful state. The degree of stability of international order is determined by the nature of the world's major powers. He concludes that if the world's major power is ruled by sage kings or hegemons, then international order is stable; but if by tyrants, then it is unstable. He also thinks that the international order can be either stable or unstable when the world is ruled by hegemons because it enjoys a stable relationship with its allies while there is instability in relation with other countries outside the alliances.

He considers the state as a most important instrument of the ruler for his governance over the society under heaven. In his view, the ruler determines the fate of the world. If the ruler finds a way to govern the world, then there is great peace and great glory, and the source of all that is praise worthy. If he does not learn how to do it, then there is great danger, which might mean that it would be better not to have the state than to have it.[157] He says, one who honors the sages may attain humane authority, one who honors the worthy may attain hegemony, one who respects the worthy will survive, whereas one who slights the worthy will perish.[158] He continues to say: "Humane authority wins over the people; hegemony wins over allies; tyranny wins over territory".[159] This implied that kings compete for talented people, hegemons compete for neighboring allies, and the rulers of great powers compete for territory.

157 Xunzi 11 humane authority and Hegemony.
158 Ibid., 24, the Prince.
159 Ibid., 9 Humane Governance.

In Xunzi's writings, the term state indicates a political unit and a tool of the ruler as well. Such an idea is consistent with the theory that states have internal sovereignty to rule within the territories and international sovereignty to be respected in the international community. He also maintains that states entail not only powers, rights, but also responsibility.[160] The domestic and international policy of a hegemonic state must serve as its principle responsibility in its strategies. Domestically it should not cheat the people and externally it should not cheat its allies.[161] Secondly, he insists that political strength plays a role as the basis for economic and military strength and that economic or military might are meaningless without the foundation of political strength. Political strength is the basis for the growth of hard power. He writes that the one who is a sage king enriches the people; the one who is a hegemon enriches the officials; a state that will survive enriches the great ministers; a dying state enriches its coffers and fills its storeroom.[162] He also believes that the political principle of foreign policy is the basis for guaranteeing state security. "If one wants to deal with norms between small and large, strong and weak states to uphold them prudently, then rites and customs must be especially diplomatic, the jade disks should be especially bright, and the diplomatic gifts particularly rich, the spokespersons sent should be gentlemen who write elegantly and speak wisely. If they keep the people's interests at heart, who will be angry with them? If they are so, then the furious will not attack. One who seeks his reputation is not so. One who seeks profit is not so. One who acts out of anger is not so. The state will be at peace, as if built on a rock, and it will last long like the stars."[163]

That is the spirit of mutual respect. If a state gently treats others with respect, the others will return it with equal esteem. Actually, this is a reciprocal principle of modern international law and international relations. It is exactly embodied in modern China's five principles of peaceful-coexistence.

He also writes: "If you serve them with wealth and treasure, then wealth and treasure will run out and your relations with them will still not be normalized. If agreements are sealed and alliances confirmed by oath, then though the agreements be fixed yet they will not last a day. If you concede your land to bribe them, then after it is conceded they will be avaricious for yet more. The more you pander to them, the more they will advance on you until you have used up your resources and the state has been given over and then there is nothing left .... Thus the intelligent prince does not do so. He must restore rites so as to unify his court, correct law so as to unify his officials, be even in governing so as to unify his people, and then customs will be unified in court, the various affair will be unified under the officials, the mass of ordinary people will be unified along with him. If you do so, then those

160 Yan Xuetong, Ancient Chinese Thoughts, Modern Chinese Power (translated by Edmund Ryden), New Jersey: Princeton University Press, 2011, p. 53.
161 Xunzi 11 Humane Authority and Hegemony.
162 Ibid., 9 Humane Governance.
163 Ibid., 10, Enriching the state.

close by will compete for affection and those far away will want to draw near. The whole country will be of one mind. The three armies will join their strength together. Your reputation will be such as to overawe them and your authority strong enough to goad them. They will come and bow down to you and accept your direction. No strong or violent state will not send ambassadors to you, like in the fight between Wu Huo [a giant] and Jiao Yao [a dwarf]."[164]

In Xunzi's thoughts, the governance of people, which today is called internal sovereignty, is fundamental for an interstate relationship. When the rulers treat their people well in resources, then their people will return the benefit so that the state will be strong and rich.[165] Thus, other states will have a good relationship with them and not invade them. If states exercise internal sovereignty in a proper manner, they will be capable of exercising external sovereignty and then achieve peaceful and good relations with other states, including strong powers. Conceding territory and paying a huge amount of protection money would not stop powerful states from capturing that state. This analysis actually happened in the 19th century when China became a semi-colony of Western countries after conceding masses of territory and paying an unbelievable amount of compensation. His idea on interstate relations could be explained that humane governance makes a harmonious world, whereas, tyranny makes a dangerous world. He also maintains: "One who uses virtue to annex others will attain humane authority; one who uses might to annex others will become weak; one who use riches to annex others will become poor. From of old until now it has always been the same." We may conclude that the thoughts of Xunzi from more than 2200 years ago have some similarities to the sovereignty principle of modern international law, for example, mutual respect among states is important; internal governance is the fundamental base of external capability; power is not just about rights but also responsibility; humane authority is the proper way to develop healthy relations with other states, otherwise, hegemony or tyranny threatens other states. However, in terms of his highest goal, which is unifying the world, and his supporting states' compliance with conditions, his idea concerning state and international relations has obvious limitations.

5.2. Mencius' Theory

Mencius (372–289 BC) was a great pre-Qin Confucian. He was recognized as the most influential Confucian after Confucius on the ground that he raised Confucianism into the Second Stage. Mencius maintains that humane authority is the best form of power in the world. He says, "if you exercise humane government, then all within the four seas would lift their heads and gaze on you and seek to have you as their prince."[166] Thus, it implies that humane authority can naturally gain political

---

164 Ibid., 10, Enriching the state.
165 Ibid., 9 Humane Governance, 10, Enriching the state.
166 Mencius, 3 Duke Wen of Teng B 5.

legitimacy without using military force because "Heaven does not speak, it simply shows itself by deeds and actions."[167] Mencius suggests that rulers should implement benevolent governance for both domestic and foreign affairs. He recommends promoting a policy of light taxation, no excessive absorption of social resource, and so guaranteeing the basic living requirements of the common people. Once the ordinary people's basic livelihood is ensured, then education must be introduced since the educated people are fundamental for a harmonious society. He stresses that five areas (which are affection between parents and children, justice between rulers and ministers, distinct roles of husbands and wives, sequential order between older and younger siblings, and trustworthiness among friends) are crucial.[168] If those five areas are performed well, society will naturally be harmonious and ordered. He emphasizes that domestic governance is the base of foreign policy. He opposes the common practice of states employing hegemonic strategies to go to war, annexing land and increasing their population. He sees wars as unjust deeds which obtain Tianxia by killing innocent people. He supports benevolence and justice as the main principles to conduct interstates' practice.[169] For Mencius the pursuit of political morality is called 'justice' and the pursuit of military and economic power is called 'profit'. If the ruler speaks of profit, proposes the hegemonic way, and implements hegemonic government, although some countries may be called hegemonic, most will descend into political chaos and a diminution of state power. Moreover, even the successful hegemony will be unable to hold onto their status for long. Their state power will decrease and they will lose their hegemonic status. Only if the ruler speaks of justice, proposed the king way, and implements benevolent government, then will the result be that political power will rise and ultimately one will become the king of Tianxia.[170]

Clearly, Mencius was a thinker of idealistic morality and was used to convert political issues into moral ones. His political views did not become the most important political strategic option of any state during his lifetime. However, his political philosophy with its moral idealism was revived during the ruling of the Wu emperor of the Han dynasty. Today, in the course of China's peaceful rise, Mencius' philosophy seemingly provides China a moral ideal means to prevent some states from misreading its rise as a serious threat to the stability of the international system. Mencius's international political philosophy may be summed up as "the benevolent has not enemies."[171] Interestingly, China's declaration of "never hegemon" and "peaceful development" can be connected with Mencius' opposition to hegemony, part of his benevolence. The greatest lesson the current Chinese government can learn from him is that China's development should be a process not only of increasing its power

---

167 Ibid., 5 Wan Zhang A5.
168 Ibid., 3 Duke Wen of Teng A 4.
169 Ibid., 6, Gaozi B 8.
170 Xu jin, The Two Poles of Confucianism, in: Ancient Chinese Thought, Modern Chinese Power (eds. Daniel A. Bell and Sun Zhe), Princeton: Princeton University Press, 2011, p. 174.
171 Mencius 1, king Hui of Liang A5.

but also of building a harmonious society with a view of securing a sound domestic environment and serving people's wellbeing. Certainly, Mencius' idea could not be completely followed by the Chinese government. Now the Chinese economy has been booming, as Mencius suggested, the Chinese government should be all the more concerned about what kind of social development and political ideals should be achieved, and try to raise a humane state and the kind of state which will win people's admiration and respect.[172]

5.3. *Han Fei*

Han Fei (280–233 BC) is one of the most influential legalists and was a student of Xunzi. Even though he was framed and forced to commit suicide, Han Fei's writings survived him and he had significant influence long after his death.

He contends that it is a waste of time for a ruler to try to make his subjects good and a ruler only needs to restrain them from doing evil since as humans we are by nature unalterably self-interested. He also argues that human behavior is determined by economic conditions rather than morality. He objects to ruling by virtue and believes that only law can offer order. In order to strictly perform law, administrative control must be removed from the feudal nobles and put into the hands of a professional bureaucracy. He believes that the autocratic system and absolute power of monarchy can lead a state to being strong and well off. He maintains that authority demands unquestioning obedience which can be achieved through harsh law by sovereign and capable bureaucrats. In interstate relations, he considers military power as being of prime importance, and military activities as essential to the survival and expansion of the political sector. He wrote:

> "Humaneness may make one shed tears and be reluctant to apply penalties, but law makes it clear that such penalties must be applied. The ancient kings allowed law to be supreme and did not give in to their tearful longings. Hence it is obvious that humaneness cannot be used to achieve order in the state."[173]

> "The best rewards are those that are generous and predictable, so that the people may profit by them. The best penalties are those that are severe and inescapable, so that the people will fear them. The best laws are those that are uniform and inflexible, so that the people can understand them."[174]

> "Therefore, in the state of an enlightened ruler there are no books written on bamboo slips; law supplies the only instruction. There are no sermons on the former kings; the officials serve as the only teachers. There are no fierce feuds of private swordsmen; cutting off the heads of the enemy is the only deed of valor. Hence, when the people of such a state make a speech, they say nothing that is in contradiction to the law;

172 Xu jin, 2011, p. 180.
173 Han Feizi, Charpter 49, "The five vermin".
174 Ibid.

when they act, it is in some way that will bring useful results; and when they do brave deeds, they do them in the army. Therefore, in times of peace the state is rich, and in times of trouble its armies are strong."[175]

His theory was fully enforced in the Qin state where the absolute authority of the king was established through law and bureaucratic system. The thoughts of Han Fei cultivated Qin into a strong state with a strong military force and eventually helped Qin create the Chinese Empire. After the Han dynasty replaced Qin, Han adopted the Qin innovation of a professional bureaucracy to run the empire even though Confucianism was indoctrinated as the national thoughts. Some even argue that various dynasties after Qin advocated Confucianism in public but ran China in actual Legalism (外儒内法).[176] Thus, Legalism continued to play a core role in the Chinese political system even after its demise as a school of thought. Even today, one might observe that some of its tenets are flourishing in modern China and foreign states as well.[177]

The era of Warring States demonstrates the anarchic world of the states where hegemony prevailed. The relations between hierarchy of internal autonomy and the anarchy of interstate relations in this period actually resemble the relations between supremacy of internal sovereignty and the anarchy of modern international community. The history that hegemons dominated with minimum limitation on the power of states is also similar to the circumstances in Westphalia era where western powers maximized their interests through their military advantage because of the lack of restriction on sovereignty.[178] Certainly, in the Warring states era, there were fewer customs and covenants imposing duties on states that were only motivated to follow those rules by self-interest or coercion by a super power. However, the unification of Qin ended the era of Warring States in which sovereignty had the best chance to emerge in China. Even though there was some evidence to show a kind of internal sovereignty and external sovereignty appearing in this era, the Tianxia theory later restrained such rules or concept from developing, after all, the creation of a single unified state (Zhongguo)by Qin completely quashed this opportunity.

Therefore, we can consider this particular period of Spring-Autumn and Warring States as a historic era in anarchic interstate society, where the stronger gobbles up the weaker. There were a few international customs, including respecting others internal jurisdiction, obeying treaties, not killing the ambassador. However, because there was nothing to prohibit wars and the strong states all aimed to achieve unification of the Tianxia (Zhongguo), states often attacked foreign states for territory and people. Lack of a lasting authority allows various states to be independent from

175 Ibid.

176 Yu Jiang, Confucian orthodoxy and the legally constituted authority in Chinese History (道统与法统在中国制度史中的体现), Beijing Culture Review, 2011, Vol. 4, pp. 86–91.

177 Cheng Hongyi, 2002, pp. 83–108.

178 Victoria Tin-bor Hui, 2004, p. 176.

other states. They actually exercised their sovereignty over their people within a certain territory, and entered into interstate relations for expansion or survival. They fought bitterly among themselves to scramble for territories from weaker neighbors and from one another. The prevalence of mutual aggression simultaneously weakened the balance-of-power mechanism and facilitated Qin's opportunistic expansion. As states could rarely do well in two-front wars, the phenomenon of mutual aggression offered Qin many opportunities to seize territory with minimal efforts.[179] Unlike the European Westphalia era which finally gave birth to a number of newly independent states with the concept of sovereignty, the Qin defeated all other states becoming the winner after hundreds of years of competitions. The emergence of sovereignty in that period had no chance to grow because of the final unification.

Certainly, the relationship between those states was not exactly like the contemporary international relationship. Some small states had to be affiliated with powerful states and had no real independent sovereignty. It did not mean that the sovereignty in the period did not exist. Actually, after two thousand years the sovereignty states formed in Europe, affiliated states stayed with sovereignty states or hegemonic states banded together. Therefore, the fact that affiliated states coexisted with hegemonic states shows that sovereignty in the modern sense had already taken shape in Spring-and-Autumn and the Warring States period in China. It indicates instead that some small states' sovereignty could not gain the respect of powerful states, a phenomenon which happens all the time. However, it cannot be said that the type of sovereignty in that era is the same as the one today. It is reasonable to conclude that this type of sovereignty assembles to an embryo of sovereignty in the period before or after Westphalia treaties.

Section 3. The Traditional Chinese Foreign Relations System

Even though the sprout of sovereignty in the interstate relations had emerged in the Spring-and Autumn period, it did not grow until the anarchic international community was replaced by the unified Imperial of Qin. It was definitely strangled by the tributary system which preached superiority of Chinese imperialism. Generally speaking, China has been predominant on the Asiatic mainland due to her vast area, immense manpower, and high civilization for thousands of years. Chinese Emperors' assertion as the son of heaven had been accepted by some neighboring princes beginning from the third century B.C. under the unique system, so-called tributary system. In return, they also received some noble titles and lavish gifts from the emperor, trade opportunities with the Chinese, and on certain occasions, his protection in the event of internal and external difficulties. Such a tributary system essentially attempted to achieve the pacification or control of the periphery usually regarded as essential to prevent attacks on Zhongguo. The system was usually established between China

179 Victoria Tin-bor Hui, 2004, p. 176.

and the neighboring countries or tribes which normally formed a security threat against Zhongguo. In some cases, for the areas not posing a significant security threat to Zhongguo, the intention was to sustain the political legitimacy and authority of the Chinese order or perhaps to deter potential adversaries.[180] Essentially, the purpose of the tributary system was to maintain the appearance of peace between China and their neighbor states under the base of unequal relations in terms of the Tianxia view which was designed for legitimizing the ruling of Chinese emperors. The presumption of harmony was most easily maintained through a thin and distant official relationship by the tributary system.[181] In other words, the tributary system was practically a defense system for Zhongguo to maintain peace with peripheral states. It differed from modern imperialism or colonialism in that China merely claimed suzerainty over these states without the intention of exploiting their economic or other resources or intervening internal affairs.

1. The Origin of Tributary System

"The sages employed the standard rule (Dao) to protect the Central States (Zhongguo) and enfeoffed the frontiers to restrain the barbarians, in order to make it clear that they [Chinese and barbarians] should not participate together."[182] However, this system failed with the fall of the Zhou dynasty. The Chinese originally developed a structure of foreign relations, partly as a defense mechanism in the Han dynasty (202 BC–220 AD), which is widely accepted as a starting-point for the tributary system. By the time of the Han dynasty, the nomad tribes in the north often raided Chinese territory. They attacked not because they wanted to claim territory or were bellicose but simply because they needed Chinese products for survival. Meanwhile, most of them were pastoral nomads, who had nomadic warriors with superior war-fighting capability and high mobility. They needed grain, medicine, craft or manufactured articles, textiles and other commodities. When China attempted to limit trade, its northern neighbors attacked Chinese border settlements to obtain by force goods they could not secure peacefully. Trade or raid seemed to be the only options in their relations with China. They raided, then just fled to the northern steppe-lands where Chinese troops normally could not pursue their enemies. China found itself in a difficult position to counter these attacks. The tributary system emerged with the roots of a defensive polity, aiming for prevention of attack by foreigners, not at active domination over them – a tendency that would be strengthened by the threat of nomadic mounted archers on the steppes. From the

180 Zhang Feng, Rethinking the 'Tribute System': Broadening the Conceptual Horizon of Historical East Asian Politics, Chinese Journal of International Politics, Vol. 2, 2009, p. 561.

181 Brantly Womack, Asymmetry and China's Tributary System, in: The Chinese Journal of International Politics, Vol. 5, 2012, p. 44.

182 Ch'en Liang, Long-chuan wen-chi (龙川文集), Beijing: the Commercial Press, 1936, 4.5b–6b.

time of this system set up, 'conciliation and blood ties'[183] was a policy used with strong nomadic tribes or countries.

Ban Gu elaborated on how to govern the frontier, when conciliatory policies or policies of loose-rein were applied: "It is not possible to till the lands of barbarians (Xiongnu), neither will barbarians subject themselves to your rule; so we should keep them outside not inside, to alienate them so as not to be close with them; we cannot administrate over the barbarians, and the edicts, decrees and our calendar cannot be applied to the barbarians; if the barbarian invades, we shall defend ourselves and punish them; if they leave away, we shall be prepared and defensive. If the barbarians desire to pay tribute to China and follow the customary rituals, their tribute shall be received properly, and we shall give to them in return. We shall appease and bind them for the long time, and never lose our propriety. This is the customary way that has prevailed since ancient times, and the accepted way of handling the barbarian peoples."[184]

This narration implies that the tributary system is basically a way of dealing with these potentially powerful and dangerous adversaries. The logic behind the tributary system is that Zhongguo intended to have a peaceful relation with strong neighbors whilst not endangering the emperor's governance as a son of heaven. Therefore, the tributary system must satisfy the peace with neighbors and conform to the Tianxia idea which emphasized superiority of the Son of Heaven. Evidently, in the early time, the tributary system is a defense stratagem to secure the periphery and maintain domestic order.

2. The Connected Concepts: Tributary System, Tianxia View, Wufu System

The tributary system is tightly linked with the *Tianxia* worldview and *Wufu* system. *Wufu* was a means to enforce *Tianxia*, and as such is often confused with the tributary system. It is necessary to clarify these three concepts for the purpose of understanding the tributary system.

As it is above mentioned, the *Tianxia* view was initiated by the Western Zhou dynasty thousands of years ago, and it has remained as the fundamental theory of other later dynasties and developed afterwards. *Tianxia* literally means "all under heaven", an extendedly-defined world. It is well established that the absolute authority of China's emperors was legitimatized under the *Tianxia* theory. This theory asserted that the ruler's power flowed from an impersonal deity (*Tian*) with the emperor being accountable to a supreme moral force that guides humanity. The core aspect of this is that the universe is dominated by an impersonal but omnipotent

183 That means that China sent royal princesses to marry the rulers of nomadic tribes and states and large gifts of fine Chinese goods, in return for their promises not to raid the frontiers.

184 Hanshu (Chronicles of the Han Dynasty), Scroll 94, Xiongnu zhuan.

Heaven, regarded as an abstract force, which people simply had to obey. However, throughout its proliferation, Chinese elites certainly knew that the *Tianxia* as "all under heaven" was an abstract concept. It was clearly impossible for China to rule the whole world.[185] As was analyzed in previous sections, *Tianxia* existed in different contexts, the *Tianxia* in the narrow sense, namely, *Zhongguo* (the Chinese name of China, meaning central kingdom), where the central dynasties could directly control directly, the *Tianxia* in the sense of culture, geography and public security, and the *Tianxia* in the broadest sense, equating *Tianxia* to all under heaven, including the world which ancient Chinese could not reach or was out of its limit. All three norms of *Tianxia* functioned for various purposes. The *Tianxia* in the broadest sense generally functioned to ideologically legitimize the Emperor's rule. The other two concepts of *Tianxia* also thrived in parallel throughout Chinese history, albeit in different spheres. The *Zhongguo* concept of *Tianxia* could be applied to both the domestic sphere, and in a larger sense to represent China's foreign policy orientation with respect to the international community. While the three different meanings of *Tianxia* were frequently found in ancient literature, these three concepts were often intertwined with the consequence that opinions regarding China's political status are rather contrasting.[186] Indeed, while the realistic geography of Chinese state authority was limited by the territorial extent of their effective control, the imaginary geography ("all under heaven") remained in theory to legitimize imperial rule.[187]

The basic framework of the Western Zhou *Tianxia* consisted of "five zones" (五服, or *Wufu*) which was, at the same time, both centrifugal and centripetal. China was the center in this world, which was viewed concentrically outward to other places and people. The Sinocentric sphere of influence in theory radiated worldwide, with greater influence exerted from its core and lesser influence on its periphery, with the effect of ensuring a harmonious world.[188] Theoretically, Chinese international relations were conducted as an extension of Chinese domestic policy under the theory of *Tianxia*. Western Zhou constantly promoted a steady cultural assimilation based on efficacy of the Chinese way of life and government. In political-geographic terms, the five zones referred to the five levels of the Zhou's mapping of their own world.[13] However, as an imaginary cosmography, the five zones comprised a worldwide order.[14] Ideally, at the center was the king's capital and region of direct control, which was surrounded by a circle of provinces ruled by princes or governors appointed by the king, and these again were surrounded by more or less independent "tributary polities." The five zone system was reflected by the extension of a civilized influence radiating from the center and the degrees of closeness to it oriented toward civilization in a centripetal manner. Clearly, the five zones constituted a complex system of relationships, a catalogue of people, and a structure of hierarchy deployed

185 Ge Zhaoguang, 2011, pp. 28–29.
186 Zhang Qixian, 2009, pp. 169–256.
187 Wang Mingming, 2012, p. 343.
188 Fairbank, 1973; Smith, 1996.

to know, to describe, and to manage the *Tianxia*. They marked out the cultural boundaries between the son of heaven and the lords of principalities, and between the principalities and the semi-cultured others. For the purpose of expanding and maintaining its supremacy, the kings made use of ritual and art, enfeoffing, warfare, writing, and family connections. The five zones system was understood as the actual tributary system to convert "barbarians" through ritual and culture. Such a system was praised as an ideal system to rule aliens by later Confucians for a long time even after it disappeared.[189]

Furthermore, *Wufu* was dismantled in the East Zhou dynasty (Ca. 770–221 BCE) and never revived afterwards. *Shi huangdi* of Qin later deployed a series of unifying measures to convert the whole of the Chinese world into a centralized state. The feudalism of Zhou was replaced, as a consequence, with an administrative hierarchy of prefectures, counties, townships, and villages. The unification of writing, transportation, money, and ways of measurement was forcefully and centrally imposed on the prefectures, counties and villages. The Qin also constructed the Great Wall on the foundations of ancient fortifications. Extending from Gansu to the Eastern part of Liaoning, the wall was intended to protect the empire against incursions from the Xiong Nu in the north.[190] The *Wufu* system thereafter disappeared from the real world, but exists in the Confucian ideal world because Confucianism idealized Zhou as the perfect social order.[191]

As discussed before, the *Wufu* system was repeatedly extolled in Confucian works and worshiped by Confucians as the perfect political system to rule the world. Unsurprisingly, it was confused with the tributary system throughout Chinese history by a number of sinologists who emphasized China as bonded by ritual or culture and conceived with the conversion of barbarians as the primary objective of the tributary system.[192] Some argue the tributary system worked as an expansion of Chinese imperialism by spreading Chinese civilization to the outside world. These perspectives incorrectly equate the tributary system with the *Wufu* system. The tributary system at a later point in history, under a different context, certainly did suit the purpose of pacifying neighboring states that frequently invaded China. The tributary system, rather than the *Wufu* system, dealt with international relations instead of China's domestic sphere. In China's foreign affairs, the ideological superiority of emperors was often symbolic and sometimes even absent. Trading, marriage,

---

189 Zhao Tingyang, Tianxia System: Introduction of the World System Philosophy ("天下体系"：世界制度哲学导论), Nanjing: Jiangsu Education Press, 2005, pp. 6–58.

190 The spheres of control of Zhou were restricted to the lower Yellow River valley, See Gu, Jiegang and Shi Nianhai. (1938) 1999. Zhongguo Jiangyu Yange Shi (A history of the changes of Chinese territories). Beijing: Shangwu Yinshuguan, p. 1.

191 Confucius said, "Zhou rite developed from Xia and Ying, it is complete and excellent, I obey it", See Ba Yi (八佾) in Lunyu (论语), Liji zhongyong (礼记中庸).

192 J. K. Fairbank, 1968, p. 2; Mark Mancall, The Persistence of Tradition in Chinese Foreign Policy, in: Annals of the American Academy of Political and Social Science 349 (1963), pp. 17–19. Martin Jacques, 2009.

military forces, cultural influence, and not just some empty rites maintained the tributary system. In other words, countries' or rulers' interests and strengths are the decisive variables, rather than the supremacy of any one sovereign.

3. Flexibility of the Tributary System

The two primary objectives of Chinese foreign policy were securing the periphery and consolidation of internal control. Both expansionism and isolationism applied throughout Chinese history. The tributary system embraced the two tendencies. Most major regimes of the imperial era were designed to placate or neutralize nearby potential threats. On the one hand, it could be exploited to extend their influence or direct control beyond the established periphery during strong Chinese imperial regimes; on the other hand, it could be a strategy to prevent foreign adversaries from invading Zhongguo in either strong Chinese imperial regimes or weak Chinese imperial regimes. As a strategy of security, the tributary system had to be flexible to apply in various situations. Certainly, various dynasties tackled foreign relations using different means. There was not an identical pattern to apply to all situations.

3.1. The Symbolic Superiority of China in the Tributary Relations

In the early Tang dynasty, as the Chinese military force grew strong, the Chinese emperor was in favor of a policy of expansionism. The Tang was praised as the peak of traditional Chinese diplomacy by controlling dangerous foreigners and demanding their ceremonial submission, using Chinese resources of wealth, bureaucratic coherence, and psychological astuteness, being attentive to detail but flexible and realistic in handling diplomatic etiquette.[193] The rulers of Tang requested acknowledgment of their superiority from all peripheral foreign states having any relation with China, including the formidable steppe empires of the Turks and the Uighurs, who formed a serious threat to the Chinese empire. They enforced their demands with astute divide-and-rule politics toward the Turks, expeditions and garrisons in the Western Regions, and the last resort of conciliation policy with the Turks and the Uighurs. Tang taizong, who is considered as the greatest emperor of China, launched a series of campaigns against the Eastern Tujue, the oasis states of the Tarim Basin, and the Western Tujue. During his reign, China annexed Karakhoja in 640, Karasahr in 644 and Kucha in 648. At the same time, the king of Tibet Songtsän Gampo sent the first ever ambassador who brought an ultimatum demanding a marriage alliance in 634 CE, but the demand was refused since Tibet did have the attention of Tang Taizhong. However, successful military attacks which Tibet launched against Tang affiliates in 637 and 638 forced Tang taizong to take Tibet seriously. Finally, Tang taizong accepted the request of Songsän Gampo, sending the Princess Wencheng to marry Songsän Gampo. Evidently, a peace treaty based on a marriage alliance was the template to

193 John E. Wills, Embassies and illusions. Dutch and Portuguese envoys to K'ang-hsi, 1666–1687, Cambridge,: Cambrige University Press, 1984, pp. 10–11.

maintain a tributary relation with a strong neighbor. The defensive character of the tributary system is obvious.

The early Ming dynasty institutionalized the tribute system even though it was impossible to put a varying pattern into a single model for the bureaucratic management of all foreign relations. The system was changed into a tendency to focus on ceremonial appearances rather than on the realities of power. Normally, foreign rulers were required to send tribute ambassadors periodically to the Chinese emperor if they wanted to deal with the Chinese. The Chinese government bore all the expenses of the ambassadors during their stay in China. Its officials taught the envoys the proper etiquette for their appearance at royal court and then they had an audience with the emperor. During the audience, they had to perform the rituals, including ketao, a symbolic recognition of their inferiority and their status as an envoy of a subordinate state. During the ritual, they offered their tribute to the emperor who bestowed valuable gifts upon them and their ruler in return. After the audience ended, they had a few days to trade with Chinese merchants. The Chinese theoretically controlled this tribute system. They determined the frequency with which ambassadors could be admitted into China, the number of men in each embassy, and the length of its stay in China. Court officials supervised the foreigners' trade with merchants, regulating the prices and profits and ensuring that neither side exploited the other. Chinese officials used the ceremonial side of foreign relations to assert formal suzerainty while avoiding the commitment of actual domination of areas outside of China.[194]

As discussed above, the tribute system often functioned as a defense system to a peripheral state with formidable military ability. It is very interesting that some foreigners with powerful military forces accepted an inferior status. Generally, they received from tributes something much more valuable than a symbolic ritual. For the Chinese emperor, the tribute system was also useful to enhance the ideological legitimacy of the Emperor's rule of *Tianxia* and peace on the frontiers. It embodied internal Chinese politics with a preference and a tendency to use Chinese wealth to buy peace from the barbarians.

It can be said that the tribute system was a compromise reached to cater different needs from the Chinese and foreigners. The purpose of the tribute system primarily concerned security and maintenance of the governance of the dynasty. It did not aim to gain financially from tribute and trade relations. Profit was not the motivation. In fact, the tributes paid from the foreigners to the court and the goods they offered to Chinese merchants were not essential to China, which was self-sufficient. Conversely, the Chinese products for the foreigners were vital and valuable. When foreigners were obstreperous, the Chinese court intentionally suspended trade and tributes as a response to the foreigners.[195]

194 Morris Rossabi, Introduction, in 'China among Equals' (ed. by Morris Rossabi), London: University of California Press, 1983, pp. 2–5.

195 Morris Rossabi, 1983, pp. 2–5.

3.2. *A Pattern of Equal Relationship*

After all, the Chinese tribute system could not always follow the same pattern from the Han dynasty to the late Qing dynasty. When China was powerful enough to make foreign states accept its inferior status, the model with China's symbolic superiority might prevail. However, when foreign states had equal or more power and sophisticated civilizations, such a model was replaced by flexible and realistic policies. Particularly, states also with self-centered conceptions of world order, such as Japan, Liao (916 AD–1125 AD), and Vietnam; they could not accept superiority from China when they had become more sophisticated in political, administrative, and technical skills mainly through close association with China, learning to employ the Chinese view, participating in a protectorate government, and using the same rhetoric and methods of 'tributary' control.[196] The views of Chinese superiority were dysfunctional in dealing with the realities of inter-states politics.[197] If the superiority of China was impossible to maintain, the Chinese government could be rather pragmatic by giving up superiority to ensure its survival.

In the early period of tributary system, the superiority of the Chinese empire was not often embodied in diplomatic activities. In early Han dynasty, because Xiongnu occasionally attacked Chinese boundaries located by the Great Wall, central dynasties could do nothing but accept the demands of the Xiongnu. The agreement between the Han dynasty and Xiongnu had four major terms: 1. The Han shall give an amount of silk, alcohol, grain, etc.; 2. The Han must send a princess to marry Chanyu[198]; 3. Xiongnu is equal to the Han; 4. The Great Wall is the official boundary between Han and Xiongnu.[199] From the content, it is clearly an agreement for peace in which the Chinese Imperial had no nominal superiority over Xiongnu. However, after 60 BC, the Han took advantage of an internal division of Xiongnu and reversed the position between them, finally forcing the ruler Huhan Xie chanyu to submit to the Han in 53 B.C.[200] Afterwards, the Han's emperor conferred Chanyu with a particular noble title and valuable rewards, Xiongnu sent an envoy and tribute to the central dynasty.[201] Notably, the substantial shift power was decisive for Chinese superiority.

The central dynasty enjoyed symbolic superiority sometimes, but had to accept an equal relationship without any superiority title at other times. When the Song came to power in 960, the emperors controlled less territory than the Tang dynasty. By the late tenth century, the Song emperors had pacified the Chinese periphery countries but still had to contend with Khitans (Qidan) who established the Liao

196 J. Wills, 1984, p. 12.
197 Ibid.
198 Changyu is a title for the king of Xiongnu.
199 Wang Qing, Two Models of Traditional China's Foreign Relations – Analysis from the Perspectives of Interests Cognition and Systematic Structure, Dissertation Submitted to Tsinghua University.
200 Hanshu (Chronicles of the Han Dynasty), Scroll 94, Xiongnu zhuan.
201 Ibid.

Dynasties (916–1125). In 1005 the Song negotiated with Khitans the Treaty of Chanyuan (澶渊之盟) in which the Song promised payment of 200,000 bolts of silk and 100,000 taels of silver in return for peace along the frontiers. The two emperors would address one another as equals and maintain friendly relations. Indeed, this treaty successfully avoided any further major wars between the two. Moreover, by signing the treaty, the Liao forced the Song to recognize Liao as peers with a supposed fraternal relationship. For the first time in Chinese history there were two Sons of Heaven, recognized by each other.[202] Chen Liang, a famous Confucian in South Song dynasty, was furious about it and wrote, "we yearly use gold and silk to buy them off, and as long as there is no war, we consider it a blessing. Moreover, giving recognition to a state of affairs where there are two emperors is something that the Han and Tang never did."[203]

The weak Chinese dynasties usually chose to pay a huge amount of treasures to threatening nomads for their quiescent or non-aggression. Such weak regimes would generally avoid the use of force for keeping peace with periphery countries of whatever type.[204] In these circumstances, Chinese dynasties had no superiority in a symbolic or substantial sense over strong adversaries. As a matter of fact, equal foreign relations prevailed in a weak Chinese regime even though it was definitely contradictory with the ideology of Tianxia view. In some cases, the relationship was even in reverse. In 1138, the founder of the Southern Sung dynasty, Gaozong, accepted the status of a "vassal" himself to Jin state.[205] His successor improved the status to that of a nephew and addressed the Jin emperor as uncle. The Sung emperors sent their powerful northern neighboring states annual presents of a large amount and value, as tribute in reverse.

3.3. *Non-application of the Tributary System for States further from China*

Ming Taizu, the first emperor of the Ming dynasty, definitely saw the use of the tribute system as something China could benefit from, not as a tool to promote Chinese culture. In his 'Ancestral Injunction', he advises his successors as follows: "The overseas foreign countries like Annan [Vietnam], Champa, Korea, Siam, Liuqiu [Ryukyu Islands], [the countries of the] Western Oceans [South India] and Eastern Oceans [Japan], and the various small countries of the southern man [barbarians] are separated from us by mountains and seas and far away in a corner. Their lands

202 Tao Jing-shen, Two Sons of Heaven: Studies in Sung-Liao Relations, University of Arizona Press, 1988, p. 192.
203 Ch'en Liang, Long-chuan wen-ji (龙川文集), Wuchang: Wuchang guan shu chu, 1912.
204 Michael D. Swaine, Ashley J. Tellis, 2000, p. 55.
205 Also known as the Jurchen dynasty (1115–1234 A.D.), it overthrew the Khitan Liao dynasty and conquered much of northern China but was defeated by the Mongol Empire.

would not produce enough for us to maintain them; their peoples would not usefully serve us if incorporated [into the empire]. If they were so unrealistic as to disturb our borders, it would be unfortunate for them. Abuse China's wealth and power and covet the military glories of the moment to send armies into the field without reason and cause a loss of life ... If they gave us no trouble and we moved troops to fight them unnecessarily, it would be unfortunate for us. I am concerned that future generations might abuse China's wealth and power and covet the military glories of the moment to send armies into the field without reason and cause a loss of life. May they be sharply reminded that this is forbidden."

This text shows a sober realization of the limits of China's capacity. When China is in a position of power it has the advantage of respect from countries in the periphery, the overall objective of its foreign policy would be defensive in nature, or it will at least be very cautious about causing aggression.[206] The key to a peaceful frontier did not lie in dominating neighbors or expedition, but rather in managing a mutually acceptable relationship.[207] For those remote and non-threatening states, it was wise to not take military actions to pursue conquests or when enforcing of the tributary system. It was viewed that the face of the dynastic court was not the most important but that peace on the frontier was the key.

For example, the Chinese regime did not try to consider Japan, India, and Russia as tributaries. The Treaty of Nerchinsk of 1689 was the first treaty between Russia and China, which established the equal relationship between the two states without any implication of a tributary system. The Qing dynasty did not show any intention of trying to contain Russia through the tributary system as a part of Tianxia. It realized Russia was a totally different empire with equal status.

Thus, the tributary system had to be relied on when China's power was strong enough to compel the neighbor states to subordination but also couple with how much China would benefit from it. It was critical that the rulers of China understood how to exploit its power and advantages on many aspects from exchanging with the peace on the frontiers to subordinating others. Chinese foreign policies had to be flexible and realistic to be prepared for various circumstances. In fact, the rhetoric of the tributary system had a rather wide spectrum in reality, in a number of cases, it was just an illusion.

The different models applied to Chinese foreign relations demonstrates that flexibility was dominant in their foreign policy which emphasized the use of different policies for different 'barbarians'. The lesser powerful foreign states could still be treated as tributaries, but the more powerful of China's neighbors, such as the Khitans, had to be dealt with as equals. Despite the rhetoric of superiority being comforting, many Chinese officials were realistic and flexible. They were able to

206 Zhou Fangyin, Equilibrium Analysis of the Tributary System. The Chinese Journal of International Politics, Vol. 4, 2011, p. 151.

207 Brantly Womack, 2012, p. 42.

make fairly reasonable appraisals of foreign affairs even if they believed in China's cultural and even military superiority.[208]

4. The Tributary System's Collapse

The Qing replaced the Ming and followed the tendency of formal Chinese dynasties to assert their sovereignty over the Inner Asia border and to assimilate their people into semi-autonomous units of Chinese military and administrative hierarchies. It did so with far greater vigor and attention to the substance of power and control than the Ming had. They also inherited, in the Ming archives and printed regulations, the singular idea that all aspects of foreign relations could be and should be managed by the regulated ceremonies. Moreover, the Qing rulers, as aliens, could hardly swallow the whole Sinocentric ideology of the tribute system. In the late Qing dynasty, they clearly lost the realism and flexible essence of the tribute system as a tool for the management of foreign relations but instead persistently pursued the ceremonies of the tribute system.[209] Qing was unable to accept the reality of the great powers intruding into its world, especially those that did not accept or even tolerate Chinese practices in foreign relations. Isolationism, ceremonialism, and a focus on symbol rather than on realities outside China were also characteristics of the institutions and regulations of the tribute system in the Qing dynasty. The Manzu who ruled China in the Qing dynasty, as non-Hanzu, cautiously copied the tributary model recorded in the Ming archives and printed regulations. They worried that their actions could expose their non-Hanzu (or barbarian) identity and tried very hard to perform the tributary system exactly as the Ming dynasty had. Eventually they lost the realistic and pragmatic approach which is fundamental to the running of the tribute system as a tool for the management of foreign relations. When the Chinese faced the Western powers, the most powerful adversaries China had ever met, the Qing dynasty tried to enforce the rite of Ketou no matter how unrealistic it was. Clearly, the Qing's rigid approach to the tributary system was far from the desired flexibility.

The Qing court's ignorance of the existence of the real external world was exposed by the Chinese defeat in the Opium War in 1843. The China-centered approach in the relations between China and Western powers completely collapsed while confronting much more powerful adversaries than they had previously. Finally, after a number of failures during the wars against Western powers and their refusal of Ketou, China realized that the stiff approach could not work out. Accepting and exploiting the sovereignty-oriental approach would benefit itself much more. The comprehensive system of the tributary system eventually ceased as China started to seek independent sovereignty to rescue China from being colonized by Western powers. They finally abandoned the isolationism and Tianxia view whilst it struggled for its equality in the Western-center order.

---

208 Morris Rossabi, 1983, pp. 7–8.
209 J. Wills, 1984, p. 24.

5. The two distinct schools of the Tributary system

Western scholars place much value on documents that might be compromised as they were written by authors who were required to flatter emperors and who were biased by their loyalty to particular Chinese dynasties and the idea of China's superiority. This is in comparison to less well-studied documents from other countries involved in the tributary system. A number of scholars represented by Fairbank and Teng view the tribute system as "the medium for Chinese international relations and diplomacy" and "the mechanism by which barbarous non-Chinese regions were given their place in the all-embracing Chinese political, and therefore ethical, scheme of things."[210] Fairbank and Teng continue, "The tributary relations were not organized by a division of territories among sovereigns of equal status but rather by the subordination of all local authorities to the central and awe-inspiring power of the emperor."[211] The hierarchy of the relations was predicated on Chinese superiority and suzerainty *vis-a-vis* foreign states' inferiority. Respect for this hierarchy and acknowledgment of Chinese superiority were absolute requirements for opening relations with China. Thus they conclude, "Outside countries, if they were to have contact with China at all, were expected and when possible obliged to do so as tributaries." They claim that China's scheme for ordering her relations with the external world clearly reflected her vision of internal order.[212] Those opinions stress that tributary relations were ubiquitous and important to an extent that they deny all other aspects of foreign relations. It maintains that Chinese rulers constructed hierarchic relations with foreign countries for reasons of prestige and political defense, and foreign rulers paid tribute to China because they needed trade and profit. Ideology constituted a main component of their foreign relationships; Chinese rulers relied chiefly on the Confucian culture and the rule of virtue to win foreigners over. Foreign rulers, meanwhile, acceded to Chinese demands and observed prescribed rituals, presumably because of their desire to trade.[213] They considered China more a civilization rather than a state seeking to use the tributary system to promote its own culture.[214]

As an opponent of Fairbank and Teng, Wang has stressed that diplomatic practice did not always conform to Confucian theory and legalists played an essential role in the Chinese political system and foreign relations. Generally, emperors and ministers acted on the basis of survival and gain. He mocked that "it was the historians who decided which policy or attitude towards foreign countries was the

210 J. K. Fairbank and S. Y. Teng, 1941, pp. 137, 139.
211 J. K. Fairbank, 1968, p. 9.
212 Ibid, p. 4.
213 Zhang Feng, 2009, pp. 545–574.
214 "China, by the standards of every other country, is a most peculiar animal", Martin Jacques, 2009, p. 196.

correct one."[215] He concludes that Confucian theory was "developed from pragmatic observations and had little directly to do with the philosophic conception of China as the center of the world."[216] The fusion of moral and physical power, the ability to triumph over invasion and catastrophe, determined China's relations with other countries. The theory of the historians became a myth that was severely shaken by the conquest of the Mongols and other neighbors, and finally undermined by the Western incursion.[217]

In agreement with Wang, it can be maintained that the theory of Fairbank and Teng was heavily influenced by Sino-centric perspectives of Confucians, who tend to portray historical East Asian politics from an idealized *Tianxia* view. In Confucianism, "all under heaven" prevailed even in the case when China was not in the position to prevail over foreign relations. They usually laud the perfection of the *Wufu* system established under the Zhou dynasty, though it had long disappeared after the rule of the first Qin emperor. Most historic documents and writing depict how the mission of any foreign envoy entered into the Chinese capital for the purposes of paying tribute to the emperor and how much they admired the Chinese civilization. They emphasized how the virtue of emperors is critical to Chinese governance, from the center outwards to the periphery. The opinion that the tribute model dominated Chinese foreign relation is heavily biased by a dependence on historical documents written with such undertones.

Moreover, scholars that heavily rely on Chinese documents, while obviously taking on a China-centered approach, may not take into account the responses of peripheral states. The disproportionate attention which it pays to the Chinese side of the story over that of other polities severely limits its interpretive power of their standpoint since Chinese bureaucrats definitely exaggerated, if not outright distorted, China's role in foreign relations in order to compliment the superiority of Chinese emperors. Scholarly work of this perspective therefore may fail to think of the tributary system as the outcome of an interactive game, which makes it difficult to consider seriously the strategic interaction among actors, thus greatly oversimplifying the analysis.

Furthermore, the wish of superiority of Chinese culture and the emperor did not inhibit them from treating powerful states as equals.[218] The model which Fairbank claims overlooks a large and important facet of the political dynamics of China's foreign relations and the reality of international relations, because the tributary system was by no means the only medium or institution of interstate relations, much

215 Wang Gung Wu, Historians and Early Foreign Relations, originally published in: The Journal of the Oriental Society of Australia, and then republished in: To Act is to Know: Chinese dilemmas, Singapore: Eastern University Press, 2003, p. 142.

216 Wang Gung Wu, 2003, p. 143.

217 Ibid, p. 127.

218 Chusei Suzuki, China's Relations with Inner Asia, in: The Chinese World Order (ed. by John King Fairbank), Harvard: Harvard University Press, 1968, pp. 180–197.

less "a scheme of things entire."[219] As Wills puts it, "the tribute system was not all of traditional Chinese foreign relations, and may not be the best key to a comprehensive understanding of these relations."[220] The Western literature represented by Fairbank on early Sino–Western relations may have given excessive emphasis to tribute embassies and the related concept of "all under heaven" as well.[221] Benjamin Schwartz, an outstanding student of Fairbank, pointed out that the decisive factor in foreign relations of the Chinese empire was not the superiority of Chinese culture, but a contestation of power. "When the empire was weak, the Chinese perception of the world had little effect on the course of events. The ultimate fact is the fact of power."[222] Fairbank gave too much credit to Chinese culture and Confucianism. He failed to realize the fact that the post-Qin Chinese political system is actually dominated by legalism under the cover of Confucian theory.[223]

Fourthly, China was clearly aware of limits to its expansion, even at the peak of her power. Its foreign policies were not limited to the tributary system. The sobering thoughts left in *Ancestral Injunction* by Ming Taizhu (discussed in para. 2.2.5) is the best example for it. Fairbank did not catch the fact that "ancient China was a real limited state where the infinite 'Tianxia' remained imagination"[224] and the concept of *Tianxia* carried multiple meanings. They confuse the imagining of "Tianxia" with the real state of China and misunderstand the tributary system as the *Wufu* system[225] which was the particular means to enforce the imaginative aspect of *Tianxia.*

Fifthly, the equal relationship between the Chinese empire and the neighboring countries normally prevailed during periods of weak Chinese rule. The Song with Khitans, the early Han with the Xiong Nu, the early Ming with Southeast Asia, definitely witnessed it even though Song and Ming rulers asserted themselves, or

219 Zhang Feng, 2009, pp. 545–574.

220 J. Wills, 1984, p. 4.

221 Ibid.

222 Benjamin Schwartz, The Chinese Perception of World Order, Past and Present, in: Chinese World Order (ed. by Fairbank), Harvard University Press, 1968, p. 278 and p. 288.

223 The various systems created by legalists in the Qin dynasty were succeeded by later dynasties although they identified Confucian as the national theory. No dynasty actually recovered Zhou's "Wufu" system.

224 Ge Zhaoguang, 2011, pp. 28–29.

225 As Zhao Tingyang comments, unlike the tributary system, the Wufu system was the one with hierarchy. See Zhao Tingyang, Tianxia System, Introduction of the World System Philosophy ("天下体系"：世界制度哲学导论), Nanjing: Jiangsu Education Press, 2005; Paul Evans, Historians and Chinese World Order: Fairbank, Wang, and the Matter of 'Indeterminate Relevance'", in China and International Relations: The Chinese View and the Contribution of Wang Gungwu (edited by Zheng Yongnian), Routledge, 2010, pp. 42–57; Wang Zhiqiang, A Review of J. K. Fairbank's On the Tributary System of the Qing Dynasty (西方朝贡制度研究的开拓与奠基之作–费正清《论清代的朝贡制度》评介), Journal of Haian Normal University (Social Sciences), Vol. 25, 2012, pp. 74–78.

at least depicted themselves, as being divinely sanctioned by Heaven to rule China and by extension "all under Heaven." This model existed not only in non-dominant dynasties, but also during the powerful Tang and Han dynasties. In fact, no single, unchanging policy or pattern of foreign relations persisted throughout China's long history and the complex realities of its foreign relations over millennia cannot be explained by a simple generalization of the tributary trading system.[226] Additionally, early dynastic rulers frequently demanded tributary relations for reasons of securing the frontier rather than prestige and legitimacy. Indeed, the tributary system was created as a strategy for maintaining border stability. Imperial China, like every other state, also had to deal with a variety of security problems that would be essential for its survival. Therefore, pragmatism often superseded Sino centrism. China could not be expected to ensure security on the frontier at all times while maintaining its self-assumed superiority without exhibiting flexibility and pragmatism in its foreign policy.[227] The foreign rulers paid tribute to China for multiple purposes beyond trade that ranged from support against internal and external adversaries, legitimacy, economic profit and military protection at one end of the scale to its use as a stepping stone to hegemony on the other. The Chinese rulers did not rely exclusively on Chinese culture or trade to expand influence, but used both "hard power" and "soft power" to obtain consent from other states. Foreign rulers, meanwhile, did not always meekly follow Chinese requirements, and at many times violated the consensus between China and them in pursuit of self-interested objectives.[228] In many cases, the superiority of China was only one side of the illusion, which was untrue for the "tributary" side. In some cases, Chinese imperials were the ones to submit tribute to the more powerful party. Therefore, a number of scholars underestimate the comprehensive scale of the imperial foreign policy; they are unable to grasp the flexibility and pragmatism of the foreign policies of the Chinese empire. They wrongly define the tributary system as a ritual, trading system for superiority of Chinese culture and oversimplify all Chinese international relations into one. Basically, they confuse the tributary system with the *Wufu* system and *Tianxia* theory, and miss the point that the tributary system was characterized by symbolism, particularly, by flexibility and pragmatism.

The tributary system theory interpreted by Teng and Fairbank has been challenged by a number of scholars. Interestingly, despite many criticisms, their ideas remained quite popular and widely cited as the standard understanding of the tributary system.[229] Their descriptions that Asia was in the Chinese-dominated

---

226 Jing-shen Tao, 1988, p. 4.
227 Zhang Feng, 2009, p. 561.
228 Ibid., p. 563.
229 For example, Wikipedia defines the tributary system as the network of trade and foreign relations between China and its tributaries, https://en.wikipedia.org/wiki/Imperial_Chinese_tributary_system.

international system[230] and "China was the superior center where its ruler had duties toward all other rulers as his inferiors"[231] are rather influential in both the political world and the academic field. The popularity of their ideas means that a misunderstood version of Chinese images might unduly affect accurate predictions of China's current trajectory.

6. The Difference between the Tributary System and the Colonial System

Indeed, in Western civilization there is no comparative concept to the tributary system, however, colonialism is often connected with it when western scholars or politicians attempt to explain it. It is a great help for grasping the key of the tributary system to compare the two.

From the title of this system, it is branded with its hierarchy. However, the hierarchy is more concerned with a symbolism than substantive context. Comprehensively, in these kinds of relations, there was hardly any substantial inequality, but relative equal relations in general. Particularly, as discussed above, the Chinese emperor initiated this type of arrangement for the pursuit of security of its frontier and meanwhile kept it theoretically consistent with China's *Tianxia* worldview. This intention provided that China must manage this arrangement to be attractive for neighboring states. It was necessary to make the rewards lucrative enough to attract potential tributary states to join the agreements. Evidently, China gained the nominal superiority, peaceful periphery area, and a number of tributes, while the tributaries gained political support from Chinese emperors and Chinese products which would usually outweigh the tributes. By means of trade, marriage alliance, rewards, etc., China made peace with its neighbors. It pursued peaceful, stable and regular bilateral relations and aimed to maintain a peaceful regional political balance, thus, it was a relatively equal transaction. Particularly in weak periods of Chinese imperial rule, it ordinarily purchased security by adopting a "pay-off" stratagem. Certainly, China did not pursue extorting profits from tributaries, but enforced a Confucian policy of "giving more and getting less" (厚往薄来).

Moreover, the tributary system usually enforced by reaching a consensus between China and the peripheral countries, normally applied to the peripherals who threaten China or might potentially threaten China. Therefore, China had not generally enforced the tributary system forcibly to non-threatening countries or non-peripheral countries. China preferred appeasement and conciliation policies in foreign relations. Meanwhile, the Chinese tributary system functioned as a useful channel to spread

230 David C. Kang, Hierarchy and Balancing in: International Relations, International Security, Vol. 28, Iss. 3, 2003, pp. 165–180.

231 John K. Fairbank, Introduction, in: Denis Twitchett and Fairbank, eds., The Cambridge History of China, Vol. 10: Late Ch'ing, 1800–1911, Part 1, Cambridge: Cambridge University Press, 1978, p. 30.

Chinese culture in a voluntary way. For example, Tang had no intention to initiate a tributary relation with Tibet until it showed its ability to threaten Tang's security. Sulu (苏录) sent envoys to China to submit its tribute in 1727, but the Qing Yongzheng emperor did not agree to have a tributary relation with it. Qing emperor Qianlong also refused the Kazak's (哈萨克) intent to become a tributary of the Qing dynasty. Zhu Yuanzhang, the Ming taizu, banned his successors from launching military expeditions against 15 countries. Interestingly, the system could also replicate itself, as demonstrated by the case of the king of Choson Korea, who acted at once as a tributary polity of the Emperor of Ming China, and as a patron in relation to smaller 'entities', constructing a Korean world order built from expedience, interaction, and Chinese concepts.[232] Korea, Japan and Vietnam, as a tributary for periods of varying duration, were gradually influenced by Chinese civilization although the Chinese imperial did not force them to establish a similar political social system with the Confucian worldview. However, many others countries with a tributary history could still keep their own cultures and languages from Chinese civilization since a tributary entity kept rather independent status from China. For example, Vietnam, Korea, Japan. China had no intention to annex tributary states or otherwise include them into the Chinese empire. Hence, the tributary system is in nature non-aggressive but more relative appeasement. Even the famous, far-ranging Zheng He naval expeditions of the Ming era (from 1405 to 1433) did not employ force against distant peoples or to conquer distant lands.[233] Following the doctrine of virtuous rule of Confucianism, overseas colonialism and material exploitation of the remote barbaric states was something almost unimaginable to the Chinese rulers. Exploiting the people beyond its political jurisdiction was furthermore immoral under Confucian principles.[234]

Furthermore, in relation to the tribute system, China usually stayed out of the internal affairs of vassal states. Colonies was tightly controlled by a colonial power in all internal affairs. After all, the tributary system is a low-key and loose reign regional arrangement, even where the outcome is an expansion of Chinese influence abroad. Certainly, Imperial China had various relations with tributaries. However, Chinese dynasties barely interfered in those countries even in Korea, the Ryukyu (琉球) which had the closest relations with Imperial China. They did not need to consult the Chinese dynasties regarding crucial affairs such as succession. Chinese dynasties conferred the titles of new kings as a recognition of the status quo, but the approval of Chinese emperors did not imply that Chinese dynasties had a substantial role in succession. For example, the king of the Ryukyu kingdom ascended to the throne in 1735, but received the investment of his title from the Qianlong emperor

232 J. Wills, 1984, p. 19.

233 The Zheng He naval expeditions rarely used force in dealing with coastal states with an exception of Ceylon. See Michael D. Swaine, Ashley J. Tellis, 2000, pp. 53–54.

234 Jerry C. Y. Liu, Does Culture Matter? The Logics and Counter-logics of Culture in State Finance, Taxation and Tributary Trade Policies during the Ming Times c. 1370–1600, in: The Icfai Journal of History and Culture, 2008, Vol. 4, pp. 28–60.

in 1756. In the late of 19th century, Japan carried ambitions to annex Korea, which was a tributary of China at that time. Thus, Japan had some diplomatic contact with China. Lord Gongqing, a minister of Qing dynasty, pointed out: "Despite that Korea is a tributary of China, China never bothers with Korean affairs which have been always conducted by Korean. Today Japan wants to have relations with Korea. Korean shall decide it by their-selves."[235]

Additionally, it was a low level arrangement when viewing the tributary relation at an institutional level as well. In this system, the Chinese empire did not establish respective political, economic, security mechanisms beyond a series of rites which could be enforced while tributary envoys met Chinese emperors.

On the other hand, European colonialism enforced their political system, economical system, religion, culture, language, and many other aspects of agency and power upon colonial subjects because the colonies were seen as integral overseas territory of the controlling state. Comparing the tributary system as a defense system for peace seeking, the colonial system is an entirely aggressive arrangement, which is normally a result of military conquest followed by a complete colonializing procedure which generally turns the colonies into an overseas territory. Western powers took advantage of their powerful militaries to conquer and colonialize territories to the best of their ability. It did not matter how far away those lands were or whether they formed a threat to Western powers. Western troops and officials were sent primarily to conquer, then govern and exploit colonies. The occupied colonies were directly under their governance as a part of their territory. Furthermore, colonialism aims to forcibly exploit colonies and to strengthen the home economy at the expense of rivals. The controlling states sent administrative bureaucrat, military forces, and preachers to rule colonies and eliminate native cultures. Even native languages within its territory were often replaced by the language of the controlling states.

Very interestingly, Hong Kong and Macao experienced both systems. They were former colonies ruled by the British and Portuguese. The current "one country, two systems" approach of China allows Hong Kong and Macau to continue to have its own political, legal, economic and financial systems, and even the ability to handle their external relations with foreign countries. The Chinese government stations troops in Hong Kong to safeguard national security, but does not interfere in Hong Kong's internal affairs. Beijing has actually promised Taiwan the ability to continue governing itself with its own military force under this "one country, two systems" policy.[236] These regions have almost exclusive jurisdiction over their lands with only one condition that they must stay within China. Hong Kong and Macao are therefore

---

235 See "Historic Documents Concerning Negotiations between Japan and China in Guang Xu of Qing dynasty" (清光绪朝中日交涉史料), Vol. 1, p. 1; Also see He Fangchuan, On the Order of Huan and Yi (华夷秩序论), in: Journal of Beijing University (Philosophy and Social Science edition), Vol. 6, 1998, pp. 30–44.

236 Deng Xiaoping's Talking, One Country, Two Systems, June 22–23, 1984, available at: http://www.china.org.cn/english/features/dengxiaoping/103372.htm.

exempt from mainland laws, mainland political and economic systems, mainland education system, mandating the use of simplified characters in publishing and Mandarin in public education and most broadcasting. Hong Kong continues to use English common law and Macau continues to use the Portuguese civil law system. The Chinese Supreme Court has no jurisdiction over Hong Kong, and the National People's Congress has no legislative rights in most of the affairs as well. Chinese people and Chinese products cannot enter into Hong Kong's territory without undergoing Hong Kong's own customs procedures. Such a high degree of autonomy makes China's sovereignty over these regions mainly symbolic. It actually shares much more similarities with the tributary system than any other form of historical governance. Undoubtedly, China enjoys much less jurisdiction in Hong Kong and Macau than their formal colonial master states. It is an extreme compromise on China's sovereignty over Hong Kong and Macao.

Conclusion

China's objectives in maintaining a regional order based on the tributary system extended to more than considerations of obtaining legitimacy. It was more often the very practical considerations of maintaining stability in the border regions at minimum cost that were China's major concerns.[237] In the different eras, under different circumstances, the hierarchic system or equal foreign relations played its role in foreign relations of Imperial China. Neither the hierarchic system nor equal foreign relations could always prevail over foreign policies during Imperial China. The equal relations method had existed between the Han dynasty and the Xiongnu, the Tang dynasty and the Tujue, the Song dynasty and the Liao or Jing; meanwhile the hierarchic system, as the favorite foreign system of Imperial China, was applied in the relations with the peripheral countries. Thus, the hierarchic system did not monopolize Chinese peripheral policy because Chinese rulers had to adopt respective strategies for various circumstances. Flexibility and pragmatism were the characteristics of Chinese foreign policies. The tributary theory of Fairbank could not reflect the flexibility and pragmatism of Chinese foreign policies. The flexible foreign policy of Imperial China embodies the multi-facet approach and pragmatism of current Chinese foreign policies. Interestingly, unlike colonialism, the Chinese tributary system was a low-level arrangement which did not aim to exploit the foreign states, neither for economic profit nor for territorial occupation.

237 Fang Tie, 'A Study on the Thoughts of Borderland Administration in Ancient China' (论中国"守中治边"、"守在四夷"传统治边思想), in: Chen Shangsheng, ed., Theory, System and Policy of Traditional Chinese Foreign Relations, Jinan: Shandong daxue chubanshe, 2007, pp. 35–48.

Chapter 3. The Emergence of Modern Sovereignty in the Late Qing Dynasty

Introduction

In the late Qing dynasty, China was confronted with an unprecedented challenge from Western states. China's position in the world and self-image was reversed from leading civilization to a subjugated and torn country. This chapter will analyze the transformation of this period. The first section discusses the history of how the concept of modern sovereignty was imported into China through cannons and guns leading to the crash of the Chinese traditional Tianxia order. The second section focuses on how Western powers imposed gross encroachment on China's sovereignty. Finally, the third section analyzes how China struggled to recover its sovereignty. It stresses that this transformation period has had an unimaginable impact on today's Chinese perceptions on sovereignty, human rights and other related political and social issues. Therefore, the analysis of this period is significant for understanding current China's identity and China's position on sovereignty.

Section 1. Evaporation of 'Chinese Traditional World Order'

1. Isolated Civilization

Before the Western powers in the nineteenth century opened the Chinese boundary with canons and guns, the Chinese grew accustomed to the notion that China was the center of the world surrounded by a host of lesser states that imbibed Chinese culture and paid tribute to China's greatness.[238] Similarly, China's international relations were based on the "tributary system", which had as its objective the maintenance of the harmony of mankind. These hierarchical principles, resembling those of the patriarchal Chinese family, assumed the inferiority of other states and ignored the view that China was but one state among equals. As a result, the idea of international law established by the consent of sovereign states in equal interrelationships could not exist in the context of China's traditional tributary system.[239] The modern concept of sovereignty did not emerge until the Opium War. However, as discussed in the previous chapter, it cannot be denied that a rather

238 Henry Kissinger, On China, New York: The Penguin Press, 2011, p. 10.

239 Suzanne Ogden, Sovereignty and International Law: The Perspective of the People Republic of China, N.Y.U. Journal of International Law and Politics, Vol. 7, Iss. 1, 1974, p. 2.

strong domestic sovereignty had existed in the long Chinese history because of its denial of others' sovereignty.

Moreover, the Chinese civilization had never had to deal with a challenge from civilizations that were able to equal it in scale and sophistication before the 19th century. In the west of China, the Himalayas, the Tibet Plateau, massive deserts of Central Asia separated China from the near eastern cultures of India, Persia, Babylonia and even the Roman Empire. In the east of China, the Pacific Ocean meant it was walled off from conflicts with other states. Japan was the closest one but contact between the two states had been heavily obstructed by the mighty ocean.[240] In Chinese history, the Chinese had expanded from their original base in the Yellow River valley into various stages of appropriation of further territory and most of the time kept a big empire with the same language and culture, which was only occasionally broken into several kingdoms. Before the industrial revolution, Chinese scientific and technological achievements equaled, and frequently outstripped, those of western Europe, India, and Arab counterparts.[241] Furthermore, China was far richer. It produced a greater share of total world GDP than any Western society in 18 of the last 20 centuries. As late as 1820, it produced over 30 percent of world GDP - an amount exceeding the GDP of Western Europe, Eastern Europe, and the United States combined.[242] Consequently, China's secure isolation, self-sufficient economy, the scale of population and territory and unique civilization nurtured a particular Chinese self-perception.[243] A letter from the Emperor of Qing dynasty to the United States said, "[h]aving, with reverence, received the commission from Heaven to rule the universe, we regard both the middle empire [China] and the outside countries as constituting one family, without distinction."[244] At the moment the letter was written, China was in danger of losing its sovereignty to Western powers. Based on such illusions, the emperor ridiculously treated these unprecedented catastrophes as similar to other barbarian invasions that were eventually overcome by China's endurance and superior civilization.[245] While Europe entered into the modern age, the traditional Chinese world order endured well into the modern era, but when later it was confronted with the Western Westphalia modality, it crashed terribly.

---

240 Henry Kissinger, 2011, pp. 12–14.

241 Joseph Needham's encyclopedic multivolume Science and Civilization in China, Cambridge: Cambridge University Press, 1954, p. 136.

242 Angus Maddison, The World Economy: A Millennial Perspective, Paris: Organization for Economic Co-operation and Development, 2006, Appendix B, pp. 261–263.

243 John King Fairbank, 1968, pp. 44–45.

244 Papers Relating to Foreign Affairs Accompanying the Annual Message of the President to the First Session of the Thirty-eighth Congress, vol. 2, Washington, D. C.: U. S. Government Printing Office, 1864, Document No. 33 (Mr. Burlingame to Mr., Seward, Peking, January 29, 1863), pp. 846–848.

245 Even in the case that China was conquered by Mongol and Manzu, Chinese culture assimilated and sinicized the non-Chinese rulers. See Henry Kissinger, On China, New York: The Penguin Press, 2011, p. 11.

2. The Acceptance of Modern Sovereignty

It was analyzed that the emperor in Confucian tradition was in some way similar to that of the sovereign described by Bodin the Emperor ruled by virtue of a mandate from heaven and related to his subjects in the manner of an absolute power. Further, the Emperor had a duty to provide his subjects with physical and spiritual nourishment in return for the subjects' loyalty, duty and obedience.[246] Due to the unitary centralized bureaucratic system and the lack of restraint from religion on Chinese emperors, the emperors' ruling could directly reach the civilians and so his superior authority established. However, the Tianxia view hindered the flowering of the concept of modern sovereignty. The Chinese traditional political conceptions were fundamentally different from the idea of the political nation and that identification with the state which is necessary for the idea of modern sovereignty to properly take root.[247] In other words, before the West forcibly opened the locked gate of China during the Qing dynasty, the Chinese government enjoyed sovereignty within its territory but denied others' sovereignty by claiming its own ruler as that of the world as the son of Heaven. Certainly, this Tianxia view was basically an illusion, and actually from time to time, China had to treat others as equal. Clearly, the Tianxia view was completely ended through Western guns and cannons. When the Western powers brought opium into China, the idea of modern sovereignty came in at the same time. The country's decline began from being the central state to a weak, poor and backward country as it encountered the West after the Opium Wars, the illusion of "all under heaven" crashed into nothing. There was no way for China to possibly continually asserts its centrality in the face of Western powerful gunboats and militia.[248]

The principle of sovereignty associated with the European intrusion into the non-European world was the very means for China to reassert its independence from colonization. In respect to the opium trade, Chinese actually invoked Vattel's Law of Nations translated into Chinese in 1839 to deal with 'the rights of states in regard to contraband' against the English.[249] The Chinese felt humiliated after their concessions to foreigners blaming China's weakness in foreign affairs on the Qing government. The Chinese began to appreciate the concept of sovereignty as well as the international legal rights and obligations of states, when their fear, shame, anger and resentment aroused with a nationalistic movement aiming to save China from destruction. The Chinese realized that the definition of state sovereignty referred to the state's exclusive supremacy over its internal affairs and external affairs, which was exactly what they wanted. Inevitably, they immediately enshrined modern sovereignty as their weapon and became its most staunch defender.

246 Jo-Anne Pemberton, Sovereignty Interpretations, Palgrave Macmillan, 2009, p. 98.
247 Ibid, p. 98.
248 John Fitzgerald, Awakening China Politics, Culture, and Class in the Nationalist Revolution, Stanford: Stanford University Press, 1998, pp. 92–93.
249 Suzaaen Ogden, 1974, p. 5.

Professor Schrecker argues that only when the Chinese understood the implications of the Western concept of sovereignty did they begin to suffer from "a sense of inferiority and even shame at the unusual position of China," which, combined with the activating force of nationalism, produced a positive and active "determination to end that inequality"[250]. In actuality, he was wrong about the causal connection since he reversed the causal relations. It was not until the foreign policy view of the reformers of the late 19th and early 20th centuries gained dominance that the Chinese took up a totally new approach to international relations, based on their new perspective of China's place within the international system as a sovereign state with equal rights before international law. It was also the reformers who, for the first time, 'adopted international law as the fundamental perspective from which to formulate and judge Chinese policy.'[251]

In 1864, Wheaton's Elements of International Law (1836) were the first works concerning international law published in Chinese at the request of the Qing dynasty. According to John E. Schrecker, the increasing frequency of sovereignty appearing in 'diplomatic documents in Qing time' embodies the gradual recognition of sovereignty by the Qing dynasty. Since 1860, Qing officials started to use the word 'sovereignty'. From 1875 to 1894, sovereignty appeared once per 100 pages, from 1895 to 1899, its appearance increased to 2.5 times per 100 pages, from 1900 to 1901 its appearance rose to 8.8 times per 100 pages, from 1902 to 1910, it showed 22 times per 100 pages.[252] This trend certainly demonstrates the process of accepting of sovereignty, meanwhile it also implies a deterioration of the Qing's sovereignty. Chinese representatives participated, from as early as 1878, in international legal symposiums among these being The Hague Peace Conferences of 1899 and 1907.[253] In the time of the early 20th century, China more vigorously asserted its right to sovereignty under international law. The Chinese government cited the principle of *'rebus sic stantibus'*, upholding that the creation of the Republic was a sign of 'change in circumstance'. It thus claimed, that China was no longer the 'old, decrepit empire' which had signed the unequal treaties with Western powers[254] but was fast becoming an effective state and one which had already gained international recognition through its involvement in international legal affairs.

3. Sovereignty and Saving China

In its final long decade of rule (1895–1911), the Qing state, for all its weaknesses vis-à-vis western powers and growing provincial or local governments, was to some

250 J. E. Schrecker, Imperialism and Chinese Nationalism: Germany in Shantung, Harvard University Press, 1971, p. 251.

251 Ibid., p. 47.

252 J. E. Schrecher, 1971, p. 253.

253 W.E.A. Hall, Treaties on International Law (ed. A. P. Higgins), Oxford: Clarendon Press, 1924, p. 49.

254 The further information of unequal treaties is in this charpter section 2.1.

extent still able to exert control over the activities of oppositional elites and other social groups trying to claim the state away from the dynasty. After 1901, Qing initiated many reforms, including abolishing the millennium-old civil service exams in 1905, in order to reassert its grip on state power and reassert the socioeconomic structure. Despite these attempts, Qing was still incapable of defending China from the allied imperialist powers and solving its essential corruption problem. Due to the impotence and corruption of the Qing dynasty, the majority of Chinese demanded a new structure of state to restore China's sovereignty. Indeed, the impression of 'wangguo' (lost the country) was rearticulated away from its traditional Chinese meaning of a change of dynasty to a modern meaning of colonization. The thought was tightly linked with the struggle of the Chinese to save the country (jiuguo) which motivated many Chinese intellectuals to begin to abandon the dynastic structure of state as the inevitable form and guarantor of China and to struggle to reconstitute themselves as national polities against western powers and Japan. Formal structures of nation-state sovereignty and enlightenment ideologies surfaced with the emergence of the Chinese nationalist movement. Accompanied with the upheaval of Chinese ideologies, the concept of revolution was named 'guomin' (nationals) replacing the old one 'cengmin' (subordinates of an emperor) by 1903. Guomin came to encompass a fundamental restructuring of the premise of political organization, which centrally included the reassessment of the relationship between the state and the people into a new concept of nation-state.[255] During that time, saving China was the most vital task. Such a priority meant that the interpretation of sovereignty during that period stressed the equality and independence of sovereignty. It also embodied a political revolution emphasizing the need to build a strong state-centre but overlooking people's sovereignty. It suppressed the enlightenment in the late Qing, which is still carrying on in today's China. Moreover, from Qin dynasty to the late Qing dynasty, the centralized governments from various dynasties had generally been absolute in strength within China for about two thousand years. In Europe, people's sovereignty is incarnated as a national state, thus modern nationalism was born with democracy and liberality at the same time. However, the modern China did not establish a nation-state under the doctrine of people sovereignty because the process of development of a nation-state was rather earlier than democratic politics. Namely, the first thing was to establish a sovereignty state, then the secondary task was to integrate the people's sovereignty into state construction. When the nation is taken to be synonymous with the state it is hence formed without enlightenment; the failure of the state to secure its own inevitability as a national embodiment invariably leads to its alleged repression of the historical other, here 'enlightenment'.[256] It made the relationship between the two extremely intricate. Consequently, it directly caused China to exceedingly focus on state strength. Inevitably, China interprets

255 Rebecca E. Karl, Staging the World: Chinese Nationalism at the Turn Twentieth Century, Durham: Duke University Press, 2002, pp. 14–15.

256 Ibid., p. 24.

sovereignty as a supreme power which is prior to human rights. It also can explain why China always emphasizes that human rights can be enjoyed only if sovereignty is guaranteed.

Section 2. The Encroachments on China's Sovereignty

1. Aggression and Imposition of Unequal Treaties

The Nanjing treaty which ended the opium war[257] in 1842 was the start of a long nightmare, followed by a large number of shameful treaties, so-called "unequal treaties", and marked the turning point for China to enter into a semi-colonial period. Hong Kong Island was yielded to the British Queen as a crown colony; five cities[258] including Shanghai had to be open for the British to trade with anyone they wished and to send consular officers. The indemnity of 21 million dollars was to be paid which included six million silver dollars for the opium lost that had been confiscated by Lin Zexu in 1839. Following the general terms of the Treaty of Nanjing, America, France, Belgium, Sweden and Norway all gained the same privileges as Britain by signing a series of unequal treaties with the Chinese government.

The Western powers were unsatisfied with the Treaty of Nanjing, they launched the Second Opium War against China. British and French occupied Guangzhou and forced the Qing government to sign the Tianjin Treaty in 1858 after their canon boats had bombarded the Dagu Forts. The French army invaded Beijing and burned down and plundered the Qing emperors' old summer palace (Yuan Ming Yuan) while the court had fled to Jehol (Rehe 熱河) in Manchuria. These military actions resulted in the Beijing Treaty (in 1860) which allowed British and French subjects free trade, travel and mission in all of China. The treaty also ceded the Kowloon Peninsula (Jiulong bandao) to Great Britain.

---

257 The first war between China and western power directly caused by banning the trade of opium. The Qing dynasty prohibited importation and domestic cultivation of opium in 1800 through its regulations mainly because of its destructive effect on the health of the people so that foreign traders had to smuggle opium. In 1836, English dealers carried Indian opium to Canton on a large scale through smuggling. It was extremely profitable so that British military officers supported the opium trade backed by force. The Chinese objection was not so strong until Lin Zexu, the Imperial High Commissioner, arrived in Canton. He ordered foreign merchants to give up all opium to the local government, and then destroyed the surrendered opium. However, the illicit traffic of the opium did not stop. English dealers did not obey Chinese rules at all. More conflicts happened. The Britain under Captain Elliott attacked some small harbors, occupied islands and threatened the port of Tianjin with canon boats. It was the beginning of the so-called Opium War. Then a British fleet, commanded by Henry Pottinger, proceeded until Nanjing, when the Chinese government finally gave in and signed the Nanjing Treaty in 1842.

258 Including Canton (Shamian Island from 1859 until 1943), Amoy (Xiamen until 1930), Foochowfoo (Fuzhou), Ningpo (Ningbo) and Shanghai (until 1943).

At the end of the 19th century, the foreign powers started to claim more colonial territories in China. In the same year of 1898, Great Britain demanded the New Territories (Xinjie), north of Hong Kong (Xianggang) as a leasehold territory for 99 years. France obtained Guangzhouwan (Zhanjiang) as a colony, Germany occupied the Jiaozhou Bay and founded Qingdao as a colony in Shandong province, Britain again could gain Weihaiwei in Shandong, and Russia claimed the Liaodong Peninsula with the harbor of Port Arthur (Lüshun and Dalian, from 1905 on Japanese territory). The deepest impact on Chinese sovereignty was the war with Japan in 1894–95 (Jiawu Zhanzheng). The Treaty of Shimonoseki (Maguan) was another treaty of shame and disgrace for the Chinese. China had no further suzerainty over the Korean kingdom, and it had to pay for a huge amount of the war damages. Japanese subjects were exempt from Chinese law and tax inside of China. The most important claim by Japan was the concession of Taiwan, the Penghu Islands, and the eastern portion of the bay of Liaodong Peninsula.

International law generally sees a treaty as being formed when contracting parties on a reciprocal basis agree with the intention for the execution of certain rights and obligations between contracting parties under a guiding of principle of equality. Contrary to standard practice, many of the treaties with harsh terms that caused huge damages to China in that period were forcibly concluded by military acts and threats, unilaterally beneficial to the foreign powers at the expense of China.[259] Through the use of force, western powers compelled China to renounce her traditional positions on former dependencies, cede and lease strategic parts of her territory, and assign specific areas of Chinese ports and cities as foreign concessions and settlement. Distinctly, the consent of China for those treaties was obtained through force and coercion contrary to its real willing and therefore should arguably be void. The external sovereignty of China was seriously impaired. Consequently, the internal sovereignty of China was highly damaged by those unequal treaties which deprived the Chinese government of ruling certain territories and internal affairs.

2. Other Encroachments of Territorial Sovereignty of China

Western powers raked profits from China in multiple forms. Besides the means mentioned above, a sphere of influence was utilized for the further territorial intention and more privileges over Chinese territory. Britain, Russia, and Japan penetrated deeply into Tibet, Xinjiang (Sinkiang), Mongolia, and Manchuria (the old name of northeast of China) and Germany and France simultaneously claimed different regions of China as well. The Chinese empire was on the verge of being dismantled.[260]

---

259 William L. Tung, China and the Foreign Powers, New York: Oceana Publications, 1970, p. 6.

260 William L. Tung, 1970, p. 8.

2.1. Foreign Concessions and Settlements

Concessions and settlements both meant 'areas set apart for foreign residence' or 'foreign residential areas'. Concessions designated foreign residential areas leased indefinitely by the Chinese government to certain foreign powers, which sub-leased divided lots to foreign residents. Normally, foreign concessions and settlements were urban areas in the ports opened to foreigners, assigned by Chinese authorities as residential quarters for foreigners. In many concessions, including those in Guangdong (Canton), Hankou, Jiujiang (Kiukiang), and Tianjin (Tientsin), the consular of the concession-holding countries was usually the officials in charge of their administration, assisted by certain agencies represented by foreign taxpayers. Japan took over Jiaodong as a leased land from Germany by force during World War I and Russia transferred Port Arthur and Dairen to Japan in 1905 even without previous consent from China. Both states absolutely violated China's sovereignty over the leased territories. The International and French Settlements in Shanghai did not regulate leasing the land, the deeds of which were directly issued by the Chinese local authorities to interested foreigners, who organized themselves into municipal councils for administrative and legislative purpose.

Despite that the sovereignty of China over the leased territories being recognized in all the treaties concerning the leases, China's authority in such areas was denied in many aspects, including the passage of Chinese police and armed forces and the right of plenary jurisdiction over Chinese nationals residing therein. Administratively, the municipal councils or organs in the concessions and settlements were controlled by foreigners, even though the residents were predominantly Chinese.[261] Those foreign leaseholds actually became 'imperium in imperio' in China. Whilst the lessees took over the local administration and jurisdiction, Chinese authority therein was heavily compromised and mainly symbolic.

2.2. Foreign Powers' Spheres of Influence in China

The concept of sphere of influence indicates that a state has exclusive or predominant control over a foreign area or territory. Such an exclusive control may be or may be not recognized as a matter of fact, or it may refer to a legal agreement by which another state or states pledge themselves to refrain from interference within the sphere of influence. That is a serious derogation for territory sovereignty. Britain, France, Germany, Russia, the USA and Japan negotiated with each other and the Qing officials to construct their own spheres of influence within China for their further interests. The growth of spheres of influence within Chinese territory created a patchwork of foreign enclaves functioning similar to a colony.

261 Ibid., p. 70.

2.2.1. Manchuria under the Domination of Russia and Japan

Since the late nineteenth century, Russia and Japan had conflicts in Manchuria. Both managed to divide as big as possible portion of Chinese territory for themselves. Manchuria was sought-after to be their spheres of influence. In 1896, Russia exploited the opportunity of the Sino-Japanese war to persuade China into consenting to let Russia to extend the Trans-Siberia Railway to Manchuria, where it was known as the Chinese Eastern Railway. However, Russia actually controlled the railway, which was nominally under the co-supervision of China and Russia stipulated in the terms of the related treaty. In 1898, Russia gained the lease of Port Arthur and Dairen using duress. Japan went further than Russian. It obtained exclusive rights of railway construction and mining interests, as well as freedom of immigration, travel and residence for Japanese subjects in Manchuria and Eastern Inner Mongolia as well as leaseholds in Shandong province according to the Twenty-one Demands presented to China by Japan in 1915. Since Russia and Japan both intended to expand their influence in Manchuria, they were mutually supportive of their respective spheres of influence (Northern part divided under Russian control and Southern part under Japan's control) according to the convention signed by the two states on July 3, 1916 when they needed each other against China, but eventually Japan invaded Machuria and declared Inner Manchuria an "independent state" in 1931.

2.2.2. British in Tibet

Britain launched the expedition to Lhasa in order to counter Russia's perceived ambitions in the east in 1904. It forced the local government to sign a convention, which compelled Tibet to establish trade relations with it, to raze all forts and fortifications, to remove all armaments between the frontier of British India and Gyantze and Lhasa of Tibet, and to pay a reimbursement for the British expedition. The convention forbade Tibet, without consent of the British, to undertake almost anything with another foreign powers, including cession, sale, lease, mortgage, or any other form of occupation of any portion of Tibetan territory, any interference in Tibetan affairs; admittance of foreign representatives; concessions for railways, roads, telegraphs, mining or other rights; and pledge or assignment of Tibetan revenues. Moreover, British troops would occupy Chumbi for a period of three years until the completion of payment of indemnity and effective opening of trade markets as specified in the Convention. The Convention effectively converted Tibet into a British protectorate or at least under its spheres of influence. The Amban, who represented Qing authority in the Buddhist theocracy of Tibet, later publicly repudiated the treaty, while Britain announced that it still accepted Chinese claims of authority over Tibet. Further negotiations between Britain and the Chinese government reached a conclusion of the Anglo-Chinese Convention of 1906.[262] It reduced the reimbursement by two-thirds

262 The declaration of Viceroy and Governor-General of India, which was appended to the ratified Convention of September 7, 1904 (MacMurry, Treaties, I, p. 581).

and considerably eased the terms in other ways. In return for British consensus "not to annex Tibetan territory or to interfere in the administration of Tibet", China undertook "not to permit any other foreign state to interfere with the territory or internal administration of Tibet". China would allow Britain to lay down telegraph lines between the trade marts in Tibet and India. China also reluctantly agreed to the Sino-British Convention of 1890 and Regulations of 1893 remaining in force in exchange of revising the 1904 Treaty.

On August 31, 1907, in St. Petersburg, Russia, the Anglo-Russian Convention of 1907 was signed. Both sides agreed to keep the "status quo" and not to take Tibet without negotiation with the Chinese government.[263] However, Britain was not satisfied with the 1904 Treaty. On April 27, 1914, an agreement was drafted but the Chinese representative refused to sign this agreement on the ground of erroneous inclusion of certain districts in the attempt to separate Outer Tibet and Inner Tibet, and for other reasons. Nonetheless, Great Britain went ahead and signed this treaty with Tibet on July 3, 1914 even though Britain recognized Tibet as a part of Chinese territory or under the suzerainty of China in the same convention. It is highly illogical that a treaty recognizing China's sovereignty and suzerainty over a territory without the consent of the Chinese government would be binding under international law.[264] Consequently, the McMahon Line provided by the 1914 convention forms a controversial boundary line which remains unsolved so far.

2.2.3. Russia in Xinjiang

Russia invaded Xinjiang (Sinkiang) in 1871 and occupied Ili by using the excuse that local disturbances had endangered the trade route to Kuldja. When the Chinese General Zuo Zongtang (also known as General Tso) reconquered the region between 1875 and 1877, China sought a peaceful settlement with Russia and ended up with the 1881 treaty of St. Petersburg, under which China recovered most of the territory of Ili, but had to pay a huge amount of compensation, nine million metallic roubles. After the Ili incident, Russia intermittently succeeded in dominating the area through her conspiracy with provincial authorities or rebel leaders whenever circumstances allowed during the period of the late Qing dynasty and the Republic of China.

3. Foreign Supervision of China's Customs, Post, and Salt Administration

British, French and American consular acted collectively as an authority to take charge of collection of customs duties in Shanghai in 1854 due to the inability of Chinese officials to collect them during the Taiping Rebellion. However, the British envoy expanded this practice with China in the agreement containing Rules of Trade on

263 Convention Between Great Britain and Russia Relating to Tibet (1907). http://www.tibetjustice.org/materials/treaties/treaties12.html.
264 William L. Tung, 1970, p. 143.

November 8, 1858. Rule X of the treaty stipulated that "the high officer appointed by the Chinese Government to superintend foreign trade will … The said high officer will be at liberty, of his own choice, and independently of the suggestion or nomination of any British authority, to select any British subject he may see fit to aid him in the administration of the Customs revenue; in the prevention of smuggling; in the definition of port boundaries; or in discharging the duties of harbor-master; also in the distribution of lights, buoys, beacons, and the like, the maintenance of which shall be provided for out of the tonnage dues." The system was extended to include domestic customs administration, postal administration, harbor and waterway management, weather reporting, and anti-smuggling operations. Despite the rhetoric of Rule X of the agreement, which said the choice of Chief of Customs was up to the Chinese government, the candidate of Inspector of General Customs was never to be under the control of the Chinese government, before 1949. It should be also noted that, until 1907, no Chinese had ever been appointed even to a full assistantship in the Maritime Customs.[265] Due to the multitude of British trade with China and privileges foreign powers and citizens had, China and Britain agreed in 1898 that the Inspector- General of Maritime Custom should in the future, as in the past, be of British nationality."[266]

The restriction on China's sovereignty on customs was not only compelling the Chinese to appoint foreigners as the head of Chinese Customs, but also on the right to set its own tariff. In fact, foreign powers had imposed on China a low-rate uniform tariff for almost a century. China did not restore its tariff autonomy until 1933 when the Republic of China published the new national regulation.

The Chinese postal service was operated by the Maritime Customs, which had been under the lead of a British from 1896 to 1911. The French Chargé d'Affaires, M.Dubail, addressed the Tsungli Yamen on April 9, 1898 and requested the Chinese government to consider French government recommendations on the candidate of the Chief of Chinese Postal Service. As a result, a Frenchman became co-director general of the Chinese postal administration. The appointment of foreigners as overseers of the Chinese salt administration originated with the Reorganization Gold Loan Agreement between China and the Five-Power Consortium on April 26, 1913. The Chinese government agreed to take immediate steps for the reorganization, with the assistance of foreigners, of the system of collecting the Chinese salt tax. The central Salt Administration under the Ministry of Finance would be headed by a Chinese Chief Inspectorate of Salt Revenues and a Foreign Associate Chief Inspectorate of Salt Revenue until February 1942. In each branch office, there would be the same

---

265 William L. Tung, 1970, p. 109.

266 The Tsungli Yamen's Note of February 13, 1898, in reply to the British Note of February 3, 1898 (MacMurray, Treaties, I, pp. 104–105). Horatio N. Lay was appointed as Inspector General of Customs in 1861 with broad powers bestowed by Rule X. In 1863, Sir Robert Hart replaced Lay and served until his death in 1911. Hart was succeeded by Sir Francis Aglen and then by his own nephew, Sir Frederick Maze. In January 1950 the last foreign Inspector-General, American Lester Knox Little resigned.

arrangement as in the central Administration.[267] It was actually not the nationality of the appointees but the forced conditions that had long irritated because somehow such a manner violated China's sovereignty.

4. Extraterritorial Jurisdiction in China

Extraterritorial jurisdiction is essentially the legal ability of a government to exercise authority beyond its normal boundaries. Generally speaking, the core of sovereignty is the territorial sovereignty on which a state has rights to rule the people in its territory. In principle, aliens are subject to the jurisdiction of the state where they reside unless international treaties provide otherwise. Thus, extraterritorial jurisdiction is normally on the contrary of territorial sovereignty except in some special circumstances, for example, diplomatic immunities and privileges and universal jurisdiction. However, Western powers imposed extraterritorial jurisdiction on some states which were different from them or not as powerful as they were. The practice was entirely unilateral in nature and totally contrary to the principle of sovereignty. Consular jurisdiction was first stated in the General Regulations for the British Trade at the Five Ports, supplemental to the Treaty of Nanking of 1842,[268] and then provided in the Sino-American Treaty of 1844, then to Sweden and Norway in the Treaty of Canton of 1847. Moreover, through the most-favored-nation clause, consular jurisdiction extends to other treaty powers, including, Austria-Hungary, Belgium, Brazil, Denmark, Germany, Italy, Mexico, the Netherlands, Peru, Portugal, Russia, Spain, and Switzerland.

Extraterritorial jurisdiction was usually exercised by consuls of the Western powers. However, following the British Crown's unilateral 1833 attempt to establish a British Court in Canton, in the Shanghai area, Britain, the United States and France jointly established settlements in the 1840s. Shanghai is but one example among many, as a plurality of foreign tribunals, mixed courts and consular arrangements gradually developed in other treaty ports and, increasingly, within the Chinese inland territories. The jurisdiction of the Court covered the adjudication of mixed

---

267 Art. V of the Reorganization Gold Loan Agreement, See John MacMurray, Treaties and Agreements with and concerning China II, New York: Oxford Univeristy Press, 1921, pp. 1007–1037.

268 'Whenever a British subject has to complain of a Chinese he must first proceed to the Consulate and state his grievance. The Consul will thereupon enquire into the merits of the case and do his utmost to arrange it amicably. In like manner, if a Chinese have reason to complain of a British subject, he shall no less listen to his complaint, and endeavor to settle it in a friendly manner...Regarding the punishment of English criminals, the English Government will enact the laws necessary to attain that end, and the Consul will be empowered to put them into force; and regarding the punishment of Chinese criminals, these will be tried and punished by their own laws, in the way provided for by correspondence which took place at Nanking, after the concluding of the peace.' (Art. XIII of the General Regulations for the British Trade at the Five Ports, supplemental to the Treaty of Nanking of 1842).

disputes and cases where both litigants were nationals of one of the governments, and subsequently extended to disputes involving citizens of other third states as well. In 1865, the British Supreme Court for China and Japan was established in Shanghai, China as a first instance consular court for cases in the Shanghai region as well as an appellate court for cases heard by consular courts in the rest of China. Additionally, in 1906, the U.S. Congress passed the United States District Court for China Act, claiming 'original jurisdiction in most civil and criminal cases where Americans were defendants, and appellate jurisdiction over cases decided first in the U.S. consular courts in China's treaty ports'. Also, the appellate body of the institution was the U.S. Circuit Court in California, an impossible choice for a Chinese plaintiff to concretely appeal a judgment.

5. The Justification of Encroachment of China's Sovereignty

Although Grotius listed wars of imperial expansion as among the unjust causes of war and Vattel condemned conquest on moral grounds, they also understood that as long as conquest was an accepted feature of state practice there was a need to legally institutionalize it. English legal publicist W.E. Hall considers international law as a product of the special civilization of modern Europe and the forming of a highly constructed system. He assumed that such a high developed system could not be supposed to be understood or recognized by countries differently civilized and they must do something with agreement with European civilization: accept European international law in its entirety.[269] Oppenheim also asserts that "the civilization of non-Christian states is essentially so different from that of the Christian States that international intercourse with them of the same kind as between Christian States has been hitherto impossible ... There should be no doubt that these States are not International Persons of the same kind and the same position within the Family of Nations as Christian States."[270] Moreover, the idea that legality, properly speaking, was a primary criterion for a country's membership in the club of Euro-American Christian civilization was prevalent among Western jurists during the nineteenth and early twentieth centuries. With regard to international law, Lassa Oppenheim asserted that 'as a law between Sovereign and equal states based on consent of these States, [it] is a product of modern Christian civilization.'[271] The French jurist, Antoine Pillet, clearly believed that only 'civilized' states could claim the privilege of sovereignty and equality.[272] Many publicists maintained that Europeans had not

269 William Edward Hall, Treatise on international law, Oxford, The Clarendon Press, 1924, p. 47.

270 Lassa Oppenheim, International Law (1st ed.), London: Longmans, Green and Co., 1905, p. 148.

271 Ibid, p. 44.

272 Antoine Pillet, Recherches Sur Les Droits Fondamentaux Des Etats Dans L'ordre des rapports internationaux et sur la solution des conflits qu'ils font naître, Paris, 1899, p. 6.

only a right but also a duty to bring a germ of civilization to barbarous lands. Conquest and colonization of 'uncivilized' peoples or lands were often justified by what they named as 'civilizing the uncivilized' because they transformed an otherwise "uncivilised" entity and its "backward natives" into the realm of "civilization" and membership of the "family of nations".[273] Accordingly, aggressing, plundering, assimilating or colonizing the uncivilized were purported into the civilizing mission of the colonizing powers for the best interest of the uncivilized peoples, therefore, the best interest of the world as a whole.[274]

Unlike the western jurists above-mentioned, Immanuel Kant suggested that a subjective element is involved in determining which state can be regarded as existing in itself and defended a country's autonomy from the ruling of European states because the autonomy of a nation means acting as an independent state which should not be ruled by another if the nation sees itself as an independent state.[275] Moreover, Kant commended that such savages for their own part may regard themselves as superior on account of the lawless freedom they have chosen. The latter likewise constitute national groups but they do not constitute states.[276] Nonetheless, even this lawless condition did not justify outside interference and entailed only limited rights of settlement. Such settlements should not be established by violence but only by treaty, and then, there must be no attempt to exploit the ignorance of the natives in persuading them to give up their territory.[277] Kant acknowledged the argument that conquest could serve "the best interests of the world as a whole, such as by civilizing the uncivilized or by purging a country of 'depraved characters', at the same time affording the hope that they or their offspring will become reformed in another continent." However, he insisted that such supposedly good intentions cannot wash away the stain of injustice from the means which are used to implement them: violence and aggression.[278] In fact, conquest did not serve in the best interest of the world as a whole but the best interest of the conquerors and would cause suffering for people of conquered nations. However, China was not without borders or lines of authorities and in fact with a great history, a splendid but different civilization, and stable domestic autonomy even while expansionist European powers confronted it. European territorialism of the earth thus involved an initial

273 Dakas C. J. Dakas, The Role of International Law in the Colonization of Africa: a Review in Light of Recent Calls for Re-conolization, 7 African Yearbook of International Law, 1999, p. 110.

274 Ibid, pp. 85–118.

275 I. Kant, Eternal Peace' in Philosophical Perspectives on Peace: An Anthology of Classical and Modern Sources (ed. by H. P. Kainz), Basinstoke: Macmillan, 1987, p. 78.

276 I. Kant, Metaphysics of Morals, in Kant's Political Writings (ed. by H. Reiss), Cambridge: Cambridge University Press, 1970, p. 164.

277 Ibid, pp. 172–173.

278 I. Kant, 1970, p. 173.

moment of deterritorialization by denying the pre-existing orders of belonging.[279] European powers competed ruthlessly against each other for colonial possessions due to perceived economic and strategic advantages that such possessions brought. They agreed not to recognize non-European political authorities' sovereignty but entered into an agreement to mutually recognize their colonial holdings.[280]

In reality, China was among those states whose "civilization had not reached that condition which was necessary to enable their Governments and their population in every respect to understand and to carry out the command of the rules of International Law".[281] The Western nations saw themselves as fully justified in demanding, with the use of force, a group of concessions and certain colonies from the Chinese.[282] Sovereignty and territorial integrity was not an issue with China. Thus, the international law and sovereignty only exist with 'Christian' states or 'civilized' states which constituted a small community, superior to all other countries. The logic was the exact same as the Chinese tribunal system, under which China treated other states as inferior uncivilized entities. However, colonialism was much worse than the tributary system which was basically a defense system with no intention of exploiting tributary parties. Sovereignty only existed in a small international society consisting of European states that shared a common history, culture, and development. China was belonging to the non-sovereignty group under the powerful military force of European states. Under those thoughts, Western powers justified their aggression and looting in China. Suzane Ogden claimed that China was a non-sovereign state because of China's own fault of a lack of internal order.[283] However, her argument is unreasonable since European powers started to treat China as a non-state nation in 19th Century while China had a rather stable internal order. The fact that China fell into parts in the early 20th Century is partly attributed to the aggression of European powers.

Strikingly, the so-called standard of civilization was exported by non-civilized means in the first place and therefore cannot justify the cruelties perpetrated by European powers under the banner of civilization.[284] Despite the fact that the European law of nations had been defined as the law of civilized or Christian nations by European, international law slowly evolved into a more neutral instrument which granted European states and non-European states or non-Christian states the same rights and imposed the same duties. Contemporary legal scholars denounced international intervention in the name of civilization, noting the horrors that had been visited upon non-European people in the name of civilizing and out of concern that

279 P. Patton, Deleuze and Political, London: Routledge, 2000, p. 92.
280 R. Jackson, 1999, p. 442.
281 L. Oppenheim, 1905, pp. 32–33.
282 Ibid, pp. 191–194.
283 Suzaaen Ogden, 1974, pp. 6–7.
284 Y. Onuma, When was the Law of International Society Born? - An Inquiry of the History of International Law from an Intercivilizational Perspective, Journal of the History of International Law, I 2000, p. 30.

it was a recipe for a universal empire.[285] Gerrit W. Gong states that the European incursion into East Asia amounted to more than a political and military conflict as it involved a clash between two different cultures each with their distinctive standards of civilization.[286] Brett Bowden emphasizes that the European 'expansion was largely an aggressive act involving violent conquest and suppression'.[287] The latter opinion has been widely confirmed by the developing states.

Section 3. Recovery of China's Sovereignty

A series of popular uprisings stirred by the Qing dynasty's failure to protect China's territorial integrity and Chinese dignity brought the demise of the Qing dynasty and the establishment of the Republic of China in 1911. The new government of China had two major objectives: eliminating the unequal treaties and extra-territorial jurisdiction and internally unifying China.[288] The successful example set by Japan of abolishing foreign extraterritorial rights through the implementation of widespread legal reforms further reinforced the Chinese Republican leaders' determination to recover Chinese sovereignty and to end the 'Humiliation'.[289] The project involved the development of criminal, civil and commercial codes, as well as codes of civil and criminal procedure. The promulgation of such codes would then have been complemented by the establishment of a considerable number of new courts in all the districts where foreigners resided in 1924. This reformation did not make a difference for the recovery of China's sovereignty. In the meantime, it was a disappointment for the Chinese that not much had changed in the concrete application of the Unequal Treaties by the end of the 1919 Paris Peace Conference.[290]

Chinese representatives submitted a memorandum entitled 'Questions for Readjustment' to the governments represented at the Peace Conference following the end

---

285 Melissa Salrin, A Family Beyond Blood: Race, Gender, and Colonialism in Action Sociale de la Femme, c. 1914–1940, Proceedings of the Western Society for French History, Vol. 33, 2005, pp. 379–391.

286 Gerrit W. Gong, The Standard of 'Civilisation' in International Society, Oxford: Clarendon, 1984, p. 172.

287 Brett Bowden, The Colonial Origins of International Law: European Expansion and the Classical Standard of Civilization, in: Journal of the History of International Law, Vol. 7, Issue 1, 2005, p. 2.

288 Joseph Esherick, Reform and Revolution in China: The 1911 Revolution in Hunan and Hubei, Berkeley: University of California Press, 1976; Jean Chesneaux, Marianne Bastid, and Marie-Claire Bergere, China from the Opium Wars to the 1911 Revolution, Florida: Harvester Press, 1977; Edmund S. K. Fung, The Military Dimension of the Chinese Revolution: The New Army and its Role in the Revolution of 1911, Vancouver: University of British Columbia Press, 1980.

289 David Scott, China and the International System, 1840–1949: Power, Presence, and Perceptions in a Century of Humiliation, New York SUNY Press, 2008, p. 34.

290 Zhang Yongjin, China's Entry into International Society: Beyond the Standard of' Civilization, in: Review of International Studies 17, No. 1, 1991, p. 13.

of the First World War.[291] By invoking general principles of international law such as territorial sovereignty and sovereign equality, Chinese representatives requested that China be treated as an equal within the international community through the implementation of measures such as the revision of their treaties with China, the abrogation of extraterritoriality, the restoration of China's tariff autonomy and the withdrawal of foreign troops and foreign post offices from China. With regard to the request to abolish extraterritorial consular jurisdiction, the final document was particularly interesting as it provided a clear statement of the Chinese dissatisfaction with the institution.

At the Washington Conference in 1922, ironically, the United States, Britain, Japan, Italy, Portugal, Belgium, the Netherlands and France jointly recognized the 'sovereignty, independence, and territorial and administrative integrity of China', but Chinese representatives of the conference were not allowed to participate actively in the substantive negotiations. By the end of the Conference, the representatives decided to not yet abolish the jurisdictional privileges enjoyed by foreigners. Interestingly, Western governments created a Special Commission on Extraterritoriality in China 'to inquire into the present practice of extraterritorial jurisdiction in China, and into [its] laws, the judicial system and the methods of judicial administration' which eventually were met in Beijing in 1926. Unfortunately, the Special Commission published an official Report on Extraterritoriality in China, justifying extraterritorial consular jurisdiction in China. Nonetheless, Austria, Hungary and Germany lost the privileges after World War I and Russia terminated consular jurisdiction on May 31 1924. It is worth mentioning that, after considerable negotiating, China finally restored its right of tariff autonomy in 1928.[292]

The turning point emerged during World War II, at a time when China was particularly weak.[293] A joint Anglo-American initiative led to the abolishment of extraterritoriality in China. Following a preliminary agreement between the British Foreign Office and the U.S. Department of State to act jointly on the issue, diplomatic negotiations began with the Chinese government.[294] In January 11, 1943, the Sino-American Treaty for the Relinquishment of Extraterritorial Rights in China was signed in Washington. Article 1 of the Treaty prescribed:

---

291 See Questions for Readjustment, Submitted by China to the Peace Conference, Paris, 1919, p. 14–18, available at: http://archive.org/details/questionsforread00paririch.

292 Franz H. Michael and George E. Taylor, The Far East in the Modern World (rev. Ed.), New York, 1964, pp. 399–401.

293 "internal political fragmentation and the Japanese occupation paralyzed the negotiations on the abolishment of the 'Unequal Treaties', and it was generally thought that the issue would not be discussed until after the conclusion of the war.", in: K. C. Chan, The Abrogation of British Extraterritoriality in China 1942–43: A Study of Anglo-American-Chinese Relations, in: Modern Asian Studies, Vol. 11, No. 2, 1977, p. 266.

294 K.C. Chan, 1977, pp. 257–291.

> "All those provisions of treaties or agreements in force between the United States of America and the Republic of China which authorize the Government of the United States of America or its representatives to exercise jurisdiction over nationals of the United States of America in the territory of the Republic of China are hereby abrogated. Nationals of the United States of America in such territory shall be subject to the jurisdiction of the Government of the Republic of China in accordance with the principles of international law and practice."

The event was marked with great celebration and the next day the Nationalist Guomindang government published a Letter to All Servicemen and Masses, announcing with triumph that

> "we, the Chinese nation, after fifty years of sanguinary revolutions and five and a half years of sacrifice in the War of Resistance, have finally transformed the history of a hundred years of the Unequal Treaties of sorrow into a glorious record of the termination of the Unequal Treaties".[295]

During the same year, Japan, Norway and Belgium consented to the termination of extraterritorial consular jurisdiction. The Netherlands and Sweden followed in 1945, while France, Portugal, Denmark and Italy all concluded new treaties for the abrogation of extraterritoriality between 1946 and 1947.[296] Thus, by the end of the 1940s, the long-abhorred institution finally vanished, with both the Nationalist Government in exile and the new People's Republic of China taking the credit for having unified the country under a single government and territorial jurisdiction.[297]

The public reasons asserted were that extraterritoriality was an 'anomaly' incompatible with 'modern international practices' and the 'generally-accepted principles of modern international law'.[298] Although the reasons behind such a dramatic turn in Anglo-American politics are assumed to actually be political intentions.[299] For instance, supporting China in order to contain Japan, the common enemy-in-war, certainly played a considerable role both for Britain and the USA. Another consideration in support of abolishment was the desire to encourage the Chinese for any

295 Wang Dong, 'The Discourse of Unequal Treaties in Modern China', Pacific Affairs, Vol. 76, No. 3, 2003, p. 399.

296 Turan Kayaoğlu, Legal Imperialism: Sovereignty and Extraterritoriality in Japan, the Ottoman Empire, and China, Cambridge: Cambridge University Press, 2010, p. 151, Table 7.

297 Pär Kristoffer Cassel, Grounds of Judgment: Extraterritoriality and Imperial Power in Nineteenth-Century China and Japan, New York: Oxford University Press, 2012, p. 179.

298 The Statement of Secretary of the State to the Ambassador in the United Kingdom (Winant). Washington, August 27, 1942, in: Foreign Relations of the United States, Diplomatic Papers, Volume China (1942), pp. 282–285, available at: http://digicoll.library.wisc.edu/cgi-bin/FRUS/FRUS-idx?type=header&id=FRUS.FRUS1942China&q1=1942%20China.

299 Ibid.

potential post-war cooperation in the East Asia.[300] Interestingly, given its historic conceptualization as a guarantee against 'backward' legal cultures, the discourse surrounding extraterritorial consular jurisdiction gradually shifted towards its categorization as an 'anomalous and anachronistic practice'. This normative shift presented extraterritoriality as an institution that increasingly clashed with modern ideas of justice and international law.[301]

Conclusion

China quickly accepted the Westphalia model after its failure against Western powers but gradually abandoned isolationist and Sino-centric attitudes while it found that sovereignty could help it from intrusion into its territory. The Opium War from 1840 to 1842 led to not only the loss of national sovereignty of imperialist powers but also the early understanding of modern sovereignty. As previously discussed, sovereignty was mainly understood as a synonym of 'equality' and 'independence' and in order for China to recover its sovereignty from Western powers it had to achieve these. However, China was denied as being a member of the international society with equal and independent sovereignty which it had struggled for a century to acquire. Moreover, this interpretation continues to be the core of today's Chinese understanding of sovereignty. Being a victim of colonization as a self-identity has an unimaginable impact on Chinese politics. Consequently, nationalism brands deeply in China's perception on sovereignty.

300 K. C. Chan, 1977, p. 267.
301 Turan, Kayaoğlu, 2010, p. 185.

Chapter 4. Nationalism in China

Introduction

As discussed previously, modern sovereignty was born with modern nationalism in China. Still today, Chinese nationalism is still deeply implanted in Chinese minds, which has been seriously influential in the interpretation of sovereignty in the perspective of China. Whenever sovereignty is involved now, Chinese nationalism rises with a mixture of xenophobia immediately and condemns any compromise with foreign states which might be accused of quisling.[302]

It is widely accepted that modern nationalism was the major source of the movements that propelled China to transform into a modern state. Yu Yingshi wrote, "various modernized theories and political movements emerged in modern China. Some of them which could instigate Chinese people all relied on nationalism and utilized nationalism".[303] Indisputably, 'nationalism was the chief stimulus behind Chinese reforming thought' in the late 19th century.[304]

Nationalism centers on loyalty and identity in a nation – "a body of people associated with a particular territory that is sufficiently conscious of its unity to seek to possess a government particularly its own".[305] In modern Europe, there developed a significant distinction between the political nationalism developed by Jean Jacques Rousseau, which was expressed throughout the French Revolution, and the romantic nationalism presented by Johann Gottfried Herder, which was exhibited in the national community movements of Central and Eastern Europe. The former model, so-called French-inspired political nationalism, has had more influence upon the American conception of nationalism; this political criterion of nation has logically led to such ideas as nation building, social mobilization, democratization, and modernization being included within the concept of nationalism. The more intertwined such concepts become with nationalism the easier it is to accept the common assertion that nationalism is a development unique to Northwestern Europe and North America during the late eighteenth and early nineteenth centuries and subsequently transmitted to others through Western political and cultural encroachment. The latter pattern, known as German-inspired romantic nationalism, evolved in Central and Eastern Europe during the nineteenth century focused on the Volk or "national

302 Junwu Pan, Chinese Philosophy and International Law, Asian Journal of International Law, Vol. 1 (2), July 2011, pages: 233–248.

303 Yu Yingshi, Chinese Modern Nationalists and Intellectual (中国现代的民族主义和知识分子), 'the supplement to United Daily News, 1st, May, 1975.

304 Paul A. Cohen, Discovering History in China: American Historical Writing on the Recent Chinese Past, New York: Columbia University Press, 1984, p. 31.

305 The Random House Dictionary of the English Language, New York: Random House Inc (T), 1973, p. 952.

community" based upon a mother tongue, ancient folk traditions, common descent, or national spirit. This somewhat vague concept of the 'folk' rejected individual liberty and decision as the basis for defining a nation and transferred the organic and unique personality of the individual to the nation. In other words, instead of thinking in terms of mass participation in a plebiscite, romantic nationalists believed that the nation was a natural and historical phenomenon and that the individual's permanent will was more accurately expressed in the national spirit than in any particular act of individual preference. This German nationalism suggests that such ideals as nation building, social mobilization, democratization, and modernization are not integral to the concept of nationalism per se.[306] In ancient times, this type of nationalism was usually activated while Hanzu was facing the danger of a foreign power attempting to subjugate China. Facing the powerful western threats, it was transformed into modern nationalism, namely, French nationalism, which drove China to seek a new political system for the purpose of its own rescue.

Section 1. Traditional Nationalism in China

Modern nationalism has existed only in modern times because national states are now capable of holding formally equal status in a world order properly composed of such states[307]; there was no such nationalism in ancient times. However, it is debatable as to whether nationalism in the German sense subsisted in premodern times. Fairbank wrote, "It would be an error ... to imagine ancient China as an embryonic nation-state. We would do better to apply the idea of culturalism and see ancient China as a complete civilization comparable to Western Christendom, within which nation-states like France and England became political sub-units that shared their common European culture."[308]

Logically, under the view of China-centric universalism (Tianxia view), the line drawn between the Chinese 'Us' and non-Chinese 'Other' was mainly a cultural division, inter-cultural relationships constituted the essence of this Chinese world order. Within this world, China did not see herself as one state among others, but as the only civilized entity that had to live with uncivilized 'barbarians'. After the opium war, the Western powers (and then Japan) rocked the very foundation of the long-lived Chinese world order first by defeating the Qing Empire militarily, and then by posing an unprecedented threat to Chinese culture. China suddenly found that it was no longer the center of the universe. Rather it was thrown out to the margins of the world as a semi-colonized land in a Eurocentric world. This

306 Hoyt Cleveland Tillman, Institute Proto-Nationalism in Twelfth-Century China? The Case of Ch'en Liang, in: Harvard Journal of Asiatic Studies, Vol. 39, No. 2, Dec., 1979, pp. 404–428.

307 James Townsend, Chinese Nationalism, The Australian Journal of Chinese Affairs, No. 27. Jan., 1992, p. 105.

308 John. Fairbank, China: A New History. Cambridge, Mass.: Harvard University Press, 1992, p. 45.

was arguably the 'biggest change in the Chinese three thousand years' history' and propelled Chinese intellectuals to search for alternative ideas to replace the Chinese dynastic system to save China. Modern nationalism emerged for the first time in Chinese history, at the same time, culturalism collapsed. The formation of modern China was the process of transformation from culturalism to modern nationalism.[309] Fairbank pointed out that Chinese thinkers before Liang Qichao were all culturalists and even the thought of anti-Manzu was also culturalism.[310]

However, an opposing opinion is that in the post-Qin and Han dynasties, traditional nationalism gradually formed and was linked to the Emperors, Huaxia ethnicity, and the unified country. It holds that Chinese views on pre-modern Tianxia order were not just one, but complex. Tianxia in a broad version and in a narrow version respectively reflected expansionism and isolationism in Chinese thoughts. The Tianxia in the narrow sense namely, Zhongguo, with isolationism was directly connected to the formation of traditional nationalism. Hence, Zhongguo has been claimed by the Chinese as evidence of nationalism in pre-modern time.[311]

1. Chinese Identity

The mainstream view represented by American scholars such as Joseph Levenson and John K. Fairbank maintains that the Chinese considered China as the only civilized entity that had to live with uncivilized 'barbarians' and had to try to convert barbarians. This system of conversion worked mainly through China's moral example - occasionally through force.[312] James Harrison also pointed out that "the traditional Chinese self-image has generally been defined as 'culturalism', based on the historical heritage and acceptance of shared values, not as nationalism, based on the modern concept of the nation-state".[313] They emphasize that the concepts of nation-state, nationalism and patriotism has never been strongly rooted in Chinese thinking since China existed not as a state but as a whole world.[314]

However, China's historical sense of identity, gradually evolving over more than two millennia following the Qin-Han imperial unification that began in 221 BC, did not preclude political or nationalistic loyalties. The long span of imperial history offered some evidence of patriotism in a sense of racial segregation and xenophobia

309 Joseph R. Levenson, Confucian China and its Modern Fate: The Problem of Intellectual Continuity, Reprinted by Routelege in 2005 (First printed in 1958), p. 95.

310 Joseph R. Levenson, Confucian China and its Modern Fate: A Trilogy, Berkeley and Los Angeles: University of California Press, 1968, p. 194.

311 Zhang Qixian, 2009, p. 241.

312 Chen Zhimin, Nationalism, Internationalism and Chinese Foreign Policy, Journal of Contemporary China, Vol. 14, Iss. 42, February 2005, pp. 35–53.

313 James Harrison, Modern Chinese Nationalism, Hunter College of the City of New York: Research Institute on Modern Asia, 1969, p. 2; Also see John King Fairbank, 1968.

314 Chen Zhimin, 2005, pp. 35–53.

and of commitments to imperial institutions and the great unified country. In other words, the Chinese identity is not only cultural, but also political-geographical, and ethnic as well. As Lucian Pye asserted, the Chinese have been generally spared the crisis of identity common to most other transitional systems because they have little doubt about their identities as Chinese and the more they have been exposed to the outside world the more self-consciously Chinese they have become.[315]

1.1. *Hua and Yi distinction*

1.1.1. *Culture as Common Identity*

It is undoubtable that culture is part of Chinese identity. As is well known, Chinese culturalism, which was the outgrowth of Confucianism, perceived China as the only true civilization and embodied a universal set of values. Its cultural superiority was believed to be unchallenged until the Opium War. Moreover, good Confucians encourage foreigners to 'come and be transformed' through their own example of creating an orderly society. Confucians held that Chinese civilization was the world's only true civilization which was unrivaled before Christian civilization crashed it. This community consisted of all those participating in the civilization, including both Han-Chinese (Hanzu)[316] and non-Han Chinese. The identity of the community was not based on ethnic background but on conducting or practicing the principles and rites of Chinese civilization. It was crucial for maintaining a huge empire with multiple-ethnicities. It justified Chinese imperial ruling non-Han people and employing them as officials[317] and it represented expansionism of the Chinese empire. Furthermore, the Hua-yi distinction, one of the core views of culturalism, demonstrated isolationism. In the view of culturalism, the isolationism implies that the culture makes the Chinese distinguished itself from others using their own identity. However, the Hua-yi distinction could be also ethnical while Han's superiority was challenged by other ethnic groups. It is worth noting that despite that the superiority of Chinese civilization being diminished after the opium war, Chinese culture was and is still a part of the Chinese identity.

1.1.2. *Ethnicity as Common Identity*

Culturalism emphasized and extolled Chinese culture permitting an easy shift from culture to ethnic nationalism since the superiority of Chinese culture was expressed from the vantage of the Huaxia culture. The culturalism justified the Hanzu as the ruling ethnicity to govern non-Han people but not *vice-versa.* The superiority of civilization was directly linked to the ascendance of the ethnicity, which embodied the distinction

315 Lucian W. Pye, The Spirit of Chinese Politics, Cambridge, Mass.: The M. I. T. Press, 1968, pp. 5–6.

316 Han Chinese, in ancient China, also known as "Hua", or "Xia", or "Huaxia", now called Hanzu.

317 James Townsend, 1992, p. 110.

of "Hua" and "Yi". It was interpreted through the traditional idea that "those who are not our kin are sure to be of a different heart."[318] It essentially conveys the nature of ethnicism since it did not treat Non-Han people as equals of the Hanzu even though the non-Han people assimilated with Chinese culture. Therefore, the culturalism is actually transformed into ethnicism which is a major character of nationalism.

As analyzed above, the traditional view of Confucianism was both universalism and isolationism. The isolationism can be easily dominated by ethnicism. The two doctrines normally functioned in different situations. When expansion was the major goal of the empire universalism certainly prevailed and the cultural isolationism only excluded Yi who did not submit to China; while the empire faced the threat from strong foreign powers universalism could not function and instead ethnic isolationism prevailed. The ethnic isolationism stressed that fundamental differences exist between Hanzu and non-Han people even if non-Han people accepted Chinese culture and performed the rites.[319]

Historically, the Hanzu was the largest of these groups and throughout imperial history it was the most powerful in every respect - although one or another of the non-Han groups held military superiority at times and established two alien dynasties in China. When the Han's ruling faced the unprecedented serious threat from powerful foreign countries in the Song dynasty, the Orthodox Theory emerged to accuse the Yi as being an illegitimate leading ethnic group. The Hanzu claimed themselves as the founder and the legitimate leaders of Chinese civilization. Therefore, a ruler's ethnic background could be a decisive factor for judging legitimacy. The legitimacy view of Hanzu intellectuals prevailed particularly over the Song dynasty.[320] It indicates that ethnic assertiveness was one of identity in ancient China. Internally, its law distinguished between Han and aliens asserting sovereignty over residents and aliens despite their status as barbarians who were not supposed to live in Chinese civilized community.[321] Aliens were sometimes recruited into the bureaucracy in significant numbers, taking Chinese names and demonstrating the idea that the empire was a community based on cultural beliefs and practices. Some non-Han people continued to be marked as foreigners long after they were almost wholly assimilated and some aliens who served with honor as imperial officials still had their households registered locally as foreigners.[322] Particularly when the dynasties were ruled by the Hanzu faced alien's threats, the legitimacy of governance emerged and emphasized that Hanzu was the only legitimate ethnicity of rulers. Fang Xiaowu (1357–1402), Gu Yanwu (1613–82) and Wang Fuzhi (1619–92) penned

318 'Zuozhuan', Chenggong 4th year.

319 James Townsend, 1992, p. 110.

320 Ge Zhaoguang, 2011, pp. 59–62.

321 R. Randle Edwards, 'Ch'ing Legal Jurisdiction over Foreigners', in Essays on China's Legal Tradition (ed. by Jerome Alan Cohen, R. Randle Edwards and Fu-mei Chang Chen), Princeton: Princeton University Press, 1980, pp. 222–269.

322 Derk Bodde and Clarence Morris, Law in Imperial China, Philadclphia: University of Pennsylvania Press, 1967, pp. 168–70.

fierce condemnation of Mongol and Manzu, comparing them to animals that were no match for the qualities of the Hanzu. The expression of Hanzu chauvinism highlights that anti-foreign sentiment played a role in conflicts with both Mongols and Manchus.[323] In the Qing dynasty, secret societies kept anti-Manchu sentiment simmering for two centuries until it surfaced again in the Taiping Rebellion (1851–64) and the burgeoning Chinese modern nationalist movement at the end of the century. Popular sentiment in those movements was laced with patriotic themes emphasizing national history and heroes.[324] Visibly, culturalism's universalism was modified and challenged by ethnic views of Yi-Xia distinction, which was embodied in imperial law and statecraft and in both elite and popular ideas about Chinese relations with other ethnic groups.[325] It emphasized the Han's dominant status in political, cultural and social aspects. When the Han's advantages were apparent universalism could be dominant, while when the Hanzu was threatened by powerful foreign countries or under an alien reign, the Han-chauvinism emerged or prevailed.

1.1.3. Geographic and Political Identity

As analyzed in Chapter 2 section 1, 2.3, "Tianxia in the broad sense and the narrow sense (Zhongguo) coexisted in ancient China. There was not only one world view but a complex layered view." 'All under heaven' was idealism and represented expansionism. The narrow sense of Tianxia was the territory where Chinese culture and Chinese ethnicity could be defended from foreign powers. The Hua-Yi distinction means more than ethnicity distinction and also connotes Imperial China as one state or one civilization surrounded by foreigners, representing isolationism. There was never pure culturalism; culturalism was modified by considerations of ethnicity and state. As Pye commented, China was a civilization state and[326] political and cultural communities were largely congruent in China.[327]

323 See the discussion of Wang's ideas in Etienne Balazs "Political Theory and Administrative Reality in Traditional China", London: School of Oriental and African Studies, 1965, pp. 37–50; Jonathan D. Spcnce and John E. Wills Jr. (eds.), Varied Manifestations of Chinese Resistance to the Manchus are Analyzed in 'From Ming to Ch'ing: Conquest Region and Continuity in Seventeenth-Century China', New Haven: Yale University Press, 1979; and Frederic Wakcman Jr. and Carolyn Grant (eds), Conflict and Control in Late Imperial China, Berkeley: University of California Press, 1975, p. 285.

324 Yuji Muramatsu, Some Themes in Chinese Rebel Ideologies, in: The Confucian Persuasion (ed. by Arthur F. Wright), Stanford: Stanford University Press, 1960, pp. 241–67; and Robert Ruhlmann, Traditional Heroes in Chinese Popular Fiction, in: Confucianism and Chinese Civilization (ed. by Arthur F. Wright), New York: Atheneum, 1964, pp. 122–57.

325 James Townsend, 1992, p. 112.

326 Lucian Pye, China: Erratic State, Frustrated Society, Foreign Affairs, Vol. 69 Iss. 4, Fall 1990, p. 235.

327 James Townsend, 1992, p. 117.

Political loyalty played a crucial role in Confucianism just as culture did. The Confucian concept of political loyalty meant a personal commitment to the emperor, it also called for a conscious devotion to the best interests of the state. Confucian held that heaven bestowed its mandate to a just ruler, the Son of Heaven, and withdraws it from a despotic ruler. In essence, it was a conflict between personal loyalty and conscientious loyalty. Theoretically, when the Emperor assumed the Mandate of Heaven loyalty to Emperor was same as loyalty to Tianxia, which was Zhongguo in reality. However, it was a conflict between personal loyalty and conscientious loyalty while if an emperor was so unjust and brutal then he lost the Mandate of Heaven.[328] Paradoxically, since Confucians stressed the emperor's absolute power, loyalty to Zhongguo was often seen as concurrent with loyalty to emperor even in the case of contradiction. Comparing European allegiance towards lords, local power, church, etc., people under Chinese various post-Qin dynasties were loyal to the Emperor and the Imperial.

Loyal to Zhongguo concerned both dynasty and territory, and both defenses interacted with each other on an equal footing that definitely violated culturalist assumptions.[329] Loyalty to the Emperor and serving your country (zhong jun ai guo) was the traditional way of describing traditional Chinese patriotism which was deeply planted in the mind of Chinese intellectuals in daily education. History witnessed that the Chinese were not just bound together through only their culture but also through their loyalty to the central dynasties and the land named "zhongyuan" (central plain) which Chinese ancestors originally resided in and was traditionally controlled by Hanzu hands.

From the Qin-Han dynasty, traditional nationalism had gradually formulated in the sense of the romantic concept of the national community and motherland.[330] Ensuing the imperial system establishment and development and the xenophobe sentiment of Hanzu, the romantic nationalism emerged with deep roots in common aspects of races, land, language, customs, and culture.

1.2. The Thought of 'Great Unification'

With the view of Hua and Yi distinction, the great unification thought constitutes the major of two national thoughts. The thought of 'Great unified country' is derived from the Tianxia view, which symbolizes the universalism. However, it transformed the infinite 'Tianxia' into a real limited state where the infinite Tianxia remained in the imagination.[331]

Chinese people are mainly from the Han who trace their ancestry from Huaxia tribes, originally living in the central plain along the Huang He or Yellow River in

---

328 James T. C. Liu, Yueh Fei (1103–41) and China's Heritage of Loyalty, in: The Journal of Asian Studies, Vol. 31, No. 2, Feb., 1972, pp. 291–297.

329 Morris Rossabi, 1983, p. 93.

330 Hoyt Cleveland Tillman, 1979, pp. 403–428.

331 Ge Zhaoguang, 2011, pp. 28–29.

northern China.[332] Jiuzhou (one ancient name of Zhonguo), which from the beginning represented the Tianxia, was located in the area around central plain. Qin Shi Huang unified Jinzhou and finally expanded China into an empire, which is recognized as the first time great unification was accomplished. He governed China with a new centralized and bureaucratic state system replacing the old feudal system and unified the country economically and culturally by decreeing a unified standard of weights, measures, currency, writing and law. Therefore, the Imperial China from Qin-Han dynasties is widely accepted as the starting point of 'self-identity' of Great Unification. In the evolution of thousands years, the thought of "Great Unification" has evolved into a major ideology in Chinese society. This thought presumed impossible in the pre-Qin dynasty came true in the Qin-Han dynasties. The former 'Tianxia' was transformed to China where the territory was effectively controlled by the emperors through one unitary centralized bureaucratic system. 'China' gradually represented the 'Great Unification', the identification of a nation collided with the state identification. Dong zongshu portrayed it as such: "Chun Qiu[333] valued 'the Great Unification', as the principle among the sky and earth, and the common sense from the past to today".[334] In this thought, the central plain was always the heartland of China of the legitimate central dynasties. During the forming and developing of the great unified state, its borders continued to expand and the idea remained and evolved both in theory and in practice. In the lengthy Chinese history, wars, conflicts and secessions happened from time to time, however, unification always followed the secessions. Just like the Chinese proverb says, 'That which is long divided must unify; that which is long unified must divide.' Consequently, since the Imperial Chinese state first took shape in the Qin dynasty (221 B.C.), the land mass that makes up the heartland of the East Asian subcontinent has remained under the roof of the great unified entity, which led to the Chinese political system being totally distinguished from European.[335] It should be noted that the great unification thought has been significantly influential on the identity of China as a nation and a state. It is the invisible unity of the Chinese in the same land. Today's China, unlike the Europe of the Roman Empire and of Charlemagne, is the only one of the ancient civilizations that has survived the test and scourge of time and continued till this day in a reinvigorated form.[336] This phenomenon is tightly connected to China's ancient thoughts.

---

332 Jia Jingyan, 'Hanren kao', in: Fei Xiaotong (ed.), Zhonghua minzu duoyuanyiti geju, Beijing: Zhongyang Minzu Xueyuan, 1989, pp. 137–138.

333 Chun Qiu was known a works of Confucius.

334 Han Book, Dong Zongshu Zhuan.

335 Liang Qichao, Comparison of Chinese and European Statecraft (论中国与欧洲国体异同), in: Nationality and Civil Morality-Liang Qichao selected works, Shanghai Far East Press, 1995, p. 21.

336 Ma Dazheng, Ancient China's Frontier Policies and Management (中国古代的边疆政策与边疆治理), in: Western Region Research, 2002, Vol. 4, pp. 1–15.

2. Traditional Nationalism in the German Sense in Chinese History

Both nationalism and German nationalism stress loyalty on a national community sustained by a shared spirit that is expressed in a common folk tradition and blood ties. Membership in a folk is determined by history and blood rather than by democratic plebiscite and is not dependent upon the process of modernization. What determined the membership of the Chinese community was actually changeable. While China was powerful enough to be dominant in its periphery, it confidently welcomed various people from foreign lands to join this community if they followed Chinese leadership. China faced threats from strong rivals and the urgent goal for China as a state to survive membership of the community was not dependent upon whether they performed the rites but their loyalty to the Han ethnicity and to the country where Han ruled. The Song dynasty is a perfect example. Ge, an influential historian, argues that as early as the Song dynasty, the notion of 'China' as a nation had emerged from the robust but troublesome international relationships between the Han Chinese and other ethnic sovereignties, such as Liao, Jin, Xia, Korea, and Japan.[337]

2.1. Traditional Nationalism Emerging While Facing Foreign Threat

Despite the Hua-Yi distinction emerging as early as the period of Spring-and-Autumn and Warring states, it was limited by the Tianxia view for a long time particularly when Imperial China and its civilization had no substantial rivals. From the beginning, the Hua-Yi distinction was mainly dependent on culture and not blood. However, the superiority of Chinese civilization certainly implied the confident faith that the Hanzu were the inventor and holder of superior civilization. When Imperial China faced threats from competitive rivals it was unable to be the center of the Tianxia and the Huan-Yi distinction simply turned into ethnicity. Chinese nationalists emerged; they demonstrated loyalty to the Chinese dynastic state, hostility to foreigners, ethnical superiority, and efforts to strengthen the Chinese dynastic state to deter foreign encroachment. The Song dynasty is a perfect example of traditional Chinese nationalism. Since the centric-view of the Tianxia was frustrated, the Han-Chinese began to see Song as a nation they belonged to.[338]

The poem of General Yue Fei,[339] 'Man Jiang Hong' (Entirely Red River) is one of the most popular poems in Chinese history so far. It reflects the raw hatred he felt towards the Jurchen-ruled Jin kingdom, as well as the sorrow he felt when his efforts to recoup northern lands lost to Jin were halted by Southern Song officials of the "Peace Faction". Such an emotion had generally permeated into literature in the Song dynasty while Zhongguo was not the dominant power but under the threats

337 Ge Zhaoguang 2011, p. 40.

338 Ibid., p. 42.

339 Yue Fei (24 March 1103 - 27 January 1142), the most popular Chinese general in history who is famous for his fighting against aggression of Jin state.

from the strong rivals, Liao, Jin, Xia, and Mongol.[340] Widely seen as a patriot and national folk hero in China since after his death, Yue Fei has evolved into a standard epitome of loyalty to his country and dynasty. The classical praise of Yue Fei was the epitome - "serve the country utmost loyalty" (Jin zhong bao guo).[341]

Cheng Liang[342] actually represented the gentry class in the time of South Song, in which China's survival was under the threat of Jin power. He clearly stresses the barbarian problem and that a reorganization of power would serve to end China having to defend against barbarians. Consistently condemning "sitting in repose" (an zuo) or "biding one's time" (dai-shi), he summons action, mobilization of financial resources, training of troops, initiation of a grand strategy, breaking the peace, marching north and restoring the heartland where the Song used to control. He spoke of "rousing the officials to action", of "shaking the cosmic forces", and of "moving the hearts of the people living in North China".[343] Chen complained bitterly about officials who exhausted themselves in administering the southeast and forgot China; here China could either be the central plain or the whole Chinese nation. It shows that the Chinese were closely bound with the central plain where their ancestors lived.[344] He complained that the Song's tribute payments to the Liao and Jin-ren were grievous insults and in violation of the ritual norms the Chinese emperor should uphold: "A Son of Heaven offering up tribute to a superior, this ritual is for ministers and subordinates!".[345] He also demonstrated his strong emotions towards the central plain, the heartland of China, but occupied by Jin. His thoughts indicated a transition of China from central states to Zhongguo as one nation; however, the passages also suggest a loss of the central plain in Chen's mind caused by loyalty to a Chinese polity that was expelled from the traditional heartland of China but ruled by Hanzu. Therefore, his love of the dynasty channeled his philosophy toward support of actively restoring the dynasty's status and territory. People, he argued, should remain within their own borders, continue their own Dao, and not

340 Ge Zhaoguang, 2011, pp. 60–62.
341 The Sung History, Yuefei Legend.
342 Chen Liang (1143–1194) represented a utilitarian orientation that was eclipsed by Neo-Confucian ethics and metaphysics during the twelfth century; but he has gained popularity in the twentieth century because most Chinese favor utilitarian approaches and disparage Neo-Confucian. His assumptions are relatively similar to modern ideas in the West as well as in China. Hoyt Cleveland Tillman, Utilitarian Confucianism: Ch'en Liang's Challenge to Chu Hsi, Harvard: Harvard University Press, 1982, p. 1.
343 Chen Liang, 1.3a.
344 Chen Liang, 4.6a. Although he did not challenge the emperor's right to all the troops and resources of t'ien-hsia, Chen urged Hsiao-tsung to stop following Wang Anshih's mistaken policy-over centralization and over concentration of these resources at court: 1.4b–5a.
345 Chen Liang, 1.4a; also 4.6b.

participate in each other's affairs.[346] Evidently, the loyalty was toward the specific territory and the particular ethnic group. His cultural view was isolationism. Just as Chen objected to foreign encroachment on China, he could not tolerate allowing foreigners to participate in Chinese culture: "The sages did not share Zhong-guo with the barbarians; therefore, Zhong-guo [should] not share rituals and culture with the barbarians".[347] His view that different ethnic groups should stay within their own borders and develop their own Dao and blood lines suggest that he was thinking in terms of today's terminology - "ethnically determined nation-states". Manifestly, Cheng Liang did not believe that the application of Confucian culture in the north could necessarily bring southerners to rejoice in the sinicization of the Jin. Zhu Xi, the founding father of neo-Confucian. Although unable to deny the achievements of Kingdom Liao and Jin which were assimilated into Chinese civilization; he believed a Chinese dynasty with Mandate of Heaven was the only source of legitimacy and a barbarian dynasty could not be legitimate no matter how they converted into Confucianism.[348] Such an idea also is reflected in the works of the most influential Confucians Wang fuzhi who compared Chinese rituals being used by barbarians to a robe on a monkey.[349] It means that the race difference (not culture) determined the final segregation between Hanzu and non-Han.

In late Yuan dynasty, Zhu Yuanzhang raised a flag of "lustrating barbarians, recovering China", and declared that "people submitting to us forever live in China safely, people against us fled to the wild world.'[350] However, when the unified state was stable he changed his policies to emphasize the harmony of various ethnicities. He announced, "I have been the sovereign of Tianxia, I see no difference between Hua and Yi. For me, Hua and Yi are different by only names, they are same for me".[351]

In the late Ming dynasty and the early Qing dynasty, the Hua and Yi distinction became the cornerstone of anti-Manzu movements when the Manzu invaded China. The traditional nationalism played a substantial role in maintaining Chinese culture. However, till the middle of the Qing dynasty, the resistance movement gradually faded away as the Qing dynasty inherited Chinese civilization and its governance was stable and strong. The fact that the Chinese accepted the governance of the Qing dynasty was not just attributed to the cultural assimilation of Qing but also to the military power and brutal suppression. For example, the Qing army slaughtered the

346 Hoyt Cleveland Tillman, 1979, p. 425.

347 Ibid, p. 424.

348 Wang Jianmei, 2006, Vol. 2, pp. 26–31.

349 Wang Fuzhi, Comments on 'History as a Mirror'(读通鉴论), Vol. 28, Five Generation (part one). Available at: http://yuedu.163.com/source/6677cbdfdca24ac49f4aea2e0f1e5d3e_4.

350 Song Lian, "Yuzhongyuanjiao" (谕中原檄), See "99 Replyes of Famous Emperors" (ed. by Huang Jing and Yao Wenjuan), Beijing: Hua Yi Publishing House, 1992, pp. 333–334.

351 Zhao Qichang ed., "Ming Document on Beijing" (明实录北京史料) (the First Part), Beijing: Beijing Antique Literature Press, 1995, p. 2.

Han-Chinese for 10 days in Yang Zhou, and committed three massacres in Jiadin and the Manzu. Moreover, the Qing dynasty was particularly notorious for their preference of 'Literary Inquisition' to smash the anti-Qing sentiments.[352] The Qing government destroyed the writings coming from Ming loyalists and sentenced them and their family members to death since their poetry and articles implied that Qing was bad or evil, etc. Certainly, for the Manzu rulers Chinese culture and the administrative system helped them to control their subjects much more easily than without them. However, illusions of superiority of their civilization could comfort Chinese even when they were in a disadvantageous situation in front of powerful foreign power. The pragmatic calculations of self-interest rather than ethnic affinity prevailed so they could survive or have a better life in alien governance. However, when the time came, xenophobia drove the Han-Chinese to overturn the alien's ruling. In the late period of Qianlong Emperor, due to increasingly serious social contradictions and conflict, anti-Manzu campaigns rose up again. The doctrine of the Hua -Yi distinction became again the stimulus for the various anti-Manzu organizations. Even in the late 19th century and the early 20th century, the Republicanism also employed the Hua-Yi distinction to arouse the nationalism needed to overthrow the Qing dynasty. Undeniably, the two dynasties ruled by aliens were toppled down by Hanzu in the name of 'Huan-Yi distinction'.

The rule is clear: When China was under serious threat of foreign powers, the Hua-Yi distinction doctrine immediately rose and prevailed over the expansionism of the Tianxia view; but if not, the stability of Chinese society required the harmony of various ethnic groups in China therefore the expansionism took priority over the distinction of different ethnic groups. Nonetheless, the doctrine of the Hua-Yi distinction was moving in the direction of the "closed" nationalism of folk rooted in ancestral soil and bonded by common blood, where biological and historical determinism dictated purity of national character and preserved it from alien invasions.[353]

The Great Unification concept and Hua-Yi distinction have served as the major stimulus for the traditional nationalism.[354] The Tianxia view was an idea but was not the principle or guideline for international relations. China was defined as a state where Han-Chinese was at the center. Clear-cut demarcations in the Song dynasty, frequent interstate transactions between equal states, and exclusive jurisdiction show a quasi-nation-state forming. For example, there were a total of 347 military treatises written during the Song period, as listed by the history text of the Song Shi (compiled in 1345).[355] Moreover, nationalism towards Hanzu and Zhongguo as a state clearly existed in the Song dynasty. Hua-Yi distinction, legitimacy of the

352 It means speech crime. It refers to systematically official persecution of intellectuals for their writings in the Qing dynasty.
353 Hoyt Cleveland Tillman, 1979, p. 425.
354 James Townsend, 1992, p. 125.
355 Schafer, Edward H., War Elephants in Ancient and Medieval China, in: Oriens, Vol. 10, Issue. 2, 1957, pp. 289–291.

rulers, the Hanzu's frustrated feeling towards the motherland (the heartland of China), and loyalty towards the Dynasty and China as a state, etc., all contributed to the emergence of nationalism in ancient China. Certainly, China is unique in its unbroken history in which the Hanzu had the common land, common culture, common moral believes, customs, life styles and common political systems.[356] The community of Hanzu was not only cultural but also political and ethnic. The fact that China was dominant in east Asia for a long time indicates that the expansionism often superseded the nationalism. However, it could not prevent the nationalism from existing. It must be noted that the traditional nationalism is not the same as the modern nationalism and that the modern one originated from the traditional one.

Section 2. The Emergence of Modern Chinese Nationalism

1. The Collapse of Traditional Chinese Culturalism

The modern Chinese nationalism arose as a passionate and somehow despondent response to the country's decline from being a powerful empire to a weak, poor and backward country as it encountered the West after the Opium Wars. The Chinese went from such a high place where Chinese elites truly believed the superiority of Zhongguo before to be the lowest of the low, the Sick Man of Asia. The difference of the modern nationalism from the traditional nationalism is that the modern nationalism no longer asked for the help of Chinese culture but was an anti-dynastic regime and aimed to establish a republic state in order to save China. The humiliation China suffered from was deployed not only in a predictably xenophobic way (anti-Manzu and western) but also in a self-critical examination of Chineseness which mobilized the Chinese to pursue a republic regime in order to save China from the governance of Manzu and aggression of the Western powers.[357]

The Opium Wars from 1839 to 1842 signified the beginning of national humiliation and the forfeit of sovereignty. Under foreign power's guns and cannons, China was coerced into signing a series of unequal treaties, compelled to open trade ports and established foreign concessions in major cities, while forced to pay unimaginable huge reparations which China could hardly afford. Under the extraterritoriality of foreign powers, Chinese courts were denied jurisdiction over foreign citizens in Chinese territory.[358] Missionaries had the privilege to come and go as they wished, proselytizing and seeking converts.[359] Foreign entities dominated the commanding heights of the economy, controlling the salt tax, postal service, customs, railways, shipping, and the

356 Ge Zhaoguang, 2011, pp. 29–32.

357 Guoguang Wu, From Post-imperial to Late Communist Nationalism: Historical Change in Chinese Nationalism from May Fourth to the 1990s, in: Third World Quarterly, Vol. 29, No. 3, 2008, p. 478.

358 Teemu Ruskola, Colonialism Without Colonies: On Extraterritorial Jurisprudence of the U.S. Court for China, Law & Contemp. Probs, Vol. 71, 2008, pp. 217–219.

359 Martin Jacques, 2009, p. 88.

manufacturing and distribution sectors.[360] Economic growth came to a standstill, and living conditions deteriorated. GDP per capita was $600 in 1829, compared to $530 in 1870, $552 in 1913, and $439 in 1950.[361] The one-century of humiliation has marked a deep memory on the collective psyche of Chinese citizens, as reminders of the great indignities at the hands of foreigners while China was too weak to have sovereignty within Chinese territory. Undeniably, the traditional political system was in doubt; its legitimacy was broken down and the Tianxia view crashed as well. Evidently, China was in both political and cultural crises. The emotions of shame the Chinese felt stimulated the birth of modern nationalism in this period.

2. The Rise of Modern Nationalism

Since the Tianxia view collapsed and the Chinese culture was crushed by Christian civilization, the legitimacy of the emperor ruling system no longer existed, and China was losing its sovereignty. The traditional political and cultural identities were confronted with a serious challenge and couldn't continue to be coherently Chinese under the same identity of political entity and Manzu as alien rulers not being recognized by Han-Chinese. It is true that Chinese modern nationalism took form as a reaction to the shock of forced contact with the West and as a tool for regaining sovereignty.[362] They redefined themselves as the 'oppressed of the world', which was put on Sun Zhongshan's deathbed in 1925.[363]

In the late 19th century, Liang Qichao wrote of his understanding of Western conquest: "I read Western newspapers and they report on ... the disorder in the Chinese polity ... This has been going on for the past few decades. Since September or October of last year [1896], they have even more openly and brazenly publicized how wild and uncivilized the Chinese are, how ignorant and dishonest, how empty Chinese Confucianism is. The meaning is clear: they will eliminate China at once".[364]

He also identified China as one among many targets of Western ambitions - with Turkey and India noted elsewhere as similar targets.[365] Liang Qichao represented Chinese elites who were aware of China being on the verge of dismemberment and reform or revolution in the urgent demand of its dilemma. He also concluded that the previous culturalism was falling apart as it was in conflict with the formal equality of states in an international system, meanwhile, other cultural or political systems as competitors seriously challenged the Chinese ones. Furthermore, the

360 Peter Stursberg, No Foreign Bones in China: Memoirs of Imperialism and its Ending, Alberta: The University of Alberta Press, 2002, pp. 85–86.

361 Martin Jacques, 2009, p. 98.

362 Jean-Pierre Cabestan, The Many Facets of Chinese Nationalism, China Perspectives, Vol. 59, May - June 2005, pp. 26–40.

363 Rebecca E. Karl, 2002, p. 200.

364 Liang Qichao, A Study on New Laws Imposing on Subjucated States (灭国新法论), published in Qingyi bao, Vol. 32, July–August 1901.

365 Ibid.

view that the common people were seen as subjects of an absolute political authority was also challenged by modern nationalism that insisted that all subjects would become citizens of the state holding equal rights and obligations within it.[366] Additionally, after the Western educational system was enforced in China, a new type of intellectuals appeared in China. The eagerness to establish a democratic republic political system and save China unified the new intellectuals as the major source of modern nationalism.

3. The Major Types of Chinese Nationalism in Modern China

3.1. The Ethnic Nationalism as One of the Earliest Forms of Nationalism

Chinese nationalism began as an ethnic one seeking movement led by the Han majority to overthrow the Qing Dynasty, under which China was ruled by the Manzu minority. The ethnic nationalism views the nation as a politicized ethnic group and often produces a state-seeking movement to create an ethnic nation-state.[367] Indeed, the ethnic nationalism has a traditional historical origin. The fact that it was not just against Western powers but also against Manzu rulers embodies the influence of the Hua-Yi distinction doctrine. Meanwhile, it was also affected by modern Western political theories because it had a political pursuit to establish a brand new government of republic. Certainly, the nationalism in a xenophobic way served to overthrow the Qing dynasty whilst the 'political' nationalism played a critical role in establishing a republic state in order to save China and re-acquire sovereignty.[368] Both ethnic nationalism and political nationalism embodied the mottos of the early time of Sun Yat-sen, first president and founding father of the Republic of China. For example: "to expel the Tatar barbarians, to revive Zhonghua, to establish a Republic, and to distribute land equally among the people." One of Sun's major legacies was the creation of his political philosophy of the Three Principles of the People. These Principles included the principle of nationalism (民族), of democracy (民權), and of welfare (民生).

3.2. The Cultural Nationalism as Part of Anti-Imperialism Movements

During the "century humiliation", the Chinese culture, which was used to being the main instrument of the Empire's expansion, lost its function and became meaningless in front of the powerful sovereign independent states. Nonetheless, Liang Qichao wanted to assert the ability of what he called 'true' Confucianism as a national essence (国粹) to combat imperialism's homogenizing tendency. It roused

366 James Townsend, 1992, p. 122.

367 Suisheng Zhao, China's Pragmatic Nationalism: Is It Manageable? In: The Washington Quarterly, Winter 2005–2006, Vol. 29, Issue. 1, p. 133.

368 Jiang Yihua, On Chinese Nationalism in 20 Century, in: Nationalism and Chinese Modernization (ed.by Liu Qingfen), Hongkong: Hongkong Chinese Press, 1994, p. 148.

the cultural nationalism for the purpose of fighting against the Western civilization. The reformism as cultural nationalism was represented by Kang Youwei and Liang Qichao who intended to reform Confucianism against Christianity.[369] The reformists established a party named "Protecting State Party" in April, 1898, and called for "Protecting the state, the race, and the culture". In the early 20th century, the new cultural nationalism named as the "national essence" school advocated for the 'preservation of national essence'. They maintained that history and culture were the most precious national essence and the root of the Chinese.[370] The cultural nationalism represented by the 'national essence' school was different from the Protecting State Party because they tried to overthrow Manzu's ruling.

3.3. Political Nationalism as the Major Source to Establish a New Nation-State

As Wu comments, 'early nationalism painfully recognized the economic backwardness of China and keenly realized the corruption of China's traditional political institutions as a response of to China's historical humiliation in the face of Western imperialism.'[371] Sun Zhongshan was the most influential politician in that period. In his six lectures on nationalism, Sun even developed a more sophisticated concept of nationalism to address the political and economic oppression from foreign countries that was turning China into a 'sub colony' - an even worse condition than a colony or a semi-colony.[372] Self-strength was the major aim of nationalism. The first priority of Chinese nationalism at the time thus was to launch a national revolution to overthrow the Manchu rulers, and to build a new national-state ruled by Han Chinese. In that period, the thought of democracy (minzhu) and nationalist patriotism (aiguo) rose as political ideas in connection with one another, thus, Chinese nationalism was anti-regime, revolutionary, and aiming to establish a nation-state. It employed ethnic nationalism and worked with cultural and political nationalism together for a common goal, namely, saving China. In any case this early idea of nationalism was an 'animating and directing power', bringing forth social reform and revolution as the degree of change preferred by different thinkers varied.[373]

---

369 Zheng Shiqu, Cultural Nationalism in Modern China, in: The Standing of Intertextual (知识分子的立场) (ed. by Li Shitao), Chang Chun: Times Literature Press, 2000, p. 263.

370 Wu Weiruo, Zhang Taiyan's Nationalism Historical Science, On Modern Thinkers: Nationalism, Florida: Times Publishing Company, 1982, p. 266.

371 Wu Guoguang, From Post-imperial to Late Communist Nationalism: Historical Change in Chinese Nationalism from May Fourth to the 1990s, in: Third World Quarterly, Vol. 29, No. 3, 2008, p. 478.

372 Sun Zhongshan, On nationalism: lecture two (民族主义六讲之第二讲), in: Sun Zhongshan wenji, Vol. I, Beijing: Unity Press, 1997, p. 78.

373 Wu Guoguang, 2008, p. 473.

4. The Nationalism Practice in the Modern History of China

The first wave of nationalism was clearly xenophobia. For example, after 1840, certain nationalist movements which appeared in China - the Taiping and the Boxers - were of social strata who perceived foreign ascendancy - respectively the Manzu and the Westerners - to be the source of their problems. Meanwhile, nationalism was the chief stimulus behind Chinese reform thought in the late 19th century and it led to re-examining the institutional foundation of the Chinese social-political order. However, after the reform failed radical alternatives increasingly occupied the mainstream in the early 20th century. Moreover, Chinese history lurched from constitutional reforms and social changes to violent revolutions as nationalism was drawn towards ever more radical positions and practices.[374]

In 1911, the Xinhai Revolution overthrew China's last imperial dynasty, the Qing Dynasty, with the abdication of the "Last Emperor" Puyi on February 12, 1912, over 2,000 years of imperial rule was formally ended and the Republic of China established. Due to the lack of the military support, the new government had no ability to hold on to the power. China was thrust into another period of warlords.

The Nationalism movement reached its peak in the May Fourth movement in Beijing in 1919 when thousands of college students protested with a manifesto denouncing the decision of the Paris Peace Conference to accept Japanese territorial rights in the Shandong province. During May Fourth, democracy served as a political and moral tutor to the students demonstrating against imperialism and the corrupt Chinese government.[375]

Chinese nationalists vented their anger not just at foreign powers but at Chinese officials for being weak in the face of foreign provocation. Prior to 1931, under the nationalistic anti-imperialism banner, the Kuomintang[376] government was able to reduce the extraterritorial privileges enjoyed by foreign powers.[377] However, Jiang Jieshi's monopoly on Chinese nationalism was eroded when his government failed to stand up to the Japanese occupation of China's Northeast provinces (Manchuria) in 1931. His decision to adopt the notorious policy of 'internal pacification before resistance to external attack' aroused nationwide protest.[378] The strong nationalism of the Chinese forced Jiang to join the anti-Japanese nationalist united front with his domestic adversary - the Chinese Communist Party (CCP) in 1936. However, after the Japanese surrendered in 1945, the united anti-Japan camp immediately lost the pressure from the nationalism. The civil war between the Guomin party and the

374 T. Bottomore, Political Sociology, Minneapolis, Minnesota: University of Minnesota Press, 1993, p. 81.

375 Wu Guoguang, 2008, pp. 467–482.

376 Kuomintang is also called Guomindang, or Guomin party because of different translation versions.

377 Selig S. Harrison, The Widening Gulf: Asian Nationalism and American Policy, New York: The Free Press, 1978, p. 70.

378 Chen Zhimin, 2005, p. 40.

Communist party erupted in 1946 and ended with the fleeing of the Guomin party to Taiwan in 1949. Clearly, nationalism had played a significant role in modern Chinese history and decided the Chinese political evolving process.

5. The State's Sovereignty Prevailing Over the People's Sovereignty

Unlike the establishment of European nation-states, China faced a tremendously dreadful international environment while Chinese attempted to establish a nation-state. Internationally, Western powers invaded China and violated Chinese sovereignty, internally, the Qing dynasty lost its legitimacy and Chinese society faced an urgent pressure of a comprehensive revolution. Since China had fallen down to a semi-colonial country from the central state, a sovereign state was the priority of modern China. When the nation faced the danger of extinction, a strong state, not democracy, was desperately needed for survival; therefore the Chinese realized that the nation could not subsist without sovereignty. In fact, after the Republic of China was founded, the major task of nationalism became how to regain the integral sovereignty but not to establish a democratic modern state. As a scholar on contemporary Chinese political thought comments:

> "Mainstream Chinese political thinking during the first decade of the century revolved around the question of how to make China into a modern nation, to forge a cohesive political system out of the organized power structure of a bureaucratic monarchy, and to ward off the threat to the country's existence in a new world where the competition for power of expansive nation-states promised to consume those societies unable to emulate their example".[379]

The saving task was overwhelmed with enlightening and establishing a national state but was not in step with the democratic process. Sovereignty of state was split with people's sovereignty. In this background, during the forging of Chinese nationalism, national sovereignty and people sovereignty reacted mutually from the beginning but gradually national sovereignty became dominant, state sovereignty replaced people sovereignty, and democracy transformed into statism. Afterward, the strength of the state overweighed the people's strength and democracy gave place to statism.[380] Consequently, the power of community surpassed the individual's political power.[381] Logically, after the national state is built, people's sovereignty should gradually develop - that is the process of democratization. It is vital to know how to reconstruct the relationship between power of state and people's

379 Wu Guoguang, 2008, pp. 467–482.

380 Zheng Yongnian, China's Nationalism and Democratic Politics, in: Nationalism and the Relationship across Taiwan Strait (Zheng Yongnian and Lin Jialong, ed), Neunaturalism Press, 2001, p. 572.

381 Ibid., p. 573.

sovereignty. How to arrange Chinese people's involvement in the state political process and how to make this process suitable for Chinese people, after a hundred years, are still the focus of Chinese nationalism.[382] It has been for a relatively long time that statism prevailed over individualism; the state sovereignty is supreme to human rights. This will be discussed mainly in Chapter 5.

Interestingly, China is unique in going into the republican eras as a centrally unified state, largely based upon the imperial territories of the previous empire.[383] Besides social intellectual, cultural and traditional politic institution factors, the conflation of nationalism and statism in China has played a critical role in the course of the transformation.

Section 3. The Influence of Nationalism on the Sovereignty of Contemporary China

There was no longer any anxiety about 'cancel[ing] [China's] global citizenship' (kaichu qiuji) which was voiced as late as the 1980s and traceable to the older patterns of nationalist thinking of the late Qing in the early 20th century.[384] Nevertheless, there was still a danger of China becoming alienated from the global society which might have been the result of the mistreatment of China by the status quo powers that dominated the capitalist world system. Historically, it is an undeniable fact that strong nationalistic feelings existed among the Chinese people throughout the PRC's history. It has had a substantial impact on the Chinese perspective of sovereignty.

1. The Nationalism and Internationalism during the Early Period of the PRC

Nationalism has a major influence on contemporary China, even in Mao's time China was more nationalist than communist. When China supported people's wars of national liberation, China had encouraged self-reliance but not conquest. As early as 1938, Mao wrote that "Chinese Communists must therefore combine patriotism with internationalism. We are at once internationalists and patriots".[385] If one were to question which one was the priority, he actually put nationalism as the priority. He comments, "Only by achieving national liberation will it be possible for the

382 Ibid., 2001, p. 570.

383 Pamela Kyle Crossley, The Late Qing Empire in Global History, Education about Asia, Vol. 13, No. 2, Fall 2008, p. 6.

384 Lu Yi (ed.), Qiuji: Yige shijiexing de xuanze (Global Citizenship: A World-Wide Choice), Shanghai: Baijia chubanshe, 1989.

385 Mao Zedong, Zhongguo Gongchandang zai minzu zhanzheng zhong de diwei (The role of the Chinese communist party in the national war, 1938), in: Mao Zedong Xuanji, Vol. II, Beijing: Renmin Press, 1991, pp. 520–521.

proletariat and other working people to achieve their own emancipation".[386] Whereas, the Soviet Union ("USSR") opposed nationalism in any socialist state. Following the lead of the Soviet Union, the Chinese government merged their nationalistic agenda with their commitment to socialist internationalism. However, Mao still attached great importance to China's full sovereignty, particularly, independence, territorial integrity and autonomy. For example, he was outraged at the Soviet's intention to set up a joint navy fleet in China in 1957.[387] His nationalist impulse propelled him to challenge the unequal relationship between the USSR and China. Moreover, China's anti-imperialistic nationalism thus was increasingly in conflict with the Soviet policy, which was seen as contrary to China's core national and ideological interests. Furthermore, the USSR even resorted to various coercive measures to force China to follow its leadership. In a dramatic move in 1960, the Soviet Union abruptly pulled its experts from China and suspended most aid projects. The coercive policy of the Soviet Union was seen as extremely insulting by China's leaders who felt much nationalist pride for winning China's independence and raising China's international status. In the meantime, the Chinese Communist Party ("CCP") rejected the Soviet version of socialist internationalism in order to maintain China's sovereignty. Notwithstanding, China launched a new international socialism to support all revolutionary struggles against imperialism and capitalism around the world on the basis of respect of other states' sovereignty. This new nationalism-through-internationalism formula allowed China to regain absolute independence from any big power.[388] While the USSR posed a serious security threat to China in 1969, Mao pragmatically decided to ally with the US in the East to resist the Soviet Union in the North.[389] Again, Mao put China's national interest ahead of internationalism. An astonishing Sino–US rapprochement came about in 1972 with the signing of the historic Shanghai Communique. Along with the rapprochement with the United States, China also normalized diplomatic relationships with most Western countries, improved its relations with developing countries, and joined the United Nations in 1971.[390] In short, the sovereignty of China was always of paramount importance and the socialist internationalism in the secondary position.

386 Mao Zedong, 1991, pp. 520–521.

387 Mao Zedong, A conversation with the Soviet Ambassador to China, 22 July 1958 (与前苏联驻华大使的谈话), in: Mao Zedong Waijiao Wenxuan, Beijing: Central Party Literature Press, 1994, p. 112.

388 Chen Zhimin, 2005, p. 44.

389 Xiong Xianghui, The prelude of the opening-up of Sino–US relationship: four veteran marshals' study of international situation and their proposals in 1969 (打开中美关系的前奏: 1969 年四位老帅对国际形势的研究与建议), in: Diplomacy of New China (新中国外交风云), Beijing: Shijie zhishi chubanshe, 1996, Vol. 4, pp. 7–34.

390 Chen Zhimin, 2005, p. 45.

2. Multiple Modalities of Nationalism after 1979

From 1978, economic modernization and improvement of the Chinese people's living standard were assigned as the 'central task' of the government, meanwhile, the impulse for world revolution was abandoned. China's relationship with other countries would no longer be decided by ideology but rather by national interest. Such nationalism is known as positive nationalism. In the 1980s, Chinese nationalism begins to lose control from the government. While liberal capitalism and democracy marched into Eastern Europe and the Soviet Union, China as the only remaining large communist state inevitably sensed an ideological insecurity. The Tiananmen Square event in 1989 aggravated such a sense of insecurity. On the one hand, the CCP started to strengthen the patriotic education of China's youth. The leaders felt that the lack of patriotic education in the 1980s allowed the rise of a romantic political liberalism among intellectuals and students, which partly caused the political instability at the end of the 1980s. A 'Campaign for National Unity' was initiated, which targeted the youth for 'patriotic education'. The CCP insists on its political legitimacy by appealing to its past credentials as the leader and defender of Chinese independence. In September 1994, the CCP's Propaganda Department issued the 'Fundamental Principles on Implementing Patriotic Education' for all people. The aim of this new campaign, as it is put in the Beijing Review, is to "take concerted effort in various quarters to create a strong atmosphere in which the entire Chinese people will be influenced by the patriotic ideas and spirit".[391] Indeed, the long history against foreign aggression and foreign powers' encroachment of Chinese sovereignty was exploited by the CCP to legitimate its governance and enforce nationalism propaganda.

Before the 1990s, the state or party had an ability to monopolize the nationalism discourse against intrusion from unofficial circles. However, a bottom-up form of nationalism emerged and gradually developed contending with the official discourse of patriotism. The 'pragmatic nationalism' emerged with China's rising, it drove the CCP's legitimacy from the economic and social realities of China, accepting and exploiting foreign influence. Another type of nationalism, so-called 'Neo-conservatism', emphasizes strong state control as well as moral values based on the conservative elements of Confucianism.[392] The Say No-ism of popular nationalism rose among Chinese people who obtained more self-confidence due to rapid economic development, and yet felt frustrated by the mistreatment and even insulting behavior of the West, in particular the United States. Its popularity came on the ground that it puts forward a nationalistic and robust view of China's foreign relations, especially with Western powers. Consequently, following the reform-opening policy nationalism was multiplied.

---

391 Zhao Shuisheng, A stateled nationalism: the patriotic education campaign in post-Tiananmen China, Communist and Post-Communist Studies, Vol. 31, Issue 3, 1998, pp. 287–302.

392 Zhao Shuisheng, Chinese nationalism and its international orientations, in: Political Science Quarterly, Vol. 115, Issue 1, 2000, p. 17.

3. The Characteristics of Present Nationalism

3.1. Humiliation as an Integral Part of Chinese Nationalism[393]

Chinese nationalistic discourse emphasizes that since the 19th century China has been treated unjustly and its territory and related sovereign rights have been exploited by other powers; China maintains its humiliation whilst in a protracted process of building power sufficient to self-protect. Present nationalism still carries on the historical humiliation even though China is rising in a world which is still dominated by the West. It is the major source of anti-western-sentiment and the rapid rise of an aggressive nationalism in China today.[394] Moreover, the century of humiliation has had an actual and substantial impact on today's Chinese foreign policy and with no sign of fading away. Since China lost sovereignty to the Western powers and Japan before 1945, now it must make sure not to lose sovereignty again to any other state.[395] In sum, the nationalistic discourse leads to a sense of 'victimization' of Chinese people and elites which is continuing to influence their interpretation of sovereignty.

3.2. Territory Sovereignty at the Core of Nationalism

Territorial integrity has been confirmed as the core of Chinese national interest. As Wang Gungwu writes, 'no leader in China can afford to let any land to go'.[396] Besides the territorial integrity, Chinese nationalists have difficulties when seeing Western states involving themselves in Chinese internal issues. As some foreign writers observe, Chinese government spokesperson even nowadays are quick to find "violations of China's sovereignty in routine differences of diplomatic opinion, whether meeting with the Dalai Lama, selling defensive arms to Taiwan, or criticizing China's internet policies."[397] Moreover, in Chinese society, whenever sovereignty is mentioned Chinese nationalism is immediately stirred up and unifies the public.[398] For example, the 2008 Carrefour boycott events happened because netizens (internet users) believed a big shareholder to be financially supporting the Tibet Independence. Nationalist protesters gathered outside Carrefour supermarkets in over a dozen

---

393 William A. Callahan, National Insecurities: Humiliation, Salvation, and Chinese Nationalism, Alternatives, Vol. 29, 2004, pp. 199–218.

394 Randall Peerenboom, China Stands up: 100 Years of Humiliation, Sovereignty Concerns, and Resistance to Foreign Pressure on PRC, Courts Emory International Law Review, Vol. 24, 2010, p. 656.

395 William A. Callahan, 2004, pp. 199–218.

396 Wang Gungwu, Joining the Modern World: Inside and Outside China, Singapore: World Scientific Publishing Company, December 4, 2000, p. 11.

397 Randall Peerenboom, 2010, p. 656.

398 Junwu Pan, Sovereignty Implication for China: Then and Now, in: Aspects of Sovereignty: Sino-Swedish Reflections (Per Sevastik ed.), Leiden: Martinus Nijhoff Publishers, 2013, p. 15.

Chinese cities, waving banners and shouting slogans about opposing Tibetan independence and boycotting French goods. The Chinese anti-Japan demonstrations of 2012 held across major cities in China during August and September 2012 developed from a series of peaceful demonstrations into violent protesting against the Japanese sovereignty claim on the Diaoyu Islands. Some protestors hoisted the portrait of Mao Zedong to express the dissatisfaction of current leaders' foreign policies.[399]

Today with the multi-polarization of Chinese society after 35 years of 'reform and opening' and the Internet as a new media source, which opened up possibilities to express popular opinion, no one can truly control public opinion and monopolize nationalism. Current circumstances are, in some aspects, similar to the eve of the overthrowing of the Qing dynasty.[400] Like the Qing court, the corruptions of officials generated mass dissatisfaction. The Chinese government does not want weak foreign policies stirring demonstrations which might trigger a regime change. Even though there are many differences between them the CCP still have to respect the public's opinions which are often aroused by issues relating to territorial sovereignty. It is undeniable that sovereignty and nationalism are frequently used interchangeably by the Chinese government as a political instrument.[401] However, some neglect the fact that the public will (Minyi) always have quite a big impact on Chinese policy and its traditional governance principles. Chinese leaders understand that inflamed nationalism can have very serious consequences which might contribute to a regime change. Particularly when Xi Jingping was in power he took a tougher stand on the territorial disputes and other issues concerning sovereignty due to the pressure of popular nationalism, resulting in a compromise with the public opinion;[402] meanwhile he carried on with harsh and wide ranging anti-corruption action.

3.3. *The View of 'Great Unification' Still Being a Part of Chinese Nationalism*

Actually, the phenomena that fragmentation has not been tolerated by many Chinese could be attributed to the traditional view of "Great Unification". Some see the PRC's position on Hong Kong as nationalistic since it has always insisted on its sovereignty there and could hardly be expected to relinquish that claim. The formula of 'one country two systems' for Hong Kong and Macao involves important concessions on matters of local autonomy although the PRC insists on the formalities of its

399 '9.18' increases anti-Japan emotion, should the hatre education promote? Voice of America. September 18, 2012.

400 Zhang Ming, The Comparison between the Dangers of Reform and the New Policies of the Late Qing Dynasty (改革危局与清末新政比较), available at: http://history.news.163.com/09/0629/07/5CV6THC2 00013 FLL.html.

401 Jean-Pierre Cabestan, 2005, pp. 26–40.

402 Wenfang Tang, Benjamin Darr, Chinese Nationalism and its Political and Social Origins, Journal of Contemporary China, Vol. 21, No. 77, September, 2012, pp. 811–826.

sovereignty over these areas.[403] Such arrangements reflect the stubbornness on the traditional idea of the "Great Unification", which is rooted in thousands of years. It helps explain why support for Chinese policies in Tibet and Xingjiang dominates in China (Further discussion seen in Chapter 6).

However, the view of the "Great Unification" does not mean a revival of the whole old empire. The major views of Chinese nationalists do not go to extreme nationalism as a western observer writes: '[Chinese] mourned not only the loss of "Our Hong Kong" but also of "Our Burma," "Our Siam [Thailand]," and "Our Annam [Vietnam]." Indeed, one of the icons of national-humiliation discourse is a map of China from 1898 showing the imperialist powers "carving the country up like a melon."... The lost "sacred territory" must be reclaimed and reunified. But as many of the maps refer back to the territories of the Qing dynasty at its peak, it is fair to ask, "What is the *status quo ante* that China is seeking to recover in cleansing its national humiliation: equality or empire?"'[404]

Such a suggestion simply comes out nowhere and goes nowhere. It is essentially against current international rules and has nothing in common with current Chinese nationalists. However, the nationalism fever in China still worries some states.

Conclusion

In conclusion, China as an ancient nation entered into modern history with nationality and nationalism both present.[405] This makes China's nationalism strong enough to influence both modern and contemporary China. Undoubtedly, nationalism dominated the modern history of China since China had been in a long period of crisis of losing its country (wangguo). Chinese nationalism was used as a powerful tool to overturn the Qing dynasty and resist imperialism and Japanese aggression. It was also a major source of a radical political change. However, Chinese traditional unified state theory affected the process of political revolution so that the task of saving the state overweighed the establishment of people's rights and people's sovereignty. Nowadays, nationalism presses China's interpretation of sovereignty into a narrow definition because of the 'century of humiliation' and the traditional idea of the 'Great Unification'. These are cautionary and show China's intention 'to bring to an end the overlong century of humiliation and subordination to the West and Japan'[406] or 'driven by nationalist sentiment' with a yearning to redeem itself

403 James Townsend, 1992, p. 122.

404 William A. Callahan, 2004, pp. 199–218.

405 Benjamin Akzin, State and Nation, London: Hutchinson, 1964, pp. 41, 46, 77–79; Royal Institute of International Affairs, Nationalism, New York: Kelley, 1966, p. xviii; Boyd C. Shatì, Nationalism: Myth and Reality, New York: Harvest, 1955, p. 10; and Louis Snyder, Global Mini-Nationalisms: Autonomy or Independence, Westport Conn.: Greenwood, 1982, p. xv.

406 Samuel P. Huntington, The Clash of Civilizations and the Remaking of World Order, New York: Simon & Schuster, 1996, p. 229.

from the humiliations of the past. Some suspect that the simple urge for international power might propel China into seeking to replace the United States as the dominant power in Asia,[407] and might endanger peace in the Pacific–Asia region.[408] Hence, Chinese leaders repeatedly promise the international sphere that it will always only insist on equal sovereignty and non-intervention policy and promise that China will not pursue hegemony[409]

407 Richard Bernstein and Ross H. Munro, 'The coming conflict with America', Foreign Affairs, March/April 1997, p. 19.

408 Edward Friedman, Chinese nationalism, Taiwan autonomy and the prospects of a larger war, Journal of Contemporary China, Vol. 6, No. 14, March 1997, p. 5.

409 Xi: There is no gene for invasion in our blood, 2014-05-16, Xihua, available at: http://usa.chinadaily.com.cn/china/2014-05/16/content_ 17511170.htm.

Chapter 5. Sovereignty and Human Rights in China

Introduction

Antonio Cassese: "At least at the normative level the international community is becoming more integrated and – what is even more important – [...] such values as human rights and the need to promote development are increasingly penetrating various sectors of international law that previously seemed impervious to them."[410]

In regards to human rights has China come a long way? At the domestic level, the Chinese human rights situation has deeply concerned Western states for a rather long time. Its particular understanding of the relationship between sovereignty rights and human rights and its rejection of humanitarian interference have been widely criticized by Western states. China has definitely taken a totally different path to human rights policy with Chinese characteristics.[411] However, it has cooperated with Western states to improve the Chinese human rights situation and has engaged in human rights dialogs with them. Notwithstanding, even though China has made constant efforts to improve its human rights and its perspective on international human rights is not static at all, Western states would still not admit it unless the 'democratic' system runs in China.

Section 1. Human Rights in the Domestic Level of China

1. The History of Human Rights in China

From the beginning of Chinese history, China assumed that the ideal order rested on a larger-scale inclusive system that unified all people under the governance of one ruler. In general, early Chinese thinkers were more concerned with peace and harmony than with the rights of individuals.[412] Indeed, human rights were not an issue in the traditional Chinese political and legal system.

In the late nineteenth and early twentieth centuries, China experienced rapid conceptual and political changes. Ensuing new modes of thought on self and society, a new vocabulary was created. The concepts of democracy, republic, sovereignty, nationalism, and natural rights arrived with Western warships and cannons. Chinese thinkers in the beginning of the twentieth century did not distinguish natural rights from human rights. In the 1920s, Sun Zhongshan (the funding father of the Republic

410 Cassese, 2005, p. 45.

411 Chen Zhishang, Rethinking on China's human rights ideology, International Critical Thought Vol. 1, No. 4, December 2011, p. 408.

412 Marina Svensson, Debating Human Rights in China: A Conceptual and Political History, Lanham: Rowman & Little field Publishers, 2002, p. 306.

of China) chose the concept of people's rights (minquan) instead of human rights (tianfu renquan) as the concept of human rights was metaphysical. The Guomin party ("GMD") basically saw human rights and people's rights as different ideas. People's rights were understood by the GMD as being conditional on people's political allegiance and given by the state with the national interest in mind. As a matter of fact, the theory of struggling for people's rights was helpful for the transformation of China when the goal was national salvation. While the concept of human rights was disseminated into China, the Chinese context was different from that of Europe in that the major worry for most Chinese was the encroachment of foreign powers and possible extinction of their race and nation.[413] It is clearly embodied in Zou Rong's writing, "Let us expand the nine generation vengeance, engage in a ten year bloody war, sharpen our knifes and raise our banners, and daringly face death in order to drive out the Manzu scoundrels who humiliate us, tyrannies us, slaughter us, and rape our women, in order to restore our cultured native land, recover our natural rights, win back the freedom which is our birth right, and restore the happiness of freedom and equality of all."[414]

He also called to fight against the white for China's sovereignty and Chinese rights in a perspective of racism.[415] Chen Tianhua described how Westerners treated the Chinese as inferiors, exemplified by their powers of extraterritoriality that had enabled them to put up a sign in a park in Shanghai reading: "Dogs and Chinese are not allowed."[416]

They saw the authoritarian political system as the main obstruction to human rights. Thus, in the early period of human rights in China, national survival rather than the freedom of the individual from an oppressive state was predominant.[417] Nationalism was the main melody. The English were said to value freedom because of its benefit to the individual and the country, whereas the French were said to value freedom as an inviolable and innate right, regardless of whether it was beneficial or not.[418] The Chinese in the early 20th century were said to value freedom for national salvation.

Nationalists like Zou Rong and Chen Tianhua used peoples' rights as a weapon against the Manzu and foreign powers. However, human rights did not figure so prominently in the revolutionary process after 1905. During this period, the GMD, the first ruling party of the Republic of China, was not a real advocate of human rights.[419] Human rights were not promoted in China after the Republic of China replaced the Qing dynasty. The opposite party, the Chinese Communist party, criticized human rights violations committed by the government and warlords. They

413 Ibid., pp. 192–193.
414 Zou Rong, Revolutionary Army, Datong Book Press, 1903.
415 Zou Rong, Revolutionary Army, Datong Book Press, 1903.
416 Chen Tianhua, Shi Zi Hou (狮子吼) (written in 1905), Qiushuo, Issue 4, 1983, p. 37.
417 Marina Svensson, 2002, p. 98.
418 Ibid., p. 86.
419 Ibid., pp. 120–121.

particularly advocated rights of women and workers, which were suppressed and deprived. Confucianism was seen as the oppressing tool used to deprive people of human rights.[420] However, they advocated revolutionary methods instead of democratic and legal methods to protect suppressed people's rights. During the 1940s, human rights issues remained as a weapon in political struggles in China. At the international level, the GMD unambiguously endorsed universal human rights which was just born but did not translate it into domestic systems. At the end of the civil war, the Communist party expelled the Nationalists out of the mainland to Taiwan.

Before the founding of the People's Republic of China in 1949, the term "human rights" was used by the Chinese Communist Party to oppose rule by the Kuomintang. During that period, the Communist Party had adopted more than 10 legal documents to guarantee human rights. After the founding of the PRC, the term "human rights" disappeared. They were replaced by "citizen's right" and "people's rights" in order to make more explicit the socialist nature of the Chinese state. Under the logic of communist ideology - that the working people are the masters in society - human rights did not make much sense. Due to the isolation during most of the Cold War period, China's human rights policy was not in the political agenda. In the late 1970s, when people started to reflect on their experiences of the Cultural Revolution of the 1960s, the term "human rights" reappeared in connection with highly publicized tragedies, such as the death of Liu Shaoqi, the Vice Chairman of the state, and other former Chinese leaders, who experienced persecution and died. People began to realize that they needed something which could protect them against arbitrary mistreatment.

When Deng Xiaoping assumed power and implemented the reform and open policy in the late 1970s, human rights ideas and knowledge of the international human rights movement reached the Chinese grassroots population. The reform and open policy has had a profound impact on the human rights discourse in China since 1979. "Class struggle" and "politics in command" have been replaced by "getting rich is glorious". The emphasis on citizens' duties to the state has been replaced by concern about citizens' basic economic needs or rights. The Chinese government divides the realization of human rights into two steps: the first step is to gain the economic and development rights, and the second step is to realize political freedom and liberal democracy.[421]

The campaign to "emancipate the mind" in the early 1980s aimed to cast off the old dogma and opened the way for reform, thus providing space for spreading human rights ideas. However, in 1984 and 1987, the government launched two political campaigns that attempted to repudiate human rights. In the first campaign, human rights were labeled as "spiritual pollution", in the second "bourgeois liberalization". China's participation in the UN human rights work gradually grew during the 1980s.

420 Ibid, pp. 152–153.

421 Information Office of the State Council of China, Progress in China's Human Rights Cause in 2012.

In 1988, during the international commemoration of the fortieth anniversary of the Universal Declaration of Human Rights, the discussion of human rights in China was limited and was used for the purposes of justifying Chinese state policies. The present-day human rights discourse in China was sparked by the Tiananmen Square Incident in 1989, as the outside world suddenly increased its pressure on the Chinese regime. Beijing began to realize the significance of human rights as a legitimate subject for both domestic and international society.[422] In response, the government published the Human Rights in The China White Paper in 1991. This was an attempt by the government to interpret Chinese laws in terms of human rights.[423] From then on, China began to work with the international society, mainly Western states, in the human rights area.

2. Chinese culture and human rights

The discussions regarding the relationship between Chinese culture and human rights are relatively controversial. They range from claiming that Chinese culture is incompatible with human rights to contending that certain human rights are more compatible with Chinese culture than others. It is true that Confucianism provided rites, not rights, as the basis of the Chinese political system. In Confucianism, the relationship between subjects and rulers, sons and fathers, women and men, were strictly hierarchical and characterized by benevolence and righteousness from above, and loyalty and obedience from below. Confucian was also attacked for suppressing women.[424] In this system people did not possess any universal rights, nor could they expect equal treatment. However, some scholars argue that even though Confucianism did not give rise to a concept of human rights, it is compatible with human rights and contains within itself ideas that are congenial to and can nurture human rights. They further argue that the Confucian humanist ethic, manifested in certain ideals such as ren (humaneness) and yi (righteousness), are quite similar to or contained in the concept of human rights.[425] They claim that the paternalistic

---

422 Yuchao Zhu, China and International 'Human Rights Diplomacy', China: An International Journal, Vol. 9, No. 2, September 2011, pp. 217–245.

423 Qian Qichen, Protecting Human Rights a Universal Ideal, in: Beijing Review, Vol. 16–22, Nov. 1998.

424 Marina Svensson, 2002, p. 119.

425 John F. Copper, Franz Michael and Yuan-li Wu, Human Rights in Post-Mao China, Colorado: Westview Press, 1985; Wm. Theodore de Bary, East Asian Civilizations: A Dialogue in Five Stages, Harvard: Harvard University Press, 1988; Du Gangjian, Two-way legal order and system of basic rights- new Benevolence perspective of Confucian Order (双向法治秩序与基本权利体系—儒家秩序观的新仁学思考), in: Studies of Law and Business, Issue 5, 1995, pp. 29–34; Xia Yong, The Origin of Human Rights: the Historical Philosophy of Rights (人权概念起源：权利的历史哲学), Chinese University of Political Science and Law Press, 1992; Xiao Yong, Public Law, Vol. 1, Law Press, 1999; William Theodore de Barry & Tu Weiming. (eds.), Confucianism and Human Rights, New York: Columbia University Press, 1998.

benevolence in imperial China wherein the emperor had the duty to secure the well being of his subjects explains the contemporary perspectives of the Chinese government's emphasis on economic rights and collective rights. The traditional concepts of society as an organ where collective rights prevail over the individual, the idea that man exists for the state rather than vice versa and that rights, rather than having any absolute value, derive from the state, have been major themes prevailing in the past as well as in contemporary China.[426]

Interestingly, there is the third voice that culture is not the necessary concern for the issue of human rights in the Chinese mainland. It holds that it is far-fetched to try to make Confucianism share the same values as human rights. It is also unnecessary to prove contradictions between Confucianism and human rights since culture in China is not static and has been always evolving. For instance, the hierarchical ideas of Chinese traditional philosophy were abandoned with the establishment of the PRC or even earlier with the birth of the RC. Moreover, the cultural revolution happening in the middle of the 20th century made a big change to Chinese traditional culture.[427] The third opinion arguably simply maintains an ignorance of Chinese traditional culture. It is a misunderstanding of the endurance of Chinese traditional culture. Despite the gradual erosion of Chinese intellectuals' faith in the viability of traditional Chinese culture in the modern era, traditional Chinese culture is still an integral part of the 'psycho-cultural construct' of the contemporary Chinese.[428] It is undeniable that the Chinese are unconsciously affected by traditional culture even though Marxism has replaced Confucianism. The discourse of human rights in China carried and carries influence from Chinese traditional culture, including Confucianism, Daoism, and Legalism.

In fact, it is extremely difficult to deny the first two ideas. The cultural arguments are not only a patent of China. It comes with Singapore, Malaysia, and other Asian states as well. All of them have questioned both the West's exploitation of the human rights issue in international relations and the relevance of the prevalent human rights concepts to their societies. They hold that the West shaped the concept of human rights and imposed them on Asia without consideration of their different cultural and historical tradition. They claim that differences with respect to human rights are justified on the ground of cultural and historical differences and on the priority of economic development.[429] It was confirmed in the Bangkok conference in 1993 by a statement, "they must be considered in the context of a dynamic and

---

426 Ann Kent, Between Freedom and Subsistence: China and Human Rights, Oxford: Oxford University Press, 1993, pp. 30–31.

427 Marina Svensson, 2002, pp. 58–59.

428 Tu Weiming, The Confucian Tradition in Chinese History, in: Heritage of China: Contemporary Perspectives on Chinese Civilization, ed. Paul S. Ropp, Berkeley: University of California Press, 1990, p. 36.

429 Marina Svensson, 2002, pp. 58–59.

evolving process of international norm-setting, bearing in mind the significance of national and regional particularities and various historical, cultural and religious backgrounds".[430]

Compared to Western societies, China places much less emphasis on individual rights and significantly more emphasis on the value of the individual in terms of his or her contribution to harmony in society. This is deeply rooted in Chinese culture. Nevertheless today, in contrast to the past, human rights is not perceived as a threat to Chinese cultural identity. Rather, engaging in the international human rights discourse is seen as a way of resisting foreign influence and keeping Chinese culture distinct.[431] The Chinese government persistently argues that the Chinese tradition emphasizes economic and social rights over civil and political rights, and the priority of collective rights over individual rights. It indicates that China recognizes human rights as universal values but also argues that the specific situation of human rights on the mainland of China was a logical and inevitable consequence of the Chinese political culture.[432]

3. The Development of Human Rights in China

For a country that had spent about one century in a state of turmoil, foreign invasion, and finally civil war, the establishment of the People's Republic of China marked much needed peace and stability. A new legal order and system of government were established, and a new socialist legal system had its heyday of development from 1954 to 1956. However, the various campaigns instigated by Mao during the late 1950s, culminating in the complete chaos of the Cultural Revolution and total isolation of nearly a quarter of the world's population, reduced China's understanding of, and engagement with, the rule of law to virtually a blank sheet of paper. The whole machinery of a judicial system had shut down in the 10 years of disorders from 1966 to 1976 when rule was almost exclusively based on administrative fiat. "Law took a back seat to politics" as the fickle will of the different factions fought for dominance in the government. In the opening-up policy led by Deng Xiaoping, from 1978 international human rights treaties were hardly at the forefront of the Chinese government's concerns. The priorities were to rejuvenate the economy and open-up relations with the outside world, and in particular the western, developed nations. Nonetheless, internal and international human rights treaties formed part of this opening up.

430 Our voice: Bangkok NGO declaration on human rights: reports of the Asia Pacific NGO Conference on Human Rights and NGOs' statements to the Asia Regional Meeting, Asian Cultural Forum on Development, 1993, pp. 244–245.

431 Xin Chunying, A Brief History of the Modern Human Rights Discourse in China, in: Human Rights Dialogue, Series 1, Number 3, Winter 1995. Available at: http://www.carnegiecouncil.org/publications/archive/dialogue/1_03/articles/515.html.

432 Qian Qichen, 1998.

The Chinese human rights discourse has its immediate background developed around domestic concerns and political contestations but it also has been shaped and inspired by development at the international human rights level.[433] In the first Constitution of the PRC that was introduced in 1954, it stated the fundamental rights and freedom that Chinese citizens could enjoy. However, influenced by ideas from the extreme left, the constitution in 1975 removed most of the rights listed in the 1954 version. Although the 1978 Constitution brought back some of the rights, it failed to restore that 'All citizens are equal in law'. After the reform and open door policy was taken at the end of 1970s, the 1982 Constitution restored a chapter on the 'fundamental rights and duties of citizens', which was based on the 1954 version. Upon making a comparison between the Chinese Constitution and the two international human rights covenants of the UN, it is not difficult to find that most of the rights mentioned in both of the covenants are listed in the Chinese Constitution. However, the two major rights that are not included are right of life and right to free movement.[434] It is worth mentioning that Article 2 of the Chinese Constitution stipulates that all power in the People's Republic of China belongs to the people. The 1982 constitution articulates that the Communist Party is to act 'within the scope of the Constitution and law, therefore restricting the Party's previously 'unlimited' control over the Chinese people and state.' In the version of the 2004 amendment of the 1982 Constitution it states that "the state respects and preserves human rights."

From the 1990s onwards, China has published a large number of domestic laws to protect human rights and abolished certain laws against human rights including the system of detention for interrogation (abolished in 1997), the system of custody and repatriation (abolished in 2003) and the system of reeducation through labor (abolished in 2013.12.28) although enforcement remains a major problem. Reforms in the last few years have greatly strengthened procedural safeguards in capital punishment cases leading to significantly fewer executions.[435] General improvements of the criminal laws, such as the recent rules to strengthen provisions for excluding illegally obtained evidence, are very useful for human rights protection.[436]

However, the major problem is not how many human rights are stipulated in Chinese laws but how to ensure their enforcement. In December 4, 2012, Chinese President Xi gave an important speech demanding full enforcement of China's

---

433 Mary Svensson, 2002, p. 306.

434 Liantai Liu, Comparison between the International Human Rights Charter and the Constitution of Our Country (国际人权宪章与我国宪法的相关比较), 1999, No. 5, Academic Journal of Chinese Communist Party School of Zhejiang Province, pp. 84–89.

435 China, Human Rights WATCH, available at: http://www.hrw.org/en/node/79301 (last visited May 17, 2014).

436 Translation: China's New Rules of Evidence in Criminal Trials, Dui Hua Human Rights Journal, May 15, 2014, available at: http://www.duihuahrjournal.org/2010/06/translation-chinas-new-rules-on_25.html.

Constitution. In October 2014, the fourth plenary session of the 18th Communist Party of China ("CPC"), as the highest level institution of decision making, unprecedentedly focuses on "comprehensively advancing the rule of law" in China. Particularly, it highlights the need to strengthen the implementation of the Constitution.[437] The 32nd anniversary of the current constitution, which was promulgated on December 4, 1982, is marked as China's first Constitution Day.[438] China has shown a greater willingness to constructively engage with domestically human rights improvement.

In a recent Human Rights White Paper put out by the Information Office of the State Council, China reported that it had signed 27 international human rights treaties.[439] The two most important UN human rights documents, the International Covenant on Economic, Social and Cultural Rights (ICESCR) and the International Covenant on Civil and Political Rights (ICCPR), have been signed by China, respectively, in 1997 and 1998. Furthermore, China ratified the ICESCR in 2001. China was one of the earliest signatories to the Convention for the Elimination of Discrimination against Women (CEDAW) in 1981 and further signed the Convention for the Elimination of Racial Discrimination (CERD) in 1982, the Convention against Torture and Other Cruel, Inhuman or Degrading Treatment or Punishment (CAT) in 1988, and the Convention on the Rights of the Child (CRC) in 1992. However, in each case, China has made reservations which reflect its concerns of state sovereignty and noninterference, or which deny individuals the right to submit individual complaints. Thus, China has made reservations to Article 22 of the CERD, Article 29 (i) of the CEDAW, Article 30 (i) of the CAT, all relating to the right whereby a dispute between two state parties can be referred to the International Court of Justice. In the case of its reservation to Article 20 of the CAT, the state party shall not be subject to outside scrutiny of the Committee against torture in the case of a complaint. China's reservation to Article 6 of the CRC, the inherent right of the child to life, limits its compliance to consistency with the provision in the Chinese Constitution on family planning.[440]

In the National Human Rights Action Plan (2012–2015), China emphasized that it will persistently advance the cause of human rights but also pointed out that China's reality would restrict the promotion of Chinese human rights. "China remains a developing country that is fraught with problems from unbalanced, uncoordinated and unsustainable development. Due to the influences and limitations of natural, historical and cultural factors, as well as the current level of economic and social

---

437 Highlights of communique of 4th plenary session of CPC Central Committee, People daily, 24th October, 2014.

438 China ratifies national Constitution Day, available at: http://www.chinadaily.com.cn/china/2014-11/01/content_18840106.htm.

439 Information Office of the State Council of China, Progress in China's Human Rights Cause in 2012.

440 Article 25 of Constitution of the People's Republic of China (1982): "The state promotes family planning so that population growth may fit the plans for economic and social development".

development, China still confronts many challenges in the development of its human rights cause and it has a long way to go before it attains the lofty goal of full enjoyment of human rights". It argues that the concept of human rights is a product of historical development and closely associated with specific social, political and economic conditions and the specific history, culture and values of a particular country. Countries at different development stages or with different historical traditions and cultural backgrounds also have a different understanding and practice of human rights.[441]

However, it does show that China has generally accepted human rights as international common values and admitted to Chinese human rights problems. The difference of culture and national conditions (guoqing) is the major argument for the current problems facing the development of human rights in China. In short, China defends itself and holds that the development of human rights shall be gradually moved forward in accordance with national conditions.

Section 2. China's Human Rights Foreign Policy and Sovereignty Principle

China generally accepts sovereignty as a limited and restricted concept.[442] The doctrine of the right to intervene emerges as a counterbalance and, according to this, the sovereignty of the state should be subordinated to a principle of extreme emergency: the need for a minimum protection of human rights.[443] Is sovereignty restricted concerning the assurance of the conditions necessary for respecting human rights? China seemingly has a different answer than the European states.

1. China's Human Rights Foreign Policy

After the Tiananmen event, within the UN human rights regime and multilateral forums, China's human rights approach has received constant attention. Since then, China has gradually developed a multi-tier strategy in its human rights diplomacy. Generally, in the multilateral international human rights arena China's approach is dominated by the sovereignty principle and organizing like-minded countries into a coalition; in bilateral diplomatic channels, China follows a combined policy of dialogue, negotiation, bargaining and supplementary economic incentives and on certain international human rights issues such as in the case of Darfur, China mainly applies ad hoc and flexible policies.[444]

---

441 The speech of Liu Huaqiu, as the head of the Chinese delegation at the UN World Conference on Human Rights in 1993.

442 Simona Tutuianu, 2012, p. 30.

443 Ibid., p. 28.

444 Yuchao Zhu, 2011, pp. 217–245.

Within the UN Human Rights Commission and later the Human Rights Council, China's activity was largely aimed at persuading others not to support draft resolutions against China that were mostly submitted by Western states. China normally argued that it was under its own jurisdiction as China's "internal affairs".[445] In multilateral international human rights diplomacy, China has persistently adhered to the sovereignty principle and has made great efforts to find like-minded states, mostly developing countries, to form a quasi-alliance to back up each other on human rights criticism to counter Western brickbats. This type of coalition in human rights diplomacy has been effectively implemented by China and many developing states in multilateral international human rights regimes.[446]

Moreover, Beijing made a big change from resistance of external criticizing to cooperation with Western states in 1996 at the bilateral level. China's human rights policy as part of its foreign policy mainly focuses on bilateral dialogues with major Western countries on the human rights issues in a long-term cooperation. It was a great compromise for the Chinese government who always held human rights as internal issues which were not subject to foreign intervention. It reveals that China turns to relative sovereignty in a cautious way. Such an approach allows it to take an advantage of flexibility in practice, meanwhile branded with some "Chinese characteristics" that bear remnants from the colonial past-century humiliation. The relative sovereignty interpretation is also embodied in its recognition of human rights protection in its White Papers. Beijing's practices show that China generally accepts that human rights are to some extent internationalized. Interestingly, the official declaration of such a shift came much later. In October 1998, at a conference commemorating the 50th anniversary of the Universal Declaration of Human Rights the Chinese Foreign Minister Qian Qichen stated that there was a global recognition of the "universality of human rights" and that all nations "observe the same international norms on human rights".[447]

After all, for China, being a target state in human rights-related resolutions is not only an embarrassment but it also puts the country in an uncomfortable position and this is certainly detrimental to China's intention to becoming a noteworthy member of the global community.[448] As a response, the Chinese government has published more than 70 White Papers since 1991 with the majority of them on human rights. China's State Council Information Office has issued White Papers on the U.S. human rights record for each of the last 15 years to show to the world that the United States has its own problems in terms of human rights and is in no position to criticize the human rights situation of countries like China.

---

445 Ann Kent, China, the United Nations, and Human Rights, Philadelphia: University of Pennsylvanzia Press, 1999, pp. 55–57.

446 Zhu Yuchao, 2011, p. 217.

447 'Qian Qichen Urges Further Promotion of International Human Rights', Xinhua News (Beijing), 20 October 2008.

448 Yuchao Zhu, China and International 'Human Rights Diplomacy', China, An International Journal, Vol. 9, No. 2, September 2011, pp. 217–245.

China's attitude to human rights diplomacy can be assessed as a process of development. Generally, China has insisted on the fundamental importance of sovereignty, "there should be no interference in any country's internal affairs" and nations have the right to "choose their own paths" on human rights.[449] Meanwhile, it also recognizes that human rights to some extent are internationalized. The double-face of human rights grants Beijing flexibility when handling its respective issues. In public, China frequently holds up the shield of sovereignty to resist the intervention and criticisms from Western countries under the umbrella of promoting human rights. When human rights are viewed as a positive integration to safeguard its sovereignty or are in accordance with China's national interests, it lays down the shield of sovereignty and welcomes human rights. What matters to China is not the human rights themselves but what is behind them. In China's view, the roles that human rights are allowed to play should be limited to the stage where China's domestic stability and development are guaranteed.

2. China's Perspective of Relationship between Sovereignty and Human Rights

As was just analyzed, China has changed its human rights policy from a strict perception of sovereignty into a relative flexible approach step by step. However, it attempts to balance sovereignty and human rights by highlighting the compatibility of two concepts while the West emphasizes that "sovereignty can no longer be used to shield the actual suppression of popular sovereignty from external rebuke and remedy".[450]

2.1. Sovereignty and Human Rights are two Fundamental Values

China has a reputation of stressing sovereignty as vital in maintaining international peace in an international order which constitutes sovereign states. It also agrees that human rights are fundamental as a universal common value. Moreover, China emphasizes that strong sovereignty is the very guarantee of human rights protection.

Chinese official documents have upheld sovereignty without reservation and viewed it as a precondition to human rights.[451] The century of humiliation did not just make nationalism influential in China but also had a far-reaching impact on China's political system and foreign policies. National sovereignty equates to group rights as without the independence of the country individuals would not enjoy

449 See U.S.-China Joint Statement, 19 January 2011, available at: <www.whitehouse.gov/the-press-office/2011/01/19/us-china-joint-statement>.

450 W. Michael Reisman, Sovereignty and Human Rights in Contemporary International Law, in: The American Journal of International Law, Vol. 84, 1990, p. 872.

451 See Information Office of the State Council of the PRC, "Human Rights in China," November 1991, http://www.china.org.cn/e-white/7/index.htm.

any right. Only after China achieved national independence could the country be respected in the world and allow its people to enjoy human rights.[452] Consequently, the Chinese put sovereignty as the foundation of human rights, thus, sovereignty prevails over human rights. It is highlighted in Deng's famous comments, "If you ask me what is more important, human rights or national rights, I would say that national rights overwhelm human rights, since the former is associated with a state's independence, sovereignty and dignity."[453] This reflects a national-interest orientated approach prevailing in Chinese foreign policy. Human rights therefore lie in second place and that is difficult for the West to understand.

It was specifically stipulated in the Chinese constitution that the "exercise by citizens of the People's Republic of China of their freedoms and rights may not infringe upon the interests of the state, of society and of the collective, or upon the lawful freedoms and rights of other citizens".[454] In the Chinese perspective, no individual should place his own rights and interests above those of the state and society. If the sovereignty of a state is not safeguarded, the human rights of its citizens are out of the question. It is reliant upon the collective principle. All societies organized into states embrace collectivist principles since sovereignty itself is a collective right, whether in the form of a collective right of punishment, taxation or conscription. However, it is a collective right which we impose on ourselves in order to promote individual wellbeing. Hence, the state shall exercise sovereignty on behalf of people because the state is established by people to take charge of the wellbeing of all. The abuse of collective rights might perhaps open a window to dictatorship. It is critical to understand how to constrain state power and reduce the risk of power abuse when there are powerful instruments in the state's hands.

China admits that there are differences between China and Western states on the issues of human rights. Evidently, Beijing believes that Western states often use human rights as a spear against China's sovereignty and worries about how far Western states go when employing human rights as a weapon against China's sovereignty. However, recent developments of human rights law both at an international level and at China's domestic level drove Beijing to accept the universality of human rights protection and acknowledge that basic human rights protection is the responsibility of sovereignty. The paradox of China's interpretation results in pragmatism prevailing over China's practices.

---

452 Junru Li, Understanding Human Rights: An Issue in EU-China Relations, EU-China Observer, Issue 4, 2009, p. 8.

453 Fu Yaozu, Some Thoughts about Building Chinese International Relations Theory (关于建设中国国际关系理论的几点思考), Foreign Affairs Review, No. 5, 2005, p. 61.

454 Article 51, the Constitution of People of Republic of China, 1982.

2.2. *China insists that human rights issues fall, by and large, within the domestic jurisdiction of each state*

China takes the general position that it agrees with the international community expressing concern in a proper way over consistent and large-scale human rights violations in a given country. However, it objects to interference in other countries' "internal affairs" under the pretext of defending human rights because "the issue of human rights is, in essence, an internal affair of a country, and should be addressed mainly by the government of that country through its own efforts"[455] China has a reputation for its sensitivity on the issue of sovereignty, along with its concerns in relation to the current distribution of global power which it sees as structurally biased in favor of the West and against China. This makes it uneasy with human rights internationalism. It always fights back protesting that western powers undertake a neo-imperialist enterprise by manipulating human rights issues into agendas that interfere with China's internal affairs.[456]

As the critics argued, while the purpose served by state sovereignty is theoretically to protect and promote the freedom of citizens too often in reality its effective purpose becomes the maintenance of national sovereignty itself, such that the rights of citizens become inferior to the claims of the state or rather those who dominate this mechanism.[457] The critical point is to what extent such a problem is an international issue.

Externally, sovereignty implies independence from outside interference. A sovereign state should be recognized by its peers as a legal independent territorial entity. As a consequence of its sovereignty, a state has the right to independently make both foreign and domestic decisions. Those governments, which have unsatisfying human rights records, may rely on sovereignty as a strong argument to fend off foreign interference in violations of human rights. Consequently, the breach of human rights may be legitimized under the principle of sovereignty. On the other hand, violation of human rights may render interference from other states and international organizations necessary, which is called humanitarian intervention or Responsibility to Protect (R2P or RtoP). The powerful states may invoke this kind of intervention to pursue their national interests because there is no real world government to protect world citizens and every state puts its own national interest as the priority. Clearly, different states hold different opinions on the priority of the two values. It is extremely hard to reach a consensus on how to achieve a balance between the respect for state sovereignty and human rights protection. China with its colonial experience holds that the true protection of human rights can only be

455 Zhu Yuchao, 2011, p. 229.

456 Carlson, 2004, p. 16; Chengqiu Wu, Sovereignty, Human Rights, and Responsibility: Changes in China's Response to International Humanitarian Crises, Journal of Chinese Political Science, Vol. 15, Iss. 1, March 2010, pp. 71–97.

457 Suzaaen Ogden, Chinese Nationalism: The Precedence of Community and Identity over Individual Rights, Asian Perspective, Vol. 25, Iss. 4, 2001, pp. 157–185.

enforced by the people's own government. However, history also witnesses that domestic governments committed unbearable atrocities against their own people. The concept of Responsibility to Protect was introduced to stop internal atrocities in 2001. During the debates concerning R2P, China reaffirmed that states had the primary responsibility to protect their populations and that the international community should focus on assisting them whilst being mindful to and respectful of their sovereignty and territorial integrity.[458] China cautiously supports the R2P, prioritizing pillar one[459] and insisting that any other measures undertaken in implementing the principle be consistent with the UN Charter.

Section 3. The Gap between EU and China in Human Rights Protection

For decades China's human rights record has always been selected as a target of criticism by the European Union (EU) and its member states. The differences between the two sides are manifest. European perceptions of China's democratic deficits and the need for improvement in human rights issues motivate the prevalence of a value-based approach on the EU side. Conversely, China claims the European value-based diplomacy is counterproductive.

Firstly, European democracy can be traced back as early as classical Athens in the 6th century B.C.E. Modern democracy emerged in Europe on the same page with state sovereignty more than two centuries ago. Without a doubt, Europe has the most developed system of human rights protection and sees itself as a noble human rights promoter. Unlike the UN which is based on the sovereignty principle, the Preamble of the Charter of Fundamental Rights of the European Union proclaims that:

> "The Union is founded on the indivisible, universal values of human dignity, freedom, equality and solidarity; it is based on the principles of democracy and the rule of law. It places the individual at the heart of its activities, by establishing the citizenship of the Union and by creating an area of freedom, security and justice."

---

458 S/PV.6066, 14 January 2009, p. 7.

459 The UN Secretary-General Ban introduced three pillars of the RtoP as follows:
1. The state carries the primary responsibility for protecting populations from genocide, war crimes, crimes against humanity and ethnic cleansing, and their incitement;
2. The international community has a responsibility to encourage and assist States in fulfilling this responsibility;
3. The international community has a responsibility to use appropriate diplomatic, humanitarian and other means to protect populations from these crimes. If a state is manifestly failing to protect its populations, the international community must be prepared to take collective action to protect populations, in accordance with the Charter of the United Nations.

Evidently, the European Union is an entity based on human rights. Moreover, human rights are not only fundamental to European states and the EU but also a major issue on their diplomatic agenda. As high moral bearers, the EU and its member states designate human rights concerns in its daily diplomatic agenda. Criticizing China's human rights situation, they also see promoting China's human rights protection as part of their diplomatic tasks. Particularly, they keep pressure on China for improving individual political rights. On the other hand, China is certainly on a different page of human rights development with a divergent perception of human rights as a target state of human rights record. The Chinese government still postulates political rights as complementary to economic rights and emphasizes state sovereignty as the foundation of human rights. Internationally, the Chinese government objects to foreign powers interfering in human rights issues within a territory, and domestically, takes a rather discreet policy on the promotion of political rights in China. China believes that a rapid political change can lead to chaos and collapse of the country, which was demonstrated in the disintegration of the former Soviet Union, as a result of prioritization of radical political reform.

Secondly, the different culture and history between China and the West led to the different understandings on human rights and how to comprehend human rights differences between China and Europe. The disparity of perception of human rights between the Chinese and Europe is extremely huge. First of all, human rights emerged in Europe as early as the 16th or 17th century. However, it appeared in China after the Qing emperor had been overthrown around the early 20th century. In China's perspective, human rights and democracy can be ensured only on the ground that the basic living needs are satisfied and it can also be guaranteed only by strong sovereignty as well; this is because of China's colonial experience. European states accumulated a number of capitals during the industrial period and emerged as advanced economical entities. China did not solve the problem of 'basic warmth and eating' until the 1980s. Consequently, the gaps of understanding result in enduring criticism from the international human rights regimes on China's human rights protection. For example, the Chinese always put collective rights ahead of individual human rights, economic rights as the foundation of political rights. Chinese traditional philosophies emphasize the primacy of family, clan, and state; therefore, Chinese traditional culture focuses on more than human rights as applicable to persons who are part of something larger than themselves as individuals.[460] Consequently, the right to development as a comprehensive collective right is one of the central pillars of China's human rights theory.[461] Beijing argues that the improvement of Chinese living conditions is still the major task of the Chinese

460 John Berthrong, Human Rights and Responsibilities: A Confucian Perspective on the Universal Declaration of Human Rights, in: Human Rights and Responsibilities in the World Religions (ed. by Runzo, Martin and Sharma), Oxford: One World Publications, 2003, pp. 199–205.

461 Zhu Yuchao, 2011, pp. 217–245.

government although China has now achieved great success in its economic development. On the other side, Europe stresses that civil and political rights must take precedence and that without such rights as to the ballot and freely elected representatives, and the freedom of religion, speech, and assembly, no one can be secure in any social, economic, or cultural rights.[462] They also argue that individual rights shall take precedence over collective rights in that individual rights are usually associated with political and economic freedom, which are fundamental for Western democracy. Whereas in a European context, collective rights are associated with social control and running the risk of forming a dictatorship when collective rights prevail over individual rights. Thus, European states are pro-liberal individualists on the one side whilst China is pro-socialist on the other side.

Thirdly, the two sides have totally different views on the relationship between sovereignty and human rights. Although EU member states might not all have the exact same understanding of it, they have a consensus in that humanitarian invention can be justified when humanitarian crises happen (concerning humanitarian further analysis in the next section). Europe interprets sovereignty as an excuse used by non-democratic regimes to suppress individuals. Therefore, it can be said that they essentially consider sovereignty as anti-human rights. Actually, they work hard to transform structures of international law from the sovereignty-oriented modality into a human rights – oriented system. On the other side, China's perception of sovereignty is manifestly pro-human rights. Meanwhile, Beijing unwaveringly sticks to sovereignty-oriented modality. The European Union and its member states always see themselves as the most dedicated promoters of human rights protection. They enjoy exporting human rights into the states that have human rights problems. For example, they aid African states with conditions regarding human rights protection or democratic process. They sanction some states that might have internal problems of violating human rights. They like to force those states to accept their values of human rights and democracy. Therefore, they advocate interventionism and consider sovereignty as an obstacle to the export of human rights to those states, which could invoke sovereignty to resist the intervention. Moreover, the history that European states had imposed colonialism on the world by preaching Christian civilization makes a number of developing states suspecting its motive of promoting human rights to the world as a new form of imperialism. Conversely, China believes that human rights can be protected only by a strong sovereign government. Beijing firmly holds that exportation cannot make a real difference but only change from the inside can truly make progress.

Fourthly, China always highlights that every state has its own system, level of economic and cultural development, religions and beliefs, national custom, way of life, ideologies, historical conditions and geographical environments, all of which

462 Rudolph Joseph Rummel, Human Rights, in: Protest, Power, and Change: An Encyclopedia of Nonviolence Action From Act-up to Women's Suffrage (ed. by William Vogele and Roger Powers), Hamden, CT: Garland Publishing, 1996, pp. 112–124.

are varied, the human rights are primarily implemented, guaranteed, and developed by the government of that particular state based on its actual conditions and its citizens' needs. On the other hand, Europe emphasizes human rights as common fundamental values of the whole world which are 'inherent in all human beings' and 'are applicable everywhere and at every time' regardless of their nation, location, language, religion, ethnic origin or any other status.[463]

Fifthly, the United Kingdom (UK), Germany and other western states try to associate human rights with the issues of Tibet and Xinjiang in many cases. China views them as territorial issues, thus, Beijing responded harshly because there is an untouchable red line which means that territorial sovereignty is nonnegotiable. On the 25th September 2007, Merkel met the 14th Dalai Lama for "private and informal talks" in Berlin in the Chancellery amid protest from China. China afterwards canceled separate talks with German officials including talks with Justice Minister, Brigitte Zypries;[464] On the 15th April 2014, Beijing canceled a human rights dialogue with Britain on the grounds that the UK made irresponsible comments and used human rights issues to interfere in its internal affairs because Britain's recent human rights report cited the forcible suppression of ethnic unrest in Tibet and Xinjiang and listed China as a country of concern.[465] Beijing cut off high-level diplomatic ties with the UK for about a year after David Cameron met the Dalai Lama in 2012. It stated that it was "a gross interference in China's domestic politics" and "a severe violation of the principles of international relations".[466]

The last but most important reason is that China is ruled by the Chinese Communist Party, which adheres to the one-party system. This is in direct conflict with the belief in the West of the multiple-party system and political democracy. For many Europeans, the Communist Party is equal to a wicked dictatorship that belongs in the past rather than nowadays and the future. Such a perception of the Chinese regime hinders mutual understanding.[467] Therefore, it is difficult for them to understand why the Chinese Communist Party is still in power after the Soviet Union collapsed

---

463 The United Nations, Office of the High Commissioner of Human Rights, What are Human Rights? Available at: http://www.ohchr.org/en/issues/pages/whatarehumanrights.aspx; Burns H. Weston, March 20, 2014, Encyclopedia Britannica, human rights, available at: http://www.britannica.com/EBchecked/topic/275840/human-rights.

464 "Merkel Meets with the Dalai Lama", Euronews, Archived from the original on 15 May 2007.

465 Tania Branigan, China Cancels Human Rights Dialogue with Britain, The Guardian, Monday 14 April 2014.

466 Leon Watson, Beijing Furious after David Cameron Meets the Dalai Lama on his Visit to Britain, 15 May 2012, Daily Mail Online, available at: http://www.dailymail.co.uk/news/article-2144711/Beijing-furious-David-Cameron-meets-Dalai-Lama-visit-Britain.html.

467 Jing Men, Between Human Rights and Sovereignty – An Examination of EU–China Political Relations, European Law Journal, Vol. 17, No. 4, July 2011, p. 544.

and Eastern Europe changed color. The European states, with an irresistible desire to serve as China's teachers, eagerly attempt to alter the Chinese political and legal system by imparting human rights and democracy into China. They remind China that rejecting their help is erratic and self-damaging because of the hypocrisy and inconsistency of the West's human rights policy and other values.[468] However, China firmly believes that only the Chinese are able to know what is the best for China and only the Chinese have rights and the capability to choose China's path to the future. China emphasizes learning from western advanced experiences but not completely copying the western system in China. As Deng Xiaoping spoke out, "China has to walk its own path".[469] Chinese academic works as well as official writings often regard the EU's value diplomacy as an interference with Chinese domestic affairs and calls upon the EU 'not to lecture China on how to rule' or 'stop imposing European political values and system into China'. They argue that the Chinese must decide a special road to develop in their particular national situation and claim that if the EU considers the strategic partnership with China a framework for collaboration among equals, the EU should avoid identifying itself as a bearer of higher moral values. The bigger problem is that Europe seemly has a problem with the fact that undemocratic sovereign states are given an equal voice to a democratic one in the current international order.[470] That worries China greatly as they are a true supporter of the current sovereignty-oriented international system. Such gaps between China and Europe in human rights make the Chinese government even firmer on upholding that human rights cannot have a supreme status over sovereignty.

Despite these differences in worldviews and at the perceptions level, it is important to mention that co-operations between the two sides have transformed into a development of human rights in China. It is worth emphasizing that China has accepted human rights as universal values as the EU regards. The Chinese generally recognize that systematically grave violations of human rights can raise international concerns. The fact that China discusses with western major powers about its own human rights situation demonstrates that China acknowledges human rights to some extent at an international level. Those discussions come to fostering and deepening cooperation and mutual understanding, the EU's value-based diplomacy towards China will gradually influence this country towards the acceptance and assimilation of Western or European values. Nowadays with successful Chinese economic developments, China is engaging in attempts to improve its human rights conditions. Therefore, with China's true intention to improve human rights, bilateral interactions

468 Marina Svensson, 2002, p. 314.

469 Deng Xiaoping, Walking our Own Path of Revolution and Construction (革命和建设都要走自己的路), the Speech in 26 October 1984, in: Deng Xiaoping Selected Works, Vol. 3, Beijing: Remin Press, 1993, p. 102.

470 Robert O. Keohane, The Contingent Legitimacy of Multilateralism' in Multilateralism Under Challenge? Power, International Order, and Structural Change (ed. by Edward Newman, Ramesh Thakur, & John Tirman), Tokyo, United Nations University Press, 2006, p. 74.

between European states and China obviously create an impact on China's human rights discourse and further deepen and yield more tangible results in human rights diplomacy.[471] Despite China still having some defects in human rights protection, it is also undeniable that step by step China has made a great progress in the human rights field. Its rigid position on the relationship between human rights and sovereignty has been slightly shifted in favor of human rights. Interestingly, China seemly insists that China's human rights development is due to the domestic sphere even though the international plane, involving co-operations with European states, have actually helped to speed up the development of Chinese human rights systems.

Section 4. China's Perspective on Humanitarian Intervention and RtoP

Following China's growth into an influential player in international community, some observers suggest that China should change their position on sovereignty. They comment that China is not a weak state any more; therefore, it is not afraid of intervention but capable of taking part in the interfering. As its power rose, its status acquired more responsibility.[472] Meanwhile, it is undeniable that with its great power and privileged position as a permanent member of the United Nations Security Council, China has considerable influence over the development of the international law of humanitarian intervention. There are some signs showing a subtle change happening in China's view on intervention. Undoubtedly, both humanitarian intervention and RtoP are the most controversial issues between China and the Western states. It is necessary to elaborate the differences in order to reconcile the differences for further development of human rights protection.

Even though China will likely remain a "persistent objector" to claims of a unilateral right of humanitarian intervention for the foreseeable future, its endorsement of RtoP implies that China may support intervention for humanitarian causes in particular cases.

However, at a more practical level, the recent trends of Chinese policies towards some troubled states suggest that the Chinese government may be willing to undertake, support, or acquiesce in military action to prevent or end atrocities, crimes against humanity, genocide, or other humanitarian catastrophes if its two preconditions - Security Council authorization and target state consent - are met. It is necessary to emphasize that China is clearly against international humanitarian intervention but partly supports the new concept of responsibility to protect under certain conditions.

---

471 Yuchao Zhu, 2011, pp. 234–235.

472 Paul M. Evans, Human Security "in Extremis": East Asia Reactions to the Responsibility to Protect, in: Sorpong Peou (ed.) Human Security in East Asia: Challenges for Collaborative Action, London: Routledge, 2009, pp. 79–93.

1. A Gap between China and Western States on Humanitarian Intervention

Non-intervention is simply a result of respecting the sovereignty of a state. However, in the period of the Westphalia system appreciation of the notion of an international system comprising sovereign equals was weak and limited; some states were not willing to recognize other states with the same status as themselves. In fact, the doctrine of sovereignty had constantly been violated. Intervention of hegemony could not be effectively stopped by the doctrine of sovereignty. For example, status of sovereign states had been only recognized in Europe. States like China, India, Egypt, etc., could not have equal status with the European countries until the end of the Second World War. The intervention doctrine was derived from the notion of a Christian universitas.[473] In practice, it continued to coexist with the sovereignty equal principle all along even though it was non-compatible with sovereignty.

The idea of 'international universalism', which was widely understood in France to mean, in the manner of Rousseau, that a nation is by definition free people led to the conclusion that revolutionary France was an ally of 'all free peoples' and thus was opposed to 'all monarchs'.[474] France would accord 'fraternity and assistance to all people who would want to recover their liberty' and charged the executive power with giving the generals the necessary orders to bring assistance to these peoples and to defend the citizens who have been or could be harassed in the cause of liberty.[475] Germany also suggested that a state might intervene in domestic crises of a foreign nation if called in to aid by the party which had justice on its side, and even without such a kind of request on the grounds of a special right or simply on the grounds of self-preservation.[476] Such decrees revealed the ambitions of Western countries and the idea of "Universal dominion"[477] which might endanger the stability of the international community. However, the propositions that were constantly made to support the doctrine of intervention were not actually accepted by the international community as a whole.

In the 1990s, the doctrine of intervention has been generally replaced by a new intervention, namely, humanitarian intervention, which is supposed to be for the purpose of humanitarian objectives. It rendered furious debates between western states and developing states. Since sovereignty can be two sides of a sword, the disagreement on it is inevitable. On the one hand, it can be a sharp weapon for weaker states to use against hegemony. On the other hand, it can be a shield from the tyranny

473 Robert Jackson, 1999, p. 319.

474 Jennifer Mori, William Pitt and the French Revolution: 1785–1795, Lodon: Palgrave Macmillan, July 1997. p. 11.

475 Ibid.

476 Arthur Nussbaum, A Concise History of the Law of Nations, New York: Macmilla, 1954, p. 83.

477 Harlod William Vazeille Temperley, Life of Canning [1905], New York: Haskell House, 1968, pp. 41, 58.

of international interference. The humanitarian intervention also can be two sides of a sword. For the positive side, humanitarian intervention might effectively stop genocides from happening or expanding. That being said it may be manipulated by the powerful states for their own interests. It is logical that weaker states uphold sovereignty while powerful states advocate humanitarian intervention.

Nonetheless, in the 1990s, humanitarian cataclysms shocked the conscience of the international community and calls for humanitarian intervention seemed compelling. Requesting to reshape the relationship between the principle of non-intervention and sovereignty drove the international community to rethink related rules. Despite extensive consideration, no consensus was reached on humanitarian intervention. The failure of the international community to take timely and effective action against the genocide happening in Rwanda in 1994 has always plagued the conscience of the world. Without the authorization of military operations from the UNSC, NATO's intervention in Kosovo in 1999 challenged contemporary international law. Due to its implications for state sovereignty and the integrity of the international legal system, humanitarian intervention is neither sanctioned by custom nor uniformly embraced by states. The Kosovo crisis unprecedentedly raised fierce quarrels on legality of humanitarian intervention. In fact, humanitarian intervention has been denied as a binding doctrine by a number of states, including China, who unwaveringly objects to legitimize it. China insists that intervention with coercive measures would be legitimated only under authorization of the UNSC and condemns the Kosovo intervention as hegemonic actions and a violation of the sovereignty of former Yugoslavia. In the Ministerial Declaration produced by the Meeting of Foreign Ministers of the Group of 77 held in New York on 24th September 1999, the 132 represented states stated that "[t]hey rejected the so-called right of humanitarian intervention, which has no basis in the UN Charter or in international law".[478] Their position has principally closed the door on humanitarian intervention.

2. China's Endorsement of RtoP

Unfortunately, mass atrocities happen from time to time and there was no legal system to stop them until the emergence of RtoP.[479] In 2001 the International Commission on Intervention and State Sovereignty (ICISS) sponsored by the Government of Canada introduced a new concept of Responsibility to Protect to prevent future mass atrocities. The drafters of R2P attempt to break the deadlock of humanitarian intervention and restrict sovereignty under human rights protection. By innovatively interpreting sovereignty as responsibility, the concept of R2P was proved to reconcile conflicts between "sovereignty" and "intervention" successfully. Ban

---

478 Ministerial Declaration of the Group of 77, para. 69, the text available at: www.g77.org/doc/Decl1999.html.

479 Peter Hilpold, Intervening in the Name of Humanity: R2P and the Power of Ideas, Journal of Conflict & Security Law, Spring, 2012, pp. 49–79.

Ki-moon highlighted this by stating, "By helping States meet one of their core responsibilities, R2P seeks to strengthen sovereignty, not weaken it."[480] The significant outcome documents of the UN World Summit in 2005 accepted the R2P by consensus and asserted the willingness "to take collective action ... through the Security Council, in accordance with the Charter ... should peaceful means be inadequate and national authorities are manifestly failing to protect their populations" from serious crimes. At most, the phrase sharpens the wording of Article 42 on authorization from the Security Council to resort to force.

Initially, during the ICISS outreach process in 2001,[481] the Chinese argued that "humanitarianism is good, interventionism is bad, and humanitarian intervention is tantamount to marrying good to evil". China pointed out that there was no basis for humanitarian intervention in the UN Charter, which recognizes only self-defense and the maintenance of international peace and security as legitimate grounds for the use of force. The use for moral reasons, Beijing argued, is dangerous and counterproductive. On one hand, it can encourage warring parties inside a country to be radical and irresponsible in the hope of internationalizing the conflict. On the other hand, it can facilitate interventions from outsiders exploiting the cloak of legality for their own purposes. Consequently, far from ending or ameliorating the effects of large-scale killings, both sets of unintended effects can prolong and aggravate crises. Surprisingly, in 2005, China's official paper on UN reforms accepted the idea of R2P: "Each state shoulders the primary responsibility to protect its own population.... When a massive humanitarian crisis occurs, it is the legitimate concern of the international community to ease and defuse the crisis."[482] China can't help but worry about the hazards brought by RtoP, which likely internationalize internal affairs and heavily weaken the independence of sovereignty since any internal turmoil can be defined as a government's failure to RtoP. Beijing expresses its concern on possible abuses of RtoP like an intervention for self-interest and so remains insistent on keeping the scope of R2P to the four narrow categories[483] specified in the 2005 World Summit's outcome document and requires Security Council authorization as a necessary precondition for any international action.[484] It emphasizes that military

480 United Nations, Department of Public Information. 'Secretary-General defends, clarifies "Responsibility to Protect" at Berlin Event on "Responsible Sovereignty: International Cooperation for a Changed World"', UN Document SG/SM/11701, available at: http://www.un.org/News/Press/docs/2008/sgsm11701.doc.htm.

481 Ramesh Thakur, The Responsibility to Protect: Norms, Laws and the Use of Force in International Politics, New York: Routledge, January 14, 2011.

482 "Full text of China's position paper on UN reforms," Xinua News Agency, June 7, 2005, available at: http://news.xinhuanet.com/english/2005-06/08/content_3056817_3.htm.

483 Four crimes are war crimes, crimes against humanity, genocide, and ethnic cleansing.

484 China Statement on Security Council Open Debate on the Protection of Civilians in Armed Conflict, 20 November 2007.

'assistance'[485] should be authorized in accordance with the UN Charter through the Security Council; be conducted in a neutral, impartial manner; and abide by the principle of the non-use of force except in self-defense. China has tried to make the concept of R2P as consistent as possible with its interpretation of sovereignty which has led to China's understanding of R2P being accused of rhetoric endorsement.[486] The main ideas of China's perspective could be concluded as follows.

2.1. The Primary Responsibility

The Responsibility to Protect is a multi-layered responsibility which explicitly indicates that a residual, fallback responsibility lies with the international community of states if a state fails that responsibility. The new interpretation imposes more constraints on sovereignty in order to allow the international society to perform the duty under any exceptional situation. However, in China's perspective, sovereignty in the sense of the 'supreme authority within a territory' has still been upheld, thus, the R2P is mainly a burden of state. Therefore, China insists that "Governments bear the primary responsibility to protect their civilians". "While the international community and outside forces can provide help, the provisions of the Charter must be followed in doing so, and care must be taken not to undermine the sovereignty and territorial integrity of the country concerned..."[487]

Moreover, Beijing recognizes the responsibility of the international community as an assistant for states.

> "The international community can provide assistance but the protection of its citizens ultimately depends on the government of the state, ... Although the world has undergone profound and complex changes, the basic status of the purposes and principles of the UN Charter remains unchanged. ... There must not be any wavering of the principles of respecting state sovereignty and non-interference of internal affairs."[488]

---

485 The preference for the term 'assistance' reflected China's opposition to coercive intervention.

486 Sarah Teitt, Assessing Polemics, Principles and Practices: China and the Responsibility to Protect, Global Responsibility to Protect, No. 2, April 2009, pp. 208–236.

487 China Statement on Security Council Open Debate on the Protection of Civilians in Armed Conflict, 04 Dec. 2006, available at: http://big5.fmprc.gov.cn/gate/big5/www.fmprc.gov.cn/ce/ceun/eng/chinaandun/securitycouncil/thematicissues/civilians_ac/t282528.htm.

488 Chinese Diplomat: Implementing "Responsibility to Protect" Must not Contravene State Sovereignty, available at: http://news.xinhuanet.com/english/2009-07/25/content_11769124.htm.

China cautiously supports the R2P prioritizing pillar one[489] and asserting that any other measures undertaken in implementing the principle be consistent with the UN Charter. Hence, Beijing has focused its main efforts towards the state capacity-building functions of the R2P mandate - which is referred to as Pillar I in the UN Secretary-General's concept paper. Specifically, Beijing has aimed to develop the norm in a direction that gives primacy to the preventative aspects of R2P in the hope of diminishing the chances of confronting the norm of non-interference. Certainly, China's position is not to remove the RtoP, simply, its interpretation of R2P lies at the conservative end of the spectrum with the positions of weak states.[490]

2.2. Consent of Host States

China has been famous for its adamant opposition to the use of force for humanitarian protection against the will of the host state. China considers the consent of host states as a way of respecting the will of sovereignty states. Beijing argues that it is up to the conflicting parties and people of host states to decide their internal and external affairs; it is also up to the host state to decide whether international society is needed or not. China holds that the international community and external players have a role to play in resolving crises by providing help and support, which should be provided with the prerequisite that the will of the government concerned must be respected and its sovereignty and territorial integrity preserved and that no arbitrary intervention should be imposed if the government concerned objects.[491] Although the host government's consent to the intervention can avoid the conflict between the intervention for the purpose of human rights protection and the host state's sovereignty, the consent of the host state is difficult to get. Beijing's position on the host state's consent is seemly rather rigid in the statements, but in practice, is flexible. For example, in the East Timor case, China supported the Australian-led intervention in East Timo to send UN force there without Indonesian consent.[492]

---

489 As the UN Secretary-General Ban suggested, pillar one states that "The State carries the primary responsibility for protecting populations from genocide, war crimes, crimes against humanity and ethnic cleansing, and their incitement".

490 Rosemary Foot, The Responsibility to Protect (R2P) and its Evolution: Beijing's Influence on Norm Creation in Humanitarian Areas, St Antony's International Review, Vol. 6, No. 2, February 2011, pp. 47–66.

491 China's Statement at the Security Council Open Debate on the Protection of Civilians in Armed Conflict, 28 June 2006, available at: http://www.china-un.org/eng/chinaandun/securitycouncil/thematicissues/civilians_ac/t260820.htm.

492 Jonathan Davis, 'From Ideology to Pragmatism: China's Position on Humanitarian Intervention in the Post-Cold War Era', Vanderbilt Journal of Transnational Law, Vol. 44, Iss. 2, 2011, p. 274.

2.3. Objectivity, Neutrality and No Regime Change

Beijing insists that non-intervention produces neutrality and objectivity and certainly means no regime change. Hence, UNSC's operations or operations under its authority should remain neutral in order to prevent the escalation of inter-state or intra-state conflicts. It stresses that implementing parties should not take sides in an internal crisis. Objectivity requires that the operations do not serve the national interests of interveners but only have the purpose of stopping atrocities. China claims that it will never take a position on the involvement of the mediations and never attempts to overturn a regime, to export revolution or to promote any political reforms as Western powers do.[493] Conversely, Western writers maintain that non-intervention in such situations does not have neutral consequences for the suffering population because stopping atrocities already picks a side against the party who causes them. Such a difference manifested in the Libya crisis. Beijing made it clear that the original intention of resolutions 1970 (2011) and 1973 (2011) was to put an end to violence and to protect civilians. Accordingly, there must be no attempt at regime change or involvement in the civil war by any party under the guise of protecting civilians.[494] China condemned the Western powers for exploiting the protection of civilians for its political agenda which led to a regime change in Libya. It contended that how to strictly and effectively monitor the implementation of Security Council resolutions has become an important and urgent issue and fully supported the concept of Responsibility while Protecting (RwP) which was brought by Brazil.[495] Additionally, China even suggested attaching equal importance to all issues on the Security Council agenda involving protection of civilians, especially including the situations in the Gaza Strip, Somalia, Afghanistan and Iraq in the light of the principle of fairness and impartiality. It pointed out that selectivity or double standards would only undermine the role and authority of the Security Council.[496] Beijing repeatedly stresses: "the strengthening of the protection of civilians in armed conflict must strictly abide by the purposes and principles of the Charter of the United Nations. The responsibility to protect civilians lies first and foremost with the Government of the

493 Michael Martina, South Sudan Marks New Foreign Policy Chapter for China: official, Feb 11, 2014, Reuters, available at: http://www.reuters.com/article/2014/02/11/us-china-southsudan-idUSBREA1A0HO20140211.

494 Statement by Ambassador Li Baodong at Security Council Open Debate on Protection of Civilians in Armed Conflict, 9 November 2011, available at: http://big5.fmprc.gov.cn/gate/big5/www.fmprc.gov.cn/ce/ceun/eng/chinaandun/securitycouncil/thematicissues/civilians_ac/t875762.htm.

495 Statement by Ambassador Li Baodong at Security Council Open Debate on Protection of Civilians in Armed Conflict, 2011/11/09, available at: http://www.china-un.org/eng/hyyfy/t875762.htm.

496 Statement by Ambassador Li Baodong at Security Council Open Debate on Protection of Civilians in Armed Conflict, 2011/11/09, available at: http://www.china-un.org/eng/hyyfy/t875762.htm.

country concerned. The international community and external organizations can provide constructive assistance, but they must observe the principles of objectivity and neutrality and fully respect the independence, sovereignty, unity and territorial integrity of the country concerned. There must be no attempt at regime change or involvement in civil war by any party under the guise of protecting civilians."[497]

Beijing is right that in principle the UNSC cannot legitimately authorize regime change neither as a goal by its own or as means for the achievement of another goal. It would shake the foundations of the international community and could destabilize international law.[498] The International Court of Justice (ICJ) in its judgment on the Nicaragua Case affirms that under customary international law there is no general right for states to intervene in support of an internal opposition in another state, even if this opposition is deemed as pursuing a politically or morally valuable cause.[499]

Undoubtedly, China's objection on regime change is unwavering since it does not want RtoP becoming a legal means to create a democracy. It underscores: "There must be no attempt at regime change or involvement in civil war by any party under the guise of protecting civilians."[500]

2.4. Intervention shall be taken in Caution

China maintains: "A cautious approach should be taken in determining whether a Government is able or willing to protect its citizens. Arbitrary and hasty intervention should be avoided. The reason behind it is that such an intervention may complicate situations and result in greater harm to innocent civilians".[501]

As is well known, China has been reluctant to permit the use of force in the resolution given its tension with the principle of non-interference and the concern that force would exacerbate the situation.[502] No war can be termed "just," and no belligerents exonerated for their participation in it, in which there is not, from the outset, a manifest intent (revealed in policy and practice) to ensure a stable peace

497 Statement by Ambassador Li Baodong, Permanent Representative of China to the United Nations, at the Security Council Open Debate on the Protection of Civilians in Armed Conflict, May 10, 2011, available at: http://www.china-un.org/eng/gdxw/t823976.htm.

498 Hugh Breakey, The Responsibility to Protect: GameChange and Regime Change, Chap. 1, in: Norms of Protection: Responsibility to Protect, Protection of Civilians and Their Interaction (ed. by Charles Sampford, Angus Francisand Vesselin Popovski), Geneva: United Nations University, 2012, pp. 11–39.

499 Military and Paramilitary Activities in and Against Nicaragua (Nicaragua v. U.S.), I. C. J., (1986) 14, paras, 108–110.

500 S/PV.6531, 10 May 2011.

501 China Statement in Security Council Open Debate on the Protection of Civilians in Armed Conflict, 9 December 2005.

502 Alex Bellamy, Paul Williams, 'The New Politics of Protection? Cote d'Ivoire, Libya and the Responsibility to Protect', *International Affairs,* Vol. 87, Issue 4, p. 843.

that provides for both long-term security and the protection of basic human rights in that war's aftermath.[503] China's representative argued that the use of force "will only complicate the situation, sharpen differences, intensify hatreds, and make it more difficult to solve the problem."[504] China maintained that Security Council action should respect the will of the host state and more focus should be on prevention and peaceful conflict resolution.[505] Beijing is not comfortable with NATO's military actions without or beyond authorization of the UNSC and insists that the UNSC is the only legal authority able to decide where to take military actions in terms of the UN Charter. China's stance on military intervention to protect populations, particularly action taken against the will of the host state, has not significantly changed.

3. China's Practices in Humanitarian Crisis

Despite China's rigid statements on humanitarian intervention and RtoP, China's strategies in humanitarian crises demonstrate an evolving flexibility when dealing with particular cases and its reluctance to sanction the use of force for humanitarian purposes.

3.1. Kosovo

During the period from 1992 to 1995, China did not block the UNSC decisions regarding the sending of UNPROFOR (The United Nations Protection Force) to Bosnia for the objective of facilitating humanitarian relief and even voted in favor of a number of resolutions enlarging UNPROFOR's mandate.[506] Plainly speaking, China supported

---

503 Brian Orend, Just War Theory and the Ethics of War and Peace, in The Ashgate Research Companion to Ethics and International Relations (Patrick Hayden ed.), New York: Routledge, 2009, p. 115, p. 117.

504 U.N. SCOR, 47th Sess., 3114th mtg. at 10–12, U.N. Doc. S/PV.3114 (Sept. 14, 1992); S.C. Res. 776, U.N. Doc. S/RES/776 (Sept. 14, 1992), para. 10.

505 'Cross-Cutting Report: Protection of Civilians No. 4,' Security Council Report, 30 Oct. 2009, p. 20, available at: www.securitycouncilreport.org/atf/cf/{65BF-CF9B-6D27-4E9C-8CD3-CF6E4FF96FF9}/XCutting%20PoC%202009.pdf.

506 China endorsed the following resolutions: S.C. Res. 758, P 8, U.N. Doc. S/RES/758 (June 8, 1992) (enlarging UNPROFOR's mandate and strength, and calling on all parties to create conditions for delivery of humanitarian supplies to Sarajevo and other destinations, including establishment of a security zone around Sarajevo's airport); S.C. Res. 761, PP 4–5, U.N. Doc. S/RES/761 (June 29, 1992) (authorizing the deployment of additional personnel to ensure the "security and functioning"of Sarajevo's airport to facilitate the delivery of humanitarian aid); S.C. Res. 807, para. 7, U.N. Doc. S/RES/807 (Feb. 19, 1993) (providing for UNPROFOR's self-defense); S.C. Res. 819, PP 1–14, U.N. Doc. S/RES/819 (Apr. 16, 1993) (declaring Srebrenica a "safe area"); S.C. Res. 824, PP 3–6, U.N. Doc. S/RES/824 (May 6, 1993) (declaring that Sarajevo and other "threatened areas," including, Tuzla, Z epa, Goraz de, Bihac, and Srebrenica, should be treated as "safe areas" by all parties); S.C. Res. 836, PP 4–11,

UN operations for the purpose of humanitarian assistance but considered the use of force for humanitarian purposes with extreme caution. The consent of the Federal Republic of Yugoslavia ("FRY") was critical for China's endorsement of UN military operations. With the consent of the FRY, China supported Resolution 743 which was not a Chapter VII enforcement measure but an ordinary Chapter VI peacekeeping mission.[507] Recognizing the situation in Bosnia as a "great threat to peace and security in the region" and noting with concern the drastic deterioration of humanitarian conditions,[508] China voted in favor of Resolution 958, an enforcement action authorizing member states to use "all necessary measures, through the use of air power, in and around the safe areas in the Republic of Bosnia and Herzegovina," for a humanitarian mandate, and emphasized that "[a]ir power should be used only for the purpose of self-defense."[509] While lacking consent of the "parties concerned" and also noting its "reservations on the invocation of Chapter VII to authorize countries to use force", China abstained from voting on Resolution 781 and 816.[510]

Indeed, the international intervention in Bosnia from 1992 to 1995 was by UN peacekeeping operations neither initially nor later primarily a humanitarian intervention.[511] Therefore, it is worth emphasizing that China seemingly took a different stance several years later in the Kosovo crisis, which was generally seen as a typical humanitarian intervention.

In early 1999, NATO launched a bombing campaign designed to drive Serbian forces from Kosovo. They claimed it was an intervention for humanitarian purposes and was to make way for an international peacekeeping force that would protect both Kosovar Albanian and Serbian communities in Kosovo. When the Western states argued that NATO's intervention in situations of overwhelming humanitarian necessity, military intervention is legally justifiable, the concerns from China for its own inviolable sovereignty and for other weak states with minority problems became much more serious. In China's perspective, the air strike on Former Yugoslavia, which US-led NATO acted without the authority of the UN, set a dangerous precedent for interfering in the internal affairs of a sovereign state. Beijing contended that the problem of this "preemption" of using force by a strong

---

U.N. Doc. S/RES/836 (June 4, 1993) (enlarging UNPROFOR's mandate to include protection of designated "safe areas").

507 China abstained from voting on the following resolutions: S.C. Res. 776, P 2, U.N. Doc. S/RES/776 (Sept. 14, 1992) (increasing UNPROFOR's strength and enlarging its mandate to include protection of International Committee of the Red Cross convoys); U.N. SCOR, 47th Sess., 3114th mtg., U.N. Doc. S/PV.3114 (Sept. 14, 1992).

508 U.N. SCOR, 48th Sess., 3228th mtg. at 48, U.N. Doc. S/PV.3228.

509 U.N. SCOR, 49th Sess., 3461st mtg. at 7, U.N. Doc. S/PV.3461 (Nov. 19, 1994).

510 U.N. SCOR, 47th Sess., 3122d mtg. at 7, U.N. Doc. S/PV.3122 (Oct. 9, 1992); U.N. SCOR, 48th Sess., 3191st mtg. at 22, U.N. Doc. S/PV.3191 (Mar. 31, 1993).

511 Jonathan E. Davis, From Ideology to Pragmatism: China's Position on Humanitarian Intervention in the Post-Cold War Era, Vanderbilt Journal of Transnational Law, Vol. 44, March, 2011, p. 239.

power (or powers) against a weak one (or ones) based on its (their) own "values" will only create disorder and hegemony. It rejected the Security Council's designation of the situation in Kosovo as a threat to international peace and security.[512] Despite the United Nations Security Council resolution 1244, adopted on 10th June 1999, basically usurping jurisdiction over Kosovo away from Yugoslav and Serb forces[513], China held that the conflict should be settled by the Federal Republic of Yugoslavia's government and its people and was opposed to external intervention. In December 1998, China stated that "Kosovo is a part of the FRY, and respect for the FRY's sovereignty and territorial integrity and noninterference in its internal affairs under any pretext are in conformity with the principles of the United Nations Charter."[514] Clearly, China was adamant that the situation in Kosovo was that Serbia was defending its sovereignty against internal challenges. Nonetheless, the Chinese representative in UNSC abstained instead of blocking the Resolution 1244 on the grounds that the Federal Republic of Yugoslavia accepted the peace proposal.[515]

Moreover, China's representative warned that "in international relations, there is a tendency to politicize humanitarian questions and to use them as a pretext to interfere in the internal affairs of sovereign countries. This can only arouse great concern."[516] China further criticized NATO's usurpation of the Security Council's exclusive prerogative to identify threats to international peace and security and to authorize corresponding enforcement actions, including the use of force.[517]

On the one side, China's permanent representative condemned, "This war, waged in the name of Humanitarianism ... in fact produced the greatest humanitarian catastrophe in post-Second-World-War Europe and ... seriously undermined peace and stability in the Balkans."[518] On the other side, the Western states claimed their operations ended violence and repression and saved the lives of tens of thousands of people.[519] Obviously, NATO's intervention in the FRY triggered the particular sensitivities against a unilateral right of humanitarian intervention which remain relevant to China's position. As a socialist country, China supported the FRY with sympathy given its own internal challenges to sovereignty, including in Tibet,

---

512 U.N. SCOR, 53d Sess., 3937th mtg. at 14, U.N. Doc. S/PV.3937 (October 24, 1998).

513 Resolution 1244 requested withdrawal of Yugoslavia from Kosovo of all military, police and paramilitary forces according to a rapid timetable, with which the deployment of the international security presence in Kosovo will be synchronized.

514 U.N. GAOR, 53d Sess., 85th plen. mtg. at 22, U.N. Doc. A/53/PV.85 (December 9, 1998).

515 "Security Council, Welcoming Yugoslavia's Acceptance of Peace Principles, Authorizes Civil, Security Presence in Kosovo", available at http://www.un.org/News/Press/docs/1999/19990610.SC6686.html.

516 U.N. SCOR, 53d Sess., 3937th mtg. at 14, U.N. Doc. S/PV.3937 (October 24, 1998).

517 U.N. SCOR, 53d Sess., 3988th mtg. at 12, U.N. Doc. S/PV.3988 ((Mar. 24, 1999).

518 U.N. SCOR, 54th Sess., 4011th mtg. at 8, U.N. Doc. S/PV.4011 (June 10, 1999).

519 NATO's role in relation to the conflict in Kosovo, available at the website of NATO: http://www.nato.int/kosovo/history.htm.

Xinjiang, and Taiwan.[520] In addition to its military presence and a strengthened US-Japan alliance, the US has increasingly expanded or strengthened its bilateral military ties with many countries surrounding China. It is reasonable that Beijing has a strong objection against unilateral military intervention invoking the humanitarian cause especially after the bombing of the Chinese Embassy in Belgrade.

In 2009, the trial chamber of the International Criminal Tribunal for the Former Yugoslavia ("ICTY") concluded that forces of the FRY and Serbia deliberately and forcibly displaced Kosovo Albanian civilians both within and outside of Kosovo during the spring of 1999. Furthermore, the chamber also verified that forces of the FRY and Serbia killed at least 600 individuals, destroyed or damaged mosques, and sexually assaulted Kosovo Albanian women during the deportation.[521] In 2014, the judgments of the appeal chamber of the ICTY affirmed the displacement and crimes committed by forces of the FRY and Serbia.[522] Nonetheless, China's stance on Kosovo has not even changed with the 2008 Kosovo Declaration of Independence on 17th February 2008. Beijing continues to back up the position of Serbia, at its first time in front of the ICJ, saying that sovereign states have a right to prevent unilateral secessions and protect their integrity.[523] Based on China's behavior and words during the Kosovo crisis, it is easy to reach a conclusion that during that time China strictly adhered to the principles of state sovereignty and non-intervention, prioritized sovereignty over human rights and objected to humanitarian intervention.

3.2. Sudan

China and Sudan's relationship developed through a framework of state-state relations in which the Chinese government has claimed, in its own terms, to have successfully pursued the principles of non-interference, mutual respect and mutual benefit. The Chinese approach is shown in practice in Sudan to pursue business as a form of applied politics since non-interference allows for 'business, not politics'. Chinese officials said, "we try to separate politics from business [...] the internal situation in the Sudan is an internal affair".[524]

---

520 Jonathan E. Davis, 2011, p. 247.

521 The judgments of the Prosecutor v. Nikola Šainović, Dragoljub Ojdanić, Nebojša Pavković, Vladimir Lazarević, Sreten Lukić & Milan Milutinović in 26 February 2009.

522 Ibid.

523 Transcript of Oral Argument, at 28, Official Transcript from Monday, December 7, 2009, International Court of Justice, available at: http://www.icj-cij.org/docket/files/141/15724.pdf.

524 The Summary of Chinese Deputy Foreign Minister Zhou Wenzhong in The New York Times, (22 August 2005).

When the Darfur crisis began in February 2003,[525] the traditional emphasis on sovereignty and noninterference prevailed in Chinese policy. China protected Sudan from the UN in September 2004, when it threatened to water down a UN resolution against Sudan, forcing the United States to forgo sanctions. In the end, the United Nations sanctioned only four officials, not the government itself. However, the negative impact of supporting pariah states on China's international image is "beginning to outweigh the economic incentives".[526] Beijing tried very hard to keep sovereignty and RtoP in balance in its own way. On the one hand, China persistently contended that "continuing to exert pressure without considering the complexity of the specific circumstances of Darfur would not help the drive for a political solution". Beijing has shown its reluctance of imposing sanctions on individual states.[527] China argued that it prevented Western countries keen on intervention from ending up in a painful predicament between their promise to undertake action and the fact that such a military intervention would be extremely risky and counterproductive without the cooperation of the national government. On the other hand, Beijing exerts its influence in Sudan to persuade Sudan to accept the UN peacekeeping force since China consistently insists on the consent of hosted states as a prerequisite for international intervention. On Resolution 1679 China argued that the agreement and cooperation of the Sudanese Government must be obtained before a peacekeeping operation could be established in Darfur.[528] Similarly, China abstained on Resolution 1706 on the expansion of the mission in Sudan to include Darfur, due to the failure to include the prerequisite of state consent.[529] However, in 2006, after intensive efforts, China successfully persuaded the Sudanese government to accept the dispatching of blue helmets to Darfur. From the perspective of the Sudanese government, China's diplomacy allowed it to save face and to secure its central position in the peace process.[530] With Sudanese consent, Beijing also supported UNMIS

525 Posor, Friederike Maria, Der Darfur-Konflikt und seine Auswirkungen auf die internationale Staatengemeinschaft: vor dem Hintergrund neuer völkerrechtlicher Rechtsfortbildung: Möglichkeiten und Grenzen der internationalen Friedenskonsolidierung, Frankfurt: Peter Lang GmbH, Internationaler Verlag der Wissenschaften; 1st ed., July 26, 2013.

526 Ken Sofer, China and the Collapse of its Noninterventionist Foreign Policy: Past Diplomatic Practices Collide with Rising Economic and Political Realities, *Center for American Progress,* 8 March 2012. Available at: https://www.americanprogress.org/wp-content/uploads/issues/2012/03/pdf/china_nonintervention.pdf.

527 Jonathan Holslag, China's Diplomatic Maneuvering on the Question of Darfur, Journal of Contemporary China, No. 1, January 2008, p. 80.

528 Ibid., p. 81.

529 Security Council Votes to Set up UN Peacekeeping Force in Darfur, available at: http://www.un.org/apps/news/story.asp?NewsID=19685&Cr=Sudan&Cr1=Darfur#.VxswMDGUe6c.

530 Jonathan Holslag, 2008, p. 84.

to play a role in the preparations for and conduct of the referendum in 2011 that would determine whether Darfur should be an autonomous region despite China's traditional resistance to secession.

China has participated in the UN Mission in Sudan (UNMIS) to support the CPA since 2005 and in the African Union (AU) – the UN Hybrid Mission in Darfur since 2007. Both have predominantly taken the form of multifunctional engineering units providing logistical support services to the UN and local areas. Beijing has also provided financial support for AU peacekeeping in Sudan. Moreover, China has sponsored humanitarian and development assistance programs, including roads and facilities. Furthermore, the economic cooperation with South Sudan is crucial for the two-state relationship. Certainly, China plays a key role in providing finance to both the central Sudanese state and South Sudan. Through the mediation of the two sides, economic cooperation, financial assistance, China's political role has grown in influence with South Sudan. China recognized South Sudan in July 2011, shortly after the new country's founding.

Manifestly, China has been playing a substantial active and decisive role in Sudan. It pressured the Sudanese government to accept UN peacekeeping troops and a referendum in order to alleviate humanitarian suffering. It was also involved in mediating between the government and rebels. Some observers comment that China is derailing from its fundamental principles of sovereignty and non-interference.[531] At least Beijing shows its flexibility on the principles of sovereignty and non-intervention.

Similarly, in November 2007, China dispatched its special envoy Wang Yi to Rangoon persuading Myanmar to cooperate with the United Nations. China urged the Myanmar government to speed up its democratization and improve its people's livelihood. Such a move can be seen as another case of how flexible China can be during the enforcement of the principle of non-intervention.

3.3. Libya Crisis

China frequently expresses its respect of the right of others to independently choose their own social system and path of development. Usually this has meant supporting whomever is in power no matter how thuggish or unpopular - "Business is Business."[532] China always attempts to separate economy from politics. During Colonel Qaddafi's rule, China had big interests in Libya's economy but much less in European countries.[533] Actually, Libya presented an unusual combination of

531 Chengqiu Wu, 2009, pp. 71–97.

532 The Summary of Chinese Deputy Foreign Minister Zhou Wenzhong, in: The New York Times, August 22, 2005.

533 In 2010 Libyan oil covered about 30 per cent of Italy's needs, 16 per cent – France, 11 per cent – China. See Azerbaijan Baku, Chinese Success in Libya's Oil Sector, Trend, March 14, 2013, available at: http://en.trend.az/capital/analytical/2129080.html.

challenges for China.[534] The widespread support among Arab countries for tough action against Muammar Qaddafi pushed China into leaving the running government in Libya. Although China has resisted permitting the use of force in a resolution of the UNSC given its tension with the principle of non-interference, and concerned that force would exacerbate the situation,[535] Beijing supported Resolution 1970 which was unanimously adopted. It recognized the seriousness of the situation in Libya, and ultimately it could not "legitimize inaction in the face of mass atrocities".[536] Resolution 1973 authorized military action for the purpose of protecting civilians without the host state's consent which has been a requirement for a military act in China's practices in the SC.[537] Its votes in favor of UN sanctions against Colonel Qaddafi are a big move from the old style of a rigid interpretation of sovereignty. As the UN representative of China, Li Baodong pointed out that "China has serious concerns over some elements of the resolution" and noted the need to respect "sovereignty, independence, unification and territorial integrity of Libya".[538] Later, China criticized that the West turned an UNSC resolution calling for all necessary means to protect civilians into a license for regime change.[539] It made very clear that it supported neither side in the Libyan internal conflict and picking one side breached the sovereignty of Libya. China required that one should "give peace a chance."[540]

Resolution 1973 authorized UN Member States to take "all necessary measures" to protect civilians with one prohibition that foreign troops cannot occupy Libyan territory. The lack of clarity on how member states should specifically act could open a door to potential abuse for self-interest. The consequence is obvious as *Gareth Evans,* one of co-drafters of the report of Responsibility to Protect, commented:

---

534 China's Evolving Foreign Policy: The Libyan Dilemma. The Economist, September 10th 2011, available at: http://www.economist.com/node/21528664.

535 Alex Bellamy, Paul Williams, The New Politics of Protection? Cote d'Ivoire, Libya and the Responsibility to Protect, in: International Affairs, Vol. 87, Issue 4, 2011, p. 843.

536 Ibid, p. 844.

537 Nicola Contessi, Multilateralism, Intervention and Norm Contestation: China's Stance on Darfur in the UN Security Council, Security Dialogue, Vol. 41, Issue 3, 2010, p. 331.

538 'Explanation of Vote by Ambassador Li Baodong after Adoption of Security Council Resolution on Libya', Permanent Mission of the People's Republic of China to the UN, 17 March 2011, available at: http://www.china-un.org/eng/hyyfy/t807544.htm.

539 Stewart M. Patrick, R2P in Crisis Following UN Syria Vote, available at: http://www.cfr.org/syria/r2p-crisis-following-un-syria-vote/p27303.

540 Steven Sotloff, China's Libya Problem: China's failure to support the rebels in Libya could hurt its investment prospects there. Time for a rethink? The Diplomats, March 14, 2012.

> "as the NATO-led intervention in Libya went on, the major Western powers overreached the civilian protection mandate they had been given by the Security Council by demanding, and achieving, nothing less than the complete destruction of the Gaddafi regime."[541]

When the actions of Western powers actually turned out a regime change, China with other states, particularly BRICS, strongly condemned operations conducted by NATO. Beijing clearly expressed its resist on regime change stating: "The efforts of the country's political resolve internal crisis, the international community can provide the necessary constructive help. China is opposed to any external forces, the military intervention, to promote regime change."[542]

The Libya situation was exceptional since the time frame for the international community to react was extremely short. It marked a clear departure away from the Chinese prior UNSC action. The members of the UNSC were never so supportive for the no-fly zone resolution called by the Gulf Cooperation Council (GCC), the Organization of the Islamic Conference (OIC), and the League of Arab States (LAS). Nonetheless, the gap on RtoP caused by the NATO intervention in Libya is so wide that some assume that Libya ended RtoP.[543]

China, with a large number of countries – led by the so-called "BRICS" (Brazil, Russia, India, China and South Africa) - assessed the Libya intervention as a typical abuse of the R2P which it would not allow again. Brazil initiated the concept of 'Responsibility while Protecting'("RwP2") as one legacy of the Libyan intervention, which focuses on prevention, strengthened accountability, and enhanced analysis and assessment.[544] However, Libya demonstrated China's biggest departure from the non-intervention principle. It implied China's acceptance of the "human rights priority over sovereignty in extreme situation".

3.4. Syria Crisis

Beijing's support for or acquiescence in UN resolutions relating to Libya was welcomed by Western society as a sign of its new willingness to allow enforcement action against states responsible for gross and systematic human rights violations. However, as China's hardline position on the crisis in Syria demonstrates, this new

---

541 Gareth Evans, After Syria: the Future of the Responsibility to Protect, available at: http://www.gevans.org/speeches/speech545.html.

542 Ambassador Li Baodong Speech in the UN Security Council Ministerial Conference in the Middle East, /2012/03/12, available at: http://www.china-un.org/eng/hyyfy/t913340.htm.

543 Jonathan E. Davis, 2011, p. 272.

544 "Responsibility while protecting: elements for the development and promotion of a concept", presented to the Security Council on 9 November 2011 by Brazil's Permanent Representative to the UN, Maria Luiza Ribeiro Viotti, during the Council's open debate on the protection of civilians.

shift was quickly reversed after NATO's bombing campaign in Libya appeared to go beyond what the Security Council resolution authorized.[545]

Regarding Syria, China has formulated a far stronger strategy. China's UNSC veto side with Russian has shielded Syria from coercive interventions and at the same time China stepped up its mediation and engagement throughout the region, lobbying for a political alternative to the military option.[546] Its policy in Syria implies that China has stepped back to its traditional perception of sovereignty and again adheres to the non-intervention principle as before. Firstly, it reiterated that the Syria crisis should be resolved in an impartial and peaceful way without any interference from the outside. It stressed that negotiation between the parties was the "only way of solving the crisis", and that China did not approve of armed interference or pushing for a "regime change" in Syria, and believes that use or threat of sanctions does not help to resolve this issue appropriately.[547] It insists that a political solution is the right one to end Syria's war. Secondly, China prefers for a traditional peacekeeping force over a member state-led force with Chapter VII enforcement powers. Beijing supported the deployment of UN monitors in Syria with Security Council Resolution 2043 strictly abided by, which set up ceasefire monitoring forces. It strongly opposes any attempt to address the Syria crisis with military interference from the outside or forcefully impose a regime change in the insurgency-ridden country.[548] Thirdly, China always concerns the consent of the conflicting parties, particularly, the governmental party which represents a sovereign state, to the deployment of the multinational force.

Conclusion

In summary, China's official stance on humanitarian intervention can be concluded as follows. Humanitarian intervention causes more harm than good, it promotes the interests of the intervening state rather than the target state's population, and it is inconsistent in the UN Charter and general principles of international law.[549] Multiple factors are influential in China's attitude towards humanitarian intervention. For instance, the hypocrisy of humanitarian intervention, Chinese historical experience during its "century of humiliation", certain characteristics of China's domestic political system (non-democratic system), China's historical positioning

---

545 Sonya Sceats, Shaun Breslin, China and the International Human Rights System, October 2012. Chatham House, available at: https://www.chathamhouse.org/sites/files/chathamhouse/public/Research/International%20Law/r1012_sceatsbreslin.pdf.

546 Yun Sun, Syria: What China Has Learned From its Libya Experience, Asia Pacific Bulletin, Number 152, February 27, 2012.

547 China Raises 6-Point Statement for Resolving Syria Issue, March 4, 2012, available at: http://china.org.cn/world/2012-03/04/content_24797150.htm.

548 China, Russia issue joint statement on Syria crisis, September 26, 2013, available at: http://news.xinhuanet.com/english/china/2013-09/26/c_132752238.htm.

549 Jonathan E. Davis, 2011, p. 272.

of itself as a defender of developing countries' rights, China's multiethnic character, its own internal challenges to sovereignty, its traditional idea of "great unification", etc. All of these factors mean that China will continue to hold onto the principle of sovereignty and non-intervention in a traditional stance.[550] However, China's growing desire to be recognized as a great power and responsible international actor and China's increasing overseas interests are shaping China's new shift on humanitarian intervention. China's endorsement of RtoP and the practices of acquiescing in or actively supporting a number of interventions in humanitarian crises in the recent decade show its willingness to embrace the development of humanitarian intervention. The cases discussed above signal that China has changed from a rather rigid position against intervention in humanitarian crises into a much more flexible one which allows Beijing to take a pro-intervention disposition case by case.[551] In some ways, its statements towards sovereignty remain occasionally almost unchanged but that paradox allows China space to react differently on a case by case basis.

550 Ibid., pp. 270–281.

551 Allen Carlson, More than Just Saying No: China's Evolving Approach to Sovereignty and Intervention Since Tiananmen, in: New Directions in the Study of China's Foreign Policy (ed. by Alastair Johnston and Robert Ross), Stanford: Stanford University Press, 2006, p. 234.

Chapter 6. China's Contemporary Perspective of Sovereignty

Introduction

The well-known Chinese scholar of international politics Wang Yizhou commented that "Sovereignty is just a historical definition of 'State'". Therefore, we must analyze it from the historical perspective in order to understand it correctly. It was born with the emergence of the modern state and it has kept varying and will keep varying with changes of the world system. Sovereignty is also a mirror of the reality, which can reflect the complexity of contemporary international politics and interactive relationships between states and entities[552]

Undoubtedly, China's perception of sovereignty reflects its own identity, which is distinct from any other states, particularly from European states. The meanings of sovereignty in various perspectives are never static but are produced and influenced through practices and interactions among states and other actors in international society.[553] This chapter generally analyzes the sovereignty interpretation of China from the founding date of the PRC to the present and the different perceptions on sovereignty of China and European states.

Section 1. Sovereignty in the PRC's Perspective

1. Sovereignty and the Evolvement of the PRC

1.1. In the Early Period of PRC

China as a newly independent state requires a bunch of international principles to maintain its sovereignty and independence. The Five Principles of Peaceful Coexistence[554] were produced precisely in response to this strong requirement of China with other newly independent nations. The core of the Five Principles is the principles of sovereignty equality and non-intervention. Premier Zhou Enlai announced China's endorsement of it at the Bandung Conference in 1955, "It is impossible to relate all the sufferings of the Chinese people under the rule of imperialism, feudalism ... As a Chinese proverb says, 'Do not do unto others what you yourself do not desire.' We are against outside interference; how could we want to interfere in the

552 Wang Yizhou, On Contemporary International Politics, Shanghai People Press, 1995, pp. 81–82.
553 Yongjin Zhang, 2008, p. 114.
554 The five principles: Mutual respect for each other's territorial integrity and sovereignty; mutual non-aggression; mutual non-interference in each other's internal affairs; equality and cooperation for mutual benefit; Peaceful co-existence.

internal affairs of others? ... Peace can only be safeguarded by mutual respect for each other's territorial integrity and sovereignty".[555] The words -"mutual respect for sovereignty"- in the Five Principles is the Chinese technique to avoid a finite stance on either of the two basic theories on sovereignty (namely absolute sovereignty and relative sovereignty) and gain popularity from developing countries besides defending against the expansionism of super powers.[556] Despite that Beijing prefers absolute sovereignty to defend itself, China also knows that absolute sovereignty may untie super powers to breach or disrespect others' sovereignty. It also allows China to have an advantage of flexibility in practice. Frequently, China invokes the sacrosanct principle of sovereignty to defend its territorial integrity and its other national interests. Generally, from the beginning of the Five Principles, they were incorporated into Chinese foreign policies and the non-intervention principle and sovereign equality have become the bedrock in China's international relations.

Moreover, Mao's new 'Three Worlds Theory', outlined in 1974, provided theoretical ground to associate China with other developing states. It categorizes the USSR and United States as the 'first world', developed capitalist and Eastern European states were the 'second world', and developing states were the 'third world', where China identified itself in. The 'three world theory' narrowed its struggle mainly to fight the Soviet Union, seeking to form a broad united-front against it and ally with developing states under a name of the same group.[557] It decided that China's stance on sovereignty shall be to stick with the weaker states. This identification has been still carried on after decades, no matter how great of a change China makes.

Furthermore, the flag of anti-hegemony was held highly against imperialism by China in earlier times. Obviously, sovereignty implies anti-hegemony from the very beginning. The Peace of Westphalia required respecting the sovereignty of small countries which had just broken away from the imperial Rome. The institution of sovereignty was exploited for the dismantling of *Respublica Christiana*. Sovereignty can alone guarantee the independence of each government and the stability of the general association therefore defends sovereigns from powerful states or empires.[558] The recognition of the sovereignty of other states is an inevitable consequence of the assertion by any one state of its own sovereignty in relation to its own territory and people.[559] If a state insists on the value of its own sovereignty then it cannot but help

---

555 The Speech of Zhou Enlai in China and the Asian-African Conference (1955), in Selection of Zhou Enlai, Vol. 2, Beijing: Remin Press, 1984, pp. 60–62.

556 Junwu Pan, Toward a New Framework for Peaceful Settlement of Chinas Territorial and Boundary Disputes, Leiden: Martinus Nijhoff Publishers, 2008, p. 83.

557 China's Foreign Policy Statements, Renmin Ribao 1 November 1977. For the English version of this document see: Peking Review, No. 45, 4 November 1977.

558 Pasquale Fiore, Edwin M. Borchard, International Law codified and its Legal Sanction or the Legal Organization of the Society of State [1890], New York: Baker, Voorhis and Company, 1918, p. 95.

559 Jo-Anne Pemberton, Sovereignty Interpretations, London: Palgrave Macmillan, 2009, p. 59.

admit its value to others. The mutual recognition implies respect of other's sovereignty and non-intervention from each other. In practice, interventions persistently happen. It shows that the implication of sovereignty cannot totally or even largely restrict states from intervention. Nonetheless, sovereignty as an anti-hegemonic weapon is essential for weaker states although it has not been always effective but it does at least have a legal base. The semi-colonial experiences push China into taking a defensive manner which heavily relies on the sovereignty principle to preclude powerful states from interfering. Consequently, China's sovereignty view always supports fighting against hegemony or imperialism. It is worth mentioning that opposition of hegemony has been written into China's constitution.[560]

In practice, China did not hesitate breaking from the Communism camp for its own sovereign integrity. Certainly, it formed an alliance with the former Soviet Union in the beginning of the PRC. However, the former Soviet Union was chauvinistic and attempted to force China to submit to its own strategic needs. For example, the Soviet Union proposed setting up a long-wave radio station that it would control in China and a joint naval fleet, showing its intent to control China militarily. To get China to submit to its control, the former Soviet Union put pressure on China by withdrawing its experts from China, tore up economic agreements it had signed with China and deployed one million soldiers along the Sino-Soviet and Sino-Mongolian borders, posing a serious threat to China. To safeguard its sovereignty and independence, China did not give in to Soviet pressure and put up a fight against the USSR. Thus, in the middle 1970s until the early 1980s, facing the serious threat from the USSR, China put forth the "one-line" strategy that extended from Japan to the U.S. and to Europe in order to counter the Soviet challenge. In 1971, the PRC replaced the Taiwan-based Kuomintang government in China's seat at the United Nations and on the Security Council. In the following decade, Beijing continued to adopt strict conceptions of sovereignty and noninterference. For example, the PRC opposed UN peacekeeping efforts by refusing to participate in Security Council deliberations or voting on peacekeeping missions, or to contribute money or resources to UN missions.[561]

During much of the Cold War, Beijing's overriding challenge was to strengthen a relatively weak state security in the face of pressing threats from the superpowers. The priority was clearly to address core survival concerns (territorial and political integrity) and the imperatives for Chinese diplomacy were correspondingly straightforward. Consequently, opposing hegemony of two super powers and sticking to non-interference has been the basic foreign policy of China during that period. Therefore, the PRC's foreign policy can be characterized largely by adherence to

560 Preamble of 1982 Constitution of China.

561 M. Taylor Fravel, China's Attitude Toward U.N. Peacekeeping Operations Since 1989, in: Asian Survey, Vol. 36, No. 11, November, 1996, p. 1102, pp. 1103–04; Bates Gill & James Reilly, Sovereignty, Intervention and Peacekeeping: The View from Beijing, Survival, Vol. 42, No. 3, Autumn 2000, p. 41, pp. 43–44.

a rigid conception of state sovereignty and steadfast insistence on the principle of noninterference in other states' internal affairs.[562] The Chinese government and Chinese people rather repulse finger-poking in the internal issues from outsiders who might be recognized as hostile parties. Most outside observers commented that Chinese foreign policies were grounded by an unrelenting attachment to sovereignty's fundamental role within international society.[563]

1.2. The 2nd Period of PRC

Since the late 1970s, China has built its central policy around economic issues, with the core goal being to enhance national power and the people's standard of living. China shifted from political struggle to economic development, from a planned economy to a socialist market economy, from a closed society and over emphasis on self-reliance to opening up and international cooperation.[564] Following Deng's 'cats' theory,[565] the CCP implemented sustainable economic, legal, and political self-reform. In that period, radical reforms were promoted internally for economic expansion, and for international society, China applied a strategy of 'low profile' which implies "concealing brilliance and cultivating internal strength". Pragmatism was dominant in both domestic policies and foreign policies. In the UNSC, China frequently abstained from voting. It even gave China the name of 'Mr. Abstention'. China changed the "one-line" strategy[566] and did not form an alliance or forge strategic relations with any big powers. On international issues, it considers the basic interests of the Chinese people and the people of the world and independently decides its own stance on the pros and cons of these issues. China particularly emphasizes an insistence on the principle of independence while opening up to the outside world. In spite of radical change in the internal sphere, China's position on sovereignty did not change within it. The Tiananmen incident forced China to invoke sovereignty more often than ever. The independence of sovereignty and non-intervention principle were rather important to pursue steady and fast economic growth. In 1988, Deng

562 Jerome Alan Cohen, China and Intervention: Theory and Practice, in: University of Pennsylvania Law Review, Vol. 121, 1973, p. 474.

563 Allen Carlson, Moving Beyond Sovereignty? A Brief Consideration of Recent Changes in China's Approach to International Order and the Emergence of the Tianxia Concept, in: Journal of Contemporary China, Vol. 20, Issue 68, 2011, p. 92.

564 Dai Bingguo, Stick to the Path of Peaceful Development, in: China Daily, 2010-12-13.

565 Deng Xiaoping said, "Whether a cat is black or white makes no difference. As long as it catches mice, it is a good cat."

566 In the early Mao time, China leaned to the USSR side. But in the late Mao time, China manifested antagonism towards the USSR and supported the USA in opposing the USSR. This one side strategy made it difficult for it to oppose the super power on the same side, and to reconcile the relations with the super power on the hostile side.

Xiaoping stated the Five Principles of Peaceful Coexistence could bear the test of time and should be the roadmap for building the new international political order.[567]

1.3. The Peaceful Rising Period

In recent years, the world has been undergoing extensive and profound changes, and China has been undergoing extensive and profound transformation. China realized the transformation of the international society, as a high-ranking official wrote,

> "Countries are more closely linked and interdependent with their interests more closely integrated than ever before. They find more areas of common interests and more issues that need joint response. They want to engage in mutually beneficial cooperation more than ever before. To some extent, the world has become a community of interests. The behavior of one country will have an impact not only on itself, but also on other countries".[568]

It also realized that more than 30 years of reform and opening-up has brought about earth-shaking changes in China from being a big, poor and weak state to being a great political, economic and military power. Beijing is no longer in the position to avoid international leadership and maintain a lower global profile. It is unrealistic for China to continue to define itself as a 'status quo' actor, given its growing global weight, and that is why it should play a more active role in global governance.[569] In a 2009 meeting between China's most senior leaders and the country's top diplomats which was largely ignored by the international media but reported in China's official newspaper, People's Daily, President Hu Jintao told China's senior diplomats "to strive to make our country more influential politically, more competitive economically, and help ensure that our country has a more friendly image, with greater moral appeal". He also told them that the global financial crisis was serving to reinforce multi-polarization and that "peace and development remain the themes of our times, but that competition for overall national strength is becoming increasingly fierce. The demand of developing countries for equal participation in international affairs is becoming increasingly strong". He emphasized that "we must defend our national development interests while also maintaining our openness to

567 Yang Jiemian, Peaceful Rise in Peaceful Coexistence: In Memory of 50th Anniversary of Fiver Principles of Peaceful Coexistence (论中国在和平共处中的和平崛起：纪念和平共处五项基本原则成立 50 周年), Journal of Study Mao and Deng, No. 6, 2004, p. 57.

568 Dai Bingguo (2010).

569 Pang Zhongying, China's Status and Role in the International System, in: Modern International Relations, No. 4, 2006, pp. 17–22; The views of Huang Ping are cited in You Nuo, Fu Jing, and Wang Bo, "China Should Play Greater Role in G-20, Expert Says," in: China Daily, March 19, 2009, http://www.chinadaily.com.cn/bizchina/2009-03/19/content_7594063.htm.

the outside world".[570] The speech opened the way for a shift in China's foreign policy from the strategy of 'low profile' toward a more proactive global stance. The official announcement came out later in 2010, written by Dai Bingguo.

Dai argues that China will not follow those selfish practices of conquering or threatening others by force, or seeking development space and resources by non-peaceful means and China considers itself as one of passengers in the same boat and wishes to cross the river peacefully together instead of fighting one another and trying to push one another off the boat. He assures that China will not engage in invasion, plundering, war or expansion that Western powers used to practice. He also accuses some countries of identifying friends and foes on the basis of ideology and ganging up under various pretexts in a quest of dominance in world affairs. He also defends the current Chinese political system as suitable for the basic national conditions and development at the current stage of the country. He defines China's strategic intention as such - harmony and development at home and peace and cooperation abroad.[571]

Logically, China's perception on sovereignty shall change from anti-interventionism to pro-interventionism as China is becoming a great power in the international community and abandoning the strategy of low profile. However, the non-intervention principle and sovereignty is still the base for Chinese foreign policy. Former Prime Minister Wen Jiabao says the policy of non-intervention isn't only a part of the past, but also the present, and it will remain long into the future. He doesn't consider non-interference as a stubborn or outdated policy but a very flexible principle.[572] His words actually show that Beijing has changed from its rigid method to a very flexible way on the principle of non-intervention although the principle is still at the core in China's foreign policy.

Recent calls from Chinese academics for a return to traditional Chinese values indicate Chinese enthusiasm to return to the role of leadership.[573] It also shows Beijing's wishes to be understood as a peaceful influential player. It requires Beijing to take an appropriate interpretation of sovereignty suitable for its new role. China has changed its discourse from opposing *hegemons* to opposing *hegemonic behavior*, since it is the latter that violates the non-intervention principle.[574] In China's eyes, the

570 Wu Qimin, Notes: China Held a Top Diplomatic Envoys Meeting, President Hu Emphasized Promoting Economic and Political Power and Building Moral Image, in: People's Daily, July 20, 2009.

571 Dai Bingguo, 2010.

572 David Cohen, China and Non-intervention, the Diplomats, December 03, 2011, available at: http://thediplomat.com/2011/12/china-and-non-intervention/.

573 For an analysis of role-playing, image, and normative concerns in the Tianxia worldview, see Shi Zhiyu and Zhang Dengji, The Epistemology of China's Rise and Its Narrative Derivatives (中国崛起的认识论及其叙事衍生), World Economics and Politics, No. 1, 2010, pp. 37–51.

574 Hung-jen Wang, Circumventing the Sovereign State? Intervention from Chinese Perspectives, Paper for 8th Pan-European Conference on International Relations: One International Relations or Many? Multiple Worlds, Multiple Crises Warsaw, Poland,

non-intervention principle might be interpreted as being influenced by the concept of 'governing by non-interference' (无为而治), in which individual states serve as a foundation for global governance. However, unlike other major international players, China still insists on the non-intervention principle but with a flexibility which was rare in the early period of the PRC. Beijing frequently repeats that the Five Principles should maintain their core status. Further, Beijing tries to convince the world that China is seeking a peaceful rise and hopes for a harmonic world and that by adhering to the Five Principles it may dispel the suspicions of China as a threat to peace and security.[575]

As Yan Xuetong and Sun Xuefeng note, China frequently quotes the Five Principles of Peaceful Coexistence in the world while it is on the stage of the international community. It believes that these principles are not only still being obeyed by China and others so far, but are also having good effect on the world. Today, the goal of China's peaceful rise policy is to develop itself instead of taking on aggressive wars against foreign countries, seizing other countries' resources, or reforming or overthrowing other countries' political regimes. The Chinese government has stated many times that China is not strong right now, and even if China becomes strong and powerful in the future, it will never seek hegemony since aggressive policy goals are not in China's interest.[576]

2. The Barometer of China's Foreign Policies - China's Aid to Africa

In practice, Beijing gradually changes its foreign policy and that started with taking active measures in its economy since the late 1990s.[577] After the Asian financial crisis and as China's economy began its dramatic climb, Beijing began to invest a growing amount of diplomatic resources into building alternative institutional options to the Bretton Woods rules, such as strengthening regional development banks across the Global South, establishing new multilateral trade arrangements, such as the China—ASEAN Free Trade Area, together with the Asian Development Bank, and the Central Asia Regional Economic Cooperation forum.[578] The dramatically

September 20, 2013, available at: http://www.eisa-net.org/be-bruga/eisa/files/events/warsaw2013/WANG_Circumventing%20the%20Sovereign%20State_%20.pdf.

575 Zheng Bijian, China's Peaceful Rise to Great Power Status, Foreign Affairs, September 2005, pp. 18–24.

576 Yan Xuetong and Sun Xuefeng, eds, Zhongguo jueqi ji qi zhanlve (The Rise of China and its Strategy), Beijing: Peking University Press, 2005, p. 152.

577 Wang Zaibang, International Situation 2008: Historic Transformations Highlight Urgent Need for Systemic Readjustments, Contemporary International Relations, Vol. 19, No. 2, March - April 2009, pp. 65–66.

578 Gregory Chin and Richard Stubbs, "China, Regional Institution-Building and the China-ASEAN Free Trade Area", Review of International Political Economy, Vol. 18, Issue 3, 2011, pp. 277–298.

growing aids from China to African states demonstrate China's desire to be an influential player. The magnitude of China's aids toward Africa is an exact barometer of Chinese foreign policy.

2.1. Free Aid for Ideological Alliance

From the establishment of the PRC to its economic opening (1949–1978), China's Africa policy heavily focused on politics. Following the wave of national independence throughout most of Africa, China treated Africa as an ally in its struggles against imperialism and hegemony.[579] From policies of exporting revolution to Africa in the 50s to using free aid as the basis to build bilateral relations in the 60s, China aimed to seek a political alliance with Africa. In 1963, Premier Zhou Enlai visited Africa and proposed the Five Principles Governing the Development of Relations with Arab and African Countries and the Eight Principles of Economic Assistance, in which equality and respect of sovereignty were integral.[580] The abandonment of the exporting revolution for China was mainly attributed to its nature of anti-intervention. Its successor, the free-aids approach, was implemented under the guidance of the Five Principles of Peaceful Co-existence. Premier Zhou especially talked about the application of the non-interference principle in international aid. He said the Chinese government should respect the sovereignty of the aided state fully; no condition should be attached to the aid; interference through international aid was unallowable.[581] The Chinese views on the non-intervention principle are that it is a useful defense for its internal issues but also means no meddling by other states. During these times of political orientation, economic aid was provided to African alliance gratis even though China's own domestic economic circumstances were far from optimal. Despite the Soviet Union supplying more arms than other states to Africa during the 1970s, its economic aid to the continent was far behind that of China.[582] Such an aid policy gained valuable supports from Africa during the early time of the PRC in a rather isolated international environment.

579 Marina Ottaway, Soviet Marxism and African Socialism, in: Journal of Modern African Studies, Volume 16, Issue 03, September 1978, pp. 477–487.

580 Li Jiasong (ed), Big Events in the History of Foreign Affairs of People's Republic of China (Vol. 2), Beijing: World Affairs Press, 2001, pp. 310–311; Full Text: China's Foreign Aid (1964), http://english.gov.cn/official/2011-04/21/content_1849913_10.htm (June 18, 2014).

581 Zhao Jianwen, Zhou Enlai's Thinking about Non-Interference Principle (周恩来关于互不干涉内政思想), Journal of Zhengzhou University, Vol. 31, No. 2, 1998, p. 47.

582 Naomi Chazan, et al., Politics and Society in Contemporary Africa, Boulder: Lynne Rienner Publishers, 1992, p. 410.

2.2. *Low Profile in Africa*

The end of the Cultural Revolution in 1976 marked a substantially shift in China's policy toward Africa from one based almost exclusively on ideological alliance to one with a far more pragmatic and diversified approach. During that period, the Chinese economy was on the edge of crashing and thus was unable to provide free aid to Africa.[583] China shifted from policies that emphasized that "economy serves diplomacy" to policies based on "diplomacy serves the economy."[584] Overall, economic pragmatism prevailed over the ideological pragmatism of the previous period. The low profile strategy was implemented in Africa by downsizing aids to Africa and abolishing free aids. In 1982, the Chinese premier visited Africa and announced the Four Principles on Economic and Technological Cooperation with Africa.[585] Chinese economic aid toward Africa was reduced. Free economic aid was replaced by preferential and discounted loans, cooperatives and joint ventures for projects in Africa, and other forms of economic support. However, such shifts were not a retreat by China from its commitment to relations with Africa but more equalized cooperation between the two sides.

2.3. *Radically Growing Cooperation with Equal Partnership for Win-Win Purpose*

The Forum on China–Africa Cooperation (FOCAC) marks a new level of cooperation between China and the states in Africa. In 2006, the third Forum of the FOCAC caught the attention of foreign observers; it convened foreign ministers from 48 African states for a summit in Beijing. China announced that in the next three years, China would double aid to Africa, provide $6 billion in preferential loans, establish a $5 billion fund to facilitate Chinese investment, and provide $1.4 billion in debt relief for overdue zero-interest loans. China would also double its grant assistance to help build hospitals as well as malaria prevention and treatment centers, assist in constructing schools in rural areas, and help to build a conference center for the African Union.[586] The large foreign aid agreement, combined with the new China - Africa Strategic Partnership Agreement signed during the Beijing FOCAC Summit, overshadowed the actual results from the G-7/8's 'historic' African Outreach announcements at Gleneagles in 2005, where the group promised $50 billion in new

---

583 See The Working Report of Chinese Government in The 1st Plenary Session of the 5th National People's Congress, People Daily, 19780307, p. 1.

584 Li Anshan, "On the Adjustments and Changes of China's Foreign Policy to Africa," West Asia and Africa, Issue 8, 2006.

585 Namely, the principle of equality, mutual benefit, efficiency, diversity and mutual development. See People's Daily, Jan. 15, 1983.

586 Hu Jintao, Speech, Opening Ceremony, Beijing Summit of the Forum on China–Africa Cooperation, November 4, 2006, http://english.focacsummit.org/2006-11/04/content_4978.htm.

aid to Africa and agreed to cancel the outstanding debt of the highly indebted poor countries. The newly created China African Development Fund alone is targeted to make $5 billion available for Chinese investment in Africa, whereas the total amount of Chinese investment in Africa for 2000–2006 had totaled $6 billion, according to China's Ministry of Commerce.[587]

Moreover, trade between Africa and China reached more than $120 billion in 2010, at a time when much of the rest of the world's economy was still in a slump. China provides more subsidized loans to Africa than the World Bank.[588] China has been Africa's biggest trade partner since 2009. In 2012, the total volume of China-Africa trade reached US$198.49 billion, a year-on-year growth of 19.3%. Of this, US$85.319 billion consisted of China's exports to Africa, up 16.7%, and US$113.171 billion was contributed by China's imports from Africa, up 21.4%.[589]

From 2000 until the present, China's aid towards Africa shows a dramatic ascension which indicates African growth to be crucial for China. While Mao gave credit to African brothers for the PRC gaining the seat of UNSC, Africa was crucial for China. Today, African states are even more important than ever. After decades of economic development, the expanding China's economy is hungry for resources. Unsurprisingly, as China evaluates its own resources security, it finds that the Americans are everywhere.[590] Such a circumstance leads China to appreciate more Africa. Although the relations between China and African states changed from political alliance to economical partners, China generally shares the same perception of sovereignty with African states, which are relatively weak and have a large amount of resources. The increasing cooperation between the two sides demonstrates that China might gain economic interests and gradually have more influence in other fields through the way of unconditional aid.

2.4. Comparison between China's Aid Policies and the EU's Aid Policies

As is well known, African states have had a special relationship with European states in the past and at present and will continue to in the future as well. European states and China, as the two major sponsors for African states, carry out rather different policies and modalities. In fact, China's engagement in Africa is highly

587 Richard Lapper, "China Deepens Links with South Africa," Financial Times, May 13, 2010; Jianye Wang, "What Drives China's Growing Role in Africa", IMF Working Paper, No. 07/211, August 2007, p. 11.

588 The Chinese in Africa: "Trying to Pull Together," The Economist, April 20, 2011, available at: <http://www.economist.com/node/18586448?story_id=18586448>.

589 White Paper of China-Africa Economic and Trade Cooperation (2013), published by Xinhua, http://www.globaltimes.cn/content/807252.shtml.

590 David Zweig, "Resource Diplomacy" under Hegemony: The Sources of Sino-American Competition in the 21st Century, Los Angeles: Pacific Council on International Policy, April 2010, pp. 35–74.

criticized by European states.[591] In spite of both having much to do with energy securing and development in Africa, Chinese objectives of development policy differ considerably in many aspects from Europe.[592]

First of all, the EU and its member states provide their loans on initiatives with typical conditions like democracy promotion, human rights protection, and corruption reduction. Unlike European states, China gives this money with little or no strings attached, based on its principles of non-intervention and respect for sovereignty. China simply declares that it "respects African countries' independent choice in political system" and developing a path suitable to their own national conditions, and supports them in their just struggles for safeguarding their independence, sovereignty and territorial integrity in terms of non-intervention and equal sovereignty.[593] On the contrary, European aid are actual tools to promote Western universalism in African states. The relationship between the EU and African states is barely equal. This political conditionality further erodes those African states' sovereignty and weakens their position.[594] China's unconditional approach has been blamed as a 'support' to tyranny but also praised for the positive effects for a number of countries, for example, Ethiopia, Zambia, South Africa, Tanzania, etc. Its rejection of the European moral supremacy becomes a legitimate challenge to the Western aid status quo.[595]

Secondly, China's non-interference and respect for sovereignty policy implies that it pays very little attention to the negative externalities that arise from its investment spending. Logically, China cooperates with authoritarian and democratic regimes whilst the former pattern would be isolated for political reasons by the EU and other Western donors. China's involvement in Africa with "rogue states" and corrupt governments has received endless criticism from Western development minds. They argue that China should use its economic leverage as a political tool and threaten to cut off financial ties to recipients who repeatedly violate human

---

591 "The EU reaffirmed its attachment to the principles of good governance and human rights, as embodied in its Africa strategy. The Chinese side emphasized the upholding of the five principles of peaceful coexistence, in particular the principle of non-interference into others' internal affairs." (Council of the European Union 2006).

592 Christine Hackenesch, "China and the EU's engagement in Africa: Setting the Stage for Cooperation, Competition, or Conflict," German Development Institute Research Project, European Policy for Global Development, Discussion Paper 16/2009, p. 54.

593 China's African Policy, available at: http://www.focac.org/eng/zt/zgdfzzcwj/t230479.htm.

594 Peter Uvin and Isabelle Biagiotti, "Global Governance and the 'New' Political Conditionality," Global Governance, Vol. 1, No. 3, 1996, p. 397.

595 Madison Condon, China in Africa: What the Policy of Non-intervention Adds to the Western Development Dilemma, Praxis: The Fletcher Journal of Human Security, Vol. 27, 2012, pp. 5–25.

rights. They claim that aids reward the behavior of dictators and actively fund the oppression of reformists. For example, China's aid towards Sudan particularly renders harsh criticism even though China finally exerted its influence leading to the referendum of South Sudan. On the other hand, the Western aid approaches with conditionality have largely been development failures.[596]

Thirdly, China considers itself as the largest and first leader of a growing band of developing countries. Without the taint of a colonial past and explicit political agenda, the relations between China and African states are devoid of the language of duty, obligation, and guilt but are for "mutual economic benefit," which is labeled as 'South-South' cooperation, a refreshingly equal partnership to development. Western states still consider Africa in terms of their "spheres of influence" from the colonial legacy and their influence on the African continent.[597] Unlike the EU and its member states, China is itself a developing country with colonized history, which in the not-too-distant past had 85 percent of its population living below the poverty line.[598] Such a common background easily bonds China with African countries without a condescending donor attitude. China has made much of this diplomacy effort, noting that it pays attention to all African countries, not just those with strategically important resources. China now has established embassies in more African countries than any European country.[599]

Fourthly, comparing the European political conditional aids pattern, Chinese aid appears in a purely economic nature.[600] However, economical influence can gradually transform into political influence when it is necessary for Chinese interests. For example, China has stepped-up the number of its blue helmets to more than 2,000, serving in 10 peacekeeping missions mainly in Africa. Furthermore, China has increasingly acknowledged and supported the work of regional organizations on security issues that affect its interests in Africa. China committed itself to providing material and financial support for the Peace and Security Council of the AU and other African security organizations and to participating in peace operations in Africa. Even though China obeys the non-intervention principle by providing

596 Madison Condon, 2012, pp. 5–25.

597 Li Anshan, China and Africa: Policy and Challenges, China Security Vol. 3 No. 3 Summer 2007, p. 83.

598 Anup Shaw, "Poverty Facts and Stats," Global Issues, January 07, 2013, available at: http://www.globalissues.org/article/26/poverty-facts-and-stats.

599 Christine Hackenesch, 2009, p. 35.

600 The three year action plan of the 2006 FOCAC meeting mentioned: Doubling aid to Africa to reach about US$ 1 billion by 2009; Establishing a China-Africa Development Fund (CADFund) to boost Chinese companies' investments in Africa; Providing US$ 3 billion preferential loans and US$ 2 billion in preferential buyer's credits to African countries; Cancelling debts for 31 African countries Opening China's market for exports to African countries; Building hospitals and schools in rural areas in Africa. Available at: http://www.focac.org/eng/ltda/dscbzjhy/DOC32009/t606841.htm.

non-conditional aids towards African states, the influence through participating in economics can legally and slowly expand to politics. The Sudan case is actually a good example to exhibit how to expand influence from economy to politics. China is therefore likely to continue reaching out to these potentially like-minded African partners who still share many of China's views when it comes to issues of sovereignty and the non-interference principle.[601]

Therefore, China's increasingly important presence in Africa arguably puts more pressure on the overly complex EU system to reform and pushes the EU to adhere more strongly to its commitments. African governments mostly welcome China's engagement in Africa since it provides greater freedom and independence from Western donors.[602] Meanwhile, more broad pressure exerted by the EU towards China certainly has an influence on China's policies *vis-à-vis* African countries.[603] In October 2008, the EU Commission took the lead in fostering trilateral dialogue mechanisms, publishing a communication on "The EU, China and Africa: Towards trilateral dialogue and cooperation". It aims to create a more comprehensive cooperation in order to reduce competition and conflict between European and Chinese development policies in regard to their external relations and their development policies on Africa.[604]

3. China's Perception of Sovereignty is in the Process of Transformation

On the one hand, economic globalization and development of information technology are making countries more closely linked and interdependent with their interests more closely integrated than ever before. No state, even the most powerful one, could stay away from other states or organizations. Globalization is understood as a process of denationalization of markets, politics, and law on the international level as well as the national level.[605] First of all, states enter into more and more treaties and transnational organizations that impose more and more duties on states. Sovereign states voluntarily accept constraints. Secondly, international organizations are growing fast and playing a significant role for countries who want to engage in mutually beneficial cooperation. Partial sovereign rights are voluntarily transferred into international organizations by states. State power is tied by many

601 Sara Van Hoeymissen, Regional Organizations in China's Security Strategy for Africa: The Sense of Supporting "African Solutions to African Problems", Journal of Current Chinese Affairs, Vol. 40, No. 4, p. 109.

602 Christine Hackenesch, 2009, p. 8.

603 Ibid p. 56.

604 Ibid, p. 9.

605 Jost Delbrilck, Structural Changes in the International System and Its Legal Order: International Law in the Era of Globalization, Swiss Review of International and European Law, No. 1, 2001, pp. 13–17.

rules. EU member states confer the EU a number of sovereignty rights, that allows the EU to exercise sovereignty rights. In eyes of many scholars or writers, the EU becomes a symbol of erosion of sovereignty. Thirdly, international human rights law is developing to reach the domestic matters which used to be purely an internal issue. The intensification of international law and the extension of the reach of human rights instruments signal the erosion of states' powers. The international society is trying legitimate interventions for a humanitarian purpose. Fourthly, international law is currently in the process of transforming, extending to states, governmental and non-governmental organizations, and other non-state corporate entities, as well as groups and individuals.[606] State powers and influence are being reduced. Some affairs which were internal issues are transforming into international concerns. For instance, environmental issues are concerning the globe's common interests. Fifthly, national identity confronts challenges coming from globalization. Globalization is increasing the exposure of all societies to foreign culture and so brings about changes in local cultures, values, and traditions. The common values are becoming universal accepted and go beyond the border of sovereign states.[607] Manifestly, sovereignty has been profoundly affected by globalization.

On the other hand, China's reform and open process has steadily enmeshed its economy with the international system, forcing Chinese policymakers to take a broader and more globalized view of China's national interests. Meanwhile, China's economic growth and military modernization process has caused concern about China's "rise", resulting in efforts to reassure neighbors that China strives to be a "responsible power".[608] By actively participating in the international community, China is making an effort to rebuild China's image as a new power that seeks to contribute to international stability through diplomatic and peaceful measures. It attempts to contribute 'creative involvement' to the international society as a new power instead of maintaining a low profile. Ensuing China's rising and transformation of the world, China's interpretation of sovereignty is in the process of change, which it embodies in every aspects of China's foreign policy, particularly in UN peacekeeping, humanitarian intervention, human rights, international trade, etc.

3.1. From Refusal to Active Engagement in UN Peacekeeping Projects

China's evolving role in peacekeeping activities demonstrates just how far its perception in sovereignty has shifted and changed in a relatively short period of time. After China joined the UN in 1971, it adamantly opposed peacekeeping operations (PKO)

---

606 Jost Delbruck, Prospects for a 'World (Internal) Law'?: Legal Development in a Changing International System, Indiana Journal of Global Legal Studies, Vol. 9, Issue 2, 2002, p. 401.

607 Yu Keping, State sovereignty in the time of Globalization, Wenhuibao (Hongkong), 2004.11.4.

608 Drew Thompson, Beijing's Participation in UN Peacekeeping Operation, China Brief Volume, Vol. 5, Iss. 11, May 10, 2005.

and refused to contribute money or resources to any operations.[609] Adhering to a strict definition of sovereignty and non-interference, China rejected international interventions that supposedly violated their notions of peaceful co-existence and potentially invited international scrutiny into China's own domestic affairs. However, during Deng's reform and the opening-up era, China's attitude towards peacekeeping started to change. Since the end of the Cold War, China has gradually become increasingly involved in multilateral interventions mandated and organized either by the UN or other appropriate regional organizations operating with the UN Security Council. In 1988, China joined the special committee on peacekeeping operations and sent its first military observers the following year and the first company of engineers to Cambodia in April 1992. As China's power is growing fast, the more active engagement in peacekeeping could enhance China's image in host countries and within the international society which is the actual goal of Beijing's charming offence policy. Meanwhile China is gradually involved with most of the multi-dimensional tasks of peacekeeping and peacebuilding, which require being handled in a much more flexible manner. Moreover, as the Chinese gradually go global for business, education, travel and employment, the Chinese government has been forced to recognize that protecting growing Chinese overseas interests requires a more outward looking and engaging foreign policy that is more flexible. It means the Chinese interpretation of sovereignty and non-intervention in its rigid manner is transforming into a more flexible one for new situations.

In the process of peaceful rising, China's participation in UN peacekeeping operations has dramatically expanded by type, numbers of personnel and location of missions. China sends military engineering, medical and transport teams, as well as military observers, civil policemen and political officials to join the UN peacekeeping missions. Up until 2013, more than 2,000 Chinese peacekeepers have been in peacekeeping operations in nine different mission zones. China has also provided the most peacekeepers among all 5 permanent members of the UN Security Council (P-5), and is the seventh largest contributor to the UN peacekeeping budget. According to the Permanent Mission of the PRC to the UN, China's contribution to the UN peacekeeping budget will increase from just over three percent of the total budget in 2013, to more than six percent by 2015.[610]

From the process of China's participation in the UN peacekeeping tasks, it can be observed that gradual involvements in peacekeeping indicate the gradual evolution of the interpretation of sovereignty

609 Samuel Kim, 'China's International Organization Behavior', in Chinese Foreign Policy: Theory and Practice (ed. by Thomas Robinson and David Shambaugh), Oxford: Oxford University Press, 1995, pp. 420–422.

610 Colleen Wong, China Embraces Peacekeeping Missions: A historical transformation is underway as China begins sending combat forces to UN operations, August 09, 2013, the Diplomat, http://thediplomat.com/2013/08/china-embraces-peacekeeping-missions/.

3.1.1. *China is in Favor of UN peacekeeping's Involvement in Humanitarian Crises instead of Humanitarian Intervention*

China has been actively engaged in deliberations on the role of UN peacekeeping missions to deter and defend attacks against civilian populations since the Council first took up Protection of Civilians ("POC") as a thematic issue in February 1999. China endorsed Resolution 1265, which expressed the Council's willingness to examine how peacekeeping operations could assist in civilian protection.[611] The following year, in April 2000, China joined the unanimous Council endorsement of Resolution 1296, which noted that "the deliberate targeting of civilian populations or other protected persons and the committing of systematic, flagrant and widespread violations of international humanitarian and human rights law in situations of armed conflict may constitute a threat to international peace and security".[612] Over the last decade the Council has explicitly mandated 10 UN peacekeeping missions to take necessary measures, including force, to "protect civilians under imminent threat of physical violence".[613] In each case, China has voted in favor, namely: UN Mission in Sierra Leone, UN Organization Stabilization Mission in the Democratic Republic of Congo (MONUC), UN Mission in Liberia, UN Operation in Burundi, UN Stabilization Mission in Haiti, UN Operation in Côte d'Ivoire, UN Mission in Sudan, UN Interim Force in Lebanon, African Union (AU)/UN Hybrid Operation in Darfur and UN Mission in the Central African Republic and Chad. China likewise endorsed POC Resolutions 1674 (2006) and 1894 (2009), both of which reaffirmed R2P. Resolution 1674 reaffirmed the practice of ensuring that UN peacekeeping missions included POC provisions and prioritized protection when making decisions on the use of available capacity and resources, while Resolution 1894 requested the Secretary-General to develop an operational concept for POC in peacekeeping operations. It is worth noting as well that China endorsed Resolution 1820 (2008), which recognized that rape and other forms of sexual violence can constitute atrocity crimes, and requested the Secretary-General to develop guidelines for UN peacekeeping operations to better protect women and girls from sexual violence. Later that year, in response to deteriorating security and increased attacks on civilians in the Kivus (Democratic Republic of Congo), China joined the Council's unanimous endorsement of Resolution 1856 to revise MONUC's robust mandate to place the highest priority on protecting civilians. It is fair to say then that China has repeatedly supported a role for peacekeeping missions to bolster

611 'Protection of Civilians', UN doc., S/RES/1265, 17 Sept. 1999.

612 'Protection of Civilians', UN doc., S/RES/1296, 19 Apr. 2000.

613 For the most part, these protection mandates have been attached with standard caveats: peacekeeping missions are authorized to protect civilians 'in the areas of deployment', 'within their capabilities' and, importantly in regard to China's support for the task, 'without prejudice to the [host] government' or 'taking into account the responsibilities of the [host] government'.

civilian protection both at the thematic level and in establishing and renewing country-specific operations.[614]

As discussed above, China shows its enthusiasm for UN peacekeeping operations instead of humanitarian intervention led by some powerful member states. Beijing seemly considers the UN peacekeeping operations as a more feasible way to cope with humanitarian crises, which may mediate the conflict between intervention and sovereignty. Legitimacy of UN peacekeeping under the UN system, comparative mature mechanism which has evolved for 40 years, and its suspicion of humanitarian intervention led China in favor of peacekeeping and peacebuilding. Additionally, China's reputation as a responsible world power can be enhanced by its involvement in peace operations. The most crucial matter is that the UN peacekeeping system is much more compatible with China's fundamental concerns on sovereignty which always obstructs Beijing's recognition of humanitarian intervention or R2P. The consent of host states, neutrality, impartiality, and respect of sovereignty have been carried on in the peacekeeping process. Clearly, the system of UN peacekeeping is much more consistent with China's current perception of sovereignty.

3.1.2. China is in Favor of Multiple Non-military Assistances instead of Military Options

The tasks are multidimensional and generally focus on maintaining peace, protecting civilians, and reconstructing post-conflict political and legal order in host states. The peacekeeping operations which China has been involved in are normally characterized as non-military. The active deployment of Chinese troops is mainly in the form of engineers, military observers, transport and logistical support units, civilian police and medical staff to UN peacekeeping operations.[615] In late 2013, Beijing sent an infantry detachment to Mali as the first overseas deployment of Chinese combat troops in a UN peacekeeping role. As an indication of its preference for non-military solutions to conflict, in December 2009 China donated US$700,000 to the UN peacekeeping fund to support mediation efforts; US$500,000 was earmarked for the Trust Fund for the AU–UN Joint Mediation Support Team for Darfur to support the political process (China had already contributed US$500,000 to the fund in March 2008), and US$100,000 was provided to both the Trust Fund for Preventive Action and the trust fund that supports UN preventive diplomacy and political mediation. At that time, China ranked seventh among UN members in financial contributions to peacekeeping.[616]

---

614 Sarah Teitt, The Responsibility to Protect and China's Peacekeeping Policy, International Peacekeeping, Vol. 18, Issue 3, 2011, pp. 298–312.

615 Chin-Hao Huang, Principles and Praxis of China's Peacekeeping, International Peacekeeping, Vol. 18, Iss. 3, 2011, p. 257.

616 Anne Tang, 'China Donates $700,000 to UN Peacekeeping Missions', Xinhua (Beijing), 2 Dec. 2009, available at: www.reliefweb.int/rw/rwb.nsf/db900sid/JBRN-7YCFEH?OpenDocument.

In August 2009, during the Security Council peacekeeping debate following the release of 'New Horizon', the Chinese delegate emphasized that "[p]eacekeeping operations must exercise caution in the use of force and avoid excessive emphasis on military options. Given the ongoing divergence of views on mandating peacekeeping operations to protect civilians, further in-depth discussions on that issue will be necessary".[617] Vice Foreign Minister He Yafei characterized the "mandate to protect civilians and robust peacekeeping" as "emerging theories", and claimed that equal importance should be attached to "the development and innovation of traditional theories such as conflict prevention, dispute mediation, crisis management and post-conflict peacebuilding".[618]

3.1.3. China's Peacekeeping Operations Highlight Respect for Sovereignty of the Host State

Firstly, in the multiple tasks of peacekeeping, Beijing has actively taken part in peacebuilding but refused to join the process of state-building. At present, UN peacekeeping operations are called upon not only to maintain peace and security but also to facilitate peace-building, including protecting civilians, assisting in the disarmament, demobilization and reintegration of former combatants, supporting the organization of elections, protecting and promoting human rights and assisting in restoring the rule of law.[619] Since most tasks of peacebuilding are generally domestic affairs in nature, China was not in favor of it. From the beginning it had reluctance for peacebuilding, yet along with the wide acceptance of peacebuilding by many states, China embraces the peacebuilding with its own terms. Due to state-building's inherently political nature and that state-building may not always automatically lead to peacebuilding, China differentiates peacebuilding and state-building. It accepts that there is a need to help a country carry out political and economic restructuring and understands that the UN needs to carry out certain administrative functions on behalf of its government. Beijing is not a supporter of peacebuilding conflated with military action or regime change, and consistently objects to any state-building operations. Thus, for the purpose of preventing peacekeeping from becoming state-building, Beijing vigorously emphasizes respect for the right of the country concerned to make its own decisions, the primary task to restore the administrative functions of state organs of the country and the full consideration of the development priorities identified independently by the country.[620]

---

617 'Security Council Open Debate on Peacekeeping Operations', UN doc., S/PV.6178, 5 Aug. 2009, p. 23.

618 Ministry of Foreign Affairs of the People's Republic of China.

619 United Nations Peacekeeping Helps Countries Torn by Conflict Create Conditions for Lasting Peace, available at: http://www.un.org/en/peacekeeping/operations/peacekeeping.shtml.

620 Permanent Mission of the People's Republic of China to the United Nations, 'Statement by Ambassador Liu Zhenmin at Security Council Open Debate on Post-

Secondly, Beijing assists peacebuilding mainly in economic developments. China holds that "poverty leads to social instability which will in turn be a threat to peace and security at the national and even regional levels".[621] It prioritizes "development" over "imposed democracy and good governance" in international peace operations.[622] Unsurprisingly, China's peacekeeping contribution mainly facilitates the host country's economic development and modernization trajectories.[623] In line with this policy, China had involved only logistical and medical personnel until 2013 when China dispatched actual security forces to help maintain the peace in Mali. Conversely, European countries pursue economic and political reform to resolve the conflict and peace because democracy is a panacea to keep peace.

Thirdly, based on the principle of sovereignty, China sticks to the principles of consent of host states, impartiality, and non-use of force in UN Peacekeeping operations.

Under the principle of respecting sovereignty of the host state, China adheres to the three principles in peacekeeping operations - never taking positions to help either party during a civil conflict, gaining the consent of the host country and using force only in self-defense. Chinese representatives at the UN and in other international settings notably intentionally omitted another exception for the use of force-defense of the mandate.[624] Its reservation on the use of force demonstrates Beijing's cautions of using force which should be monopolized within a territory by the sovereign.

Due to its concerns about the sovereignty of host states, Beijing tackles its peacekeeping task very dedicatedly. Unlike other delegations that have expressed concern that traditional peacekeeping principles - principles of neutrality, respect for state sovereignty, consent of the parties and non-use of violence except in cases of self-defense - are unable to meet the challenges of peacekeeping environments and offer support for recommendations to clearly define and further develop the role of UN peacekeepers in civilian protection, China has been hesitant to endorse such proposals and maintains that the new peacekeeping doctrine should be based on traditional peacekeeping principles.[625] Despite that it has no intention to alter them

---

conflict Peacebuilding', 22 July 2009, available at: www.china-un.org/eng/hyyfy/t575181.htm.

621 Permanent Mission of the People's Republic of China to the United Nations, Statement by Ambassador Shen Guofang, Deputy Permanent Representative of China to UN at the Security Council on the Topic of 'Peace-Building: Towards a Comprehensive Approach', 5 Feb. 2001, Available at: www.china-un.org/eng/chinaandun/securitycouncil/thematicissues/peacekeeping/t29428.htm).

622 Zhao Lei, 2011, p. 352.

623 Miwa Hirono & Marc Lanteigne, Introduction: China and UN Peacekeeping, International Peacekeeping, Vol. 18, Issue 3, 2011, p. 249.

624 Sarah Teitt, 2011, p. 305.

625 'Special Committee Members Commend Performance of United Nations Peacekeepers Faced with Complex Mandates, Lacking Key Capabilities: Delegates Express

or add any new principles, Beijing accepts the 2008 UN 'Principles and Guidelines'.[626] According to the UN 'Principles and Guidelines' of January 2008, consent of host states, impartiality and the non-use of force remain the cornerstones of UN peacekeeping, and it also asserts that force may be used in self-defense as well as the defense of the mandate.[627]

Certainly, the 2008 Guidelines deliberately alter some words in order to give the UN peacekeeping forces some space to carry out its tasks effectively. For example, 'impartiality' instead of 'neutrality' allows the UN blue helmets to pick sides for the protection of civilians. Such a shift suggests that China may continue to liberalize its position on the role of the United Nations in intervening to end mass atrocities or gross violations of human rights.[628]

3.2. *China's Endorsement of RtoP*

As "a growing tendency to recognize that the principle of state sovereignty finds its limits in the protection of human security",[629] China has conceded to the universality of human rights principles; and increasingly supports the respect of basic human rights as a responsibility of a sovereign state. Such acceptance led to China's public acknowledgment of the need for international intervention under the UN auspices in cases of massive violations of human rights at the 2005 World Summit. China acknowledged that, "When a massive humanitarian crisis occurs, it is the legitimate concern of the international community to ease and defuse the crisis". It implies that China has made a fundamental turn to accept human rights' higher status over that of sovereignty in exceptional cases.

Views on Early Peacebuilding, Civilian Protection, "Robust Peacekeeping" as General Debate Concludes', UN doc., GA/PK/204, 23 Feb. 2010.

626 China's delegate noted, adhering to the three principles of the consent of the country concerned, impartiality and the non-use of force except in self-defense is the key to the success of peacekeeping operations. Any deviation from those basic principles will cause more conflicts and problems, even to the point of jeopardizing the success of the peacekeeping operation concerned, rather than help to protect civilians. See 'Security Council Open Debate on Protection of Civilians in Armed Conflict', UN Doc., S/PV.6354, 7 July 2010, p. 28.

627 UN DPKO and Department of Field Support, 'United Nations Peacekeeping Operations: Principles and Guidelines', 2008.

628 Jonathan E. Davis, 2011, p. 283.

629 The Outcome Document is qualified by some as a milestone in the relationship between sovereignty and human rights. See the abstract dated July 28, 2006, of the online version of Alex J. Bellamy, Whither the Responsibility to Protect? Humanitarian Intervention and the 2005 World Summit, ETHICS & INT'LA FF., Vol. 20, Issue 143, 2006, available at: <http://www.cceia.org/resources/journal/20_2/articles/5384.htmiln>, which Bellamy's article is described as taking a different view.

"Sovereignty as responsibility" as the core of RtoP indicates that a government can no longer "hide behind the shield of sovereignty, claiming non-intervention by other states in its internal affairs, if it fails to protect the people under its jurisdiction from massive violations of human rights".[630] China's endorsement of RtoP embodies that China recognizes that human rights protection imposes more restrictions on sovereignty and in some extreme exceptions it overpowers sovereignty. Meanwhile, China also attempts to reconcile potential conflicts between the RtoP and sovereignty. It underscores the primary responsibility of states and stresses that only strong sovereignty can ensure protection of human rights. The international community has a complementary responsibility only existing in case of national authorities manifestly failing to protect their populations from genocide, war crimes, ethnic cleansing and crimes against humanity.[631] China holds that such control of crisis should be accomplished within the UN framework by maximizing the use of all peaceful means. It points out that R2P's application is very controversial and needs further discussion to reach a consensus in the UN General Assembly.[632] As discussed above, China is in favor of employing the UN peacekeeping mechanism to pursue the responsibility to protect.

3.3. Globalization and Transferable Sovereign Rights

China's fascination with Westphalian sovereignty was a notorious label of China's in international society. Due to self-identifying as a victim of imperialism, Beijing had unwaveringly guarded sovereignty and was opposed to various types of hegemony. Unsurprisingly, the obsession of sovereignty did not impede China embracing globalization which definitely erodes sovereignty from economic, social, cultural and political aspects. The global economic governance through international institutions, such as the World Trade Organizations and International Monetary Fund, undermines the traditional role of states in exercising economic sovereignty. Embracing globalization led to China redefining China's perception of sovereignty, reconsidering and adapting China's international behavior in the transforming world.[633] On the one hand, China's uncompromising rhetoric on sovereignty and non-intervention in territorial issues has very often been evoked as clear evidence that China is still stuck in the Westphalian anarchy. On the other hand, although

630 Ved P. Nanda, The Protection of Human Rights Under International Law: Will the U.N. Human Rights Council and the Emerging New Norm "Responsibility To Protect" Make a Difference?, Denver Journal. International Law & Policy, Vol. 35, 2007, pp. 353, 373.

631 2005 World Summit Outcome Document', UN doc., A/60/L.1, 15 Sep. 2005, para.139.

632 Wang Guangya, China's Statement at the 59th Session of the United Nations General Assembly, on 6 April 2005.

633 Yongjin Zhang, Ambivalent Sovereignty: China and Re-Imagining the Westphalian Ideal, in Re-envisioning Sovereignty: The End of Westphalia? Vermont: Ashgate Publishing Limited Company, 2008, p. 110.

Chinese analysts and policy-makers are fully aware that globalization poses serious challenges to the traditional sovereignty, China does not hesitate to make significant political and economic concessions in order to gain China's membership in the World Trade Organization ("WTO") compromising China's economic sovereignty. Obviously, the monitoring mechanisms and measures under the WTO system can be regarded as a clear infringement of Chinese sovereignty, as traditionally conceived. Sovereign rights transference theory emerges to reconcile contradictions on China's policies about sovereignty. Chinese analysts argue that indivisibility of sovereignty decides that sovereignty is nontransferable because "sovereignty over the same territory cannot reside simultaneously in two different authorities."[634] However, indivisibility of sovereignty does not prohibit sovereign rights being transferred to international institutions. Therefore, sovereignty is an abstract symbol of supreme authority while specific sovereign powers can be divided from sovereignty, specific sovereign rights can be reassigned to international organizations.[635] As the German Constitution Court holds, the critical sovereign rights concerning democratic formative action cannot be transferred to anybody but only those in the transferable areas[636]; China also considers that only part of sovereign rights are transferable but never clarifies which part. Indisputably, economic sovereign rights are acknowledged as transferable by China. Obviously, such a theory solves China's contradictory policies on state sovereignty and allows China to staunchly defend its core national interests meanwhile China's engagement with globalization makes China a winner in its economic development and further encourages China to reconsider the concept of sovereignty.

3.4. The Concept of Core National Interest and Sovereignty

Two major leitmotifs have begun simultaneously to inform the role of Chinese foreign policy in 2005, the 'harmonious world', and 'core national interest'.[637] The concept of core national interests coming into being by no means denotes the uncompromised volition of China to protect its national security and territorial integrity. It was first adopted in China's foreign policy around 2005 when the Chinese foreign affairs officials mentioned it in a response to the Taiwan question in order to express China's firm stance on upholding the country's national unity and territorial integrity. When some Western leaders successively met with the Dalai Lama in their

---

634 Hans J. Morgenthau, "The Problem of Sovereignty Reconsidered," Columbia Law Review, Vol. 48, no. 3, 1948, pp. 350.

635 Zhang Junqi, Three Points of the Legal Meanings of Transfer of Sovereignty, Modern Law Science, Vol. 27, No. 1, 2005, pp. 98–102.

636 Judgment of German Constitution Court in Lisbon Treaty Case, BVerfG, 2 BvE 2/08 from 30 June 2009, para. 224.

637 Shih Chih-yu and Yin Jiwuy, Between Core National Interest and a Harmonious World: Reconciling Self-role Conceptions in Chinese Foreign Policy, The Chinese Journal of International Politics, Vol. 6, 2013, pp. 59–84.

offices and some foreign governments sold weapons to Taiwan, Chinese officials have repeatedly asserted that the Taiwan and Tibet questions concern China's sovereignty and territorial integrity, and that these provocations have "hurt the feelings of the Chinese people". On 6th September 2011, China's State Council released a White Paper named China's Peaceful Development, which defined China's core national interests as state sovereignty, national security, territorial integrity and national reunification, China's political system established by the Constitution, overall social stability, and the basic safeguards for ensuring sustainable economic and social development. China has stressed the importance of safeguarding China's core national interests at many occasions. Moreover, it also implies that some national interests other than core national interests can be compromised.

The relationship between sovereignty and national interests is clear. For Beijing, "sovereignty is not synonymous with national interests, rather it should be subject to overall national interests, not protected at all costs".[638] The formula of 'one country, two systems' that has facilitated the handover of Hong Kong and Macau reflects a substantial, negotiated compromise of China's sovereignty and demonstrates how far China's concession on sovereignty can reach for national reunification. The instrumental nature of sovereignty determines flexibility of interpretation on sovereignty to pursue China's national interests. Such flexibility often presents discursive even paradoxical engagement with the changing sovereignty.

While China did not veto the UNSC intervention of Côte d'Ivoire, Foreign Ministry Spokesperson said: "China has been following the situation in [Côte] d'Ivoire since the election. Adhering to the principle of non-interference in other[s'] internal affairs, China upholds respecting the sovereignty of [Côte] d'Ivoire and hope[s] parties in the country properly settle their disputes through dialogue and consultation to realize political reconciliation and jointly safeguard state stability and national solidarity".[639] It implies that China does not approve this action but there are not enough national interests affected to veto against the decision. China's actions in Libya seemly also fall into this pattern. Due to China's image as a benign and responsible global power overcoming its economic interests in Sudan, China shifts its stance to support the UN peacekeeping operation. Those cases suggest that China's rigid position on sovereignty and the non-intervention principle seemly shift to a pro-intervention tendency. Nevertheless, China's uncompromising rhetoric on sovereignty and non-intervention in internal affairs has frequently been used to defend its policies in Taiwan.

Likewise, China admits openly that human rights protection could be an international affair and discusses its human rights situation with Western states. However,

---

638 Bates Gill and James Reilly, Sovereignty, Intervention and Peacekeeping: The View from Beijing', Survival, Vol. 42, No. 3, Autumn 2000, pp. 41–59.

639 Jiang Yu, Foreign Ministry Spokesperson, Consulate-General of China in N.Y., Press Conference on December 9, 2010, available at: http://newyork.china-consulate.org/eng/fyrth/t777253.htm.

when Western states associate human rights with the issues of Tibet, Xinjiang, which China maintains as territorial issues, Beijing always invokes sovereignty against Western states and condemns them for interfering in Chinese internal affairs. Consequently, the policy of core national interests gives Beijing more space to employ sovereignty to safeguard China's interest and thus promotes more variations in China's practices regarding sovereignty. Variations and contradictions in China's interpretations and practices of sovereignty represent that both perceptions of the classic sovereignty and eroded sovereignty coexist and serve for national interests in China's practices. Such a paradox reflects perpetual agony in coming to terms with sovereignty as a dynamic institution constantly reconstituted and reconstructed.[640]

4. China's Current Major Views on Sovereignty

4.1. State Remains the Key Player in International Plane and Sovereignty Remains the Base of International Relations

As Xue Hanqing wrote, China realizes the concept of sovereignty is transforming, "While Europe has been undergoing a process of integration, in this process the concept of sovereignty is "undeniably changing, but not diminishing".[641]

It is true that it is said that it is this very capability of sovereignty states to limit themselves by the creation of new binding laws is the cause of the alleged decline of sovereignty but that such limitations do not affect the quality of the sovereignty state as such. The state maintains its sovereignty in international law and continues to be able to guide its future destiny within the limits that it has itself accepted. As the comments Sir Jennings made, sovereignty states, by undertaking treaty obligations and by becoming members of international organizations and also in other ways, "use their powers to limit their powers"; at the same time and by the same act they also "use their power to acquire new and different powers". Such changes to sovereignty power do not amount to the disappearance of sovereignty but, on the contrary, it does show how external sovereignty works in different planes for different purposes.[642] No doubt, no surrogates of states could exercise as identifiable, responsible agents in the sense of democracy or by being subject to the popular will.[643] The sovereign state is not perfect, and the change is mounting significant challenges but it still provides the best framework for the current organization of collective political life.[644] It is still sovereign states that make, and ultimately also

640 Yongjin Zhang, 2008, p. 114.

641 Xue Hanqing, Chinese observations on international law, Chinese Journal of International Law, Vol. 6, 2007, p. 84.

642 Robert Jennings, 2002, p. 36.

643 Chris Brown, Foreword of Politics without Sovereignty (ed. by Christopher J. Bickerton, Philip Cunliffe and Alexander Gourevitch), New York: Routledge, 2007.

644 Robert Jennings, 2002, p. 41.

enforce, international law.[645] As the former President of China Jiang said once, "sovereignty still stays or will stay as long as states exist."[646]

4.2. Sovereignty and Non-intervention Remains the Base of China's Foreign Policy

From the initial opening and reforming policy in the late 1970s, China has steadily yielded into a slow erosion of its strict sovereignty perception.[647] Particularly, the globalization and evolvements of human rights system progressively and significantly change China's position on sovereignty. Nonetheless, Beijing recalcitrantly holds that there must not be any wavering of the principles of respecting state sovereignty and non-interference of internal affairs. It emphases, "Although the world has undergone profound and complex changes, the basic status of the purposes and principles of the UN Charter remains unchanged".[648]

First of all, a victim's attitude branded by the colonial experiences remains in China's mind and it has influenced China's position at present. Despite that, China becomes much stronger and more confident and its concerns about external powers intervening in China's domestic affairs does not disappear. The century humiliation as a part of China's identity bolsters a strong nationalism in China's understanding of sovereignty. Secondly, China has been aware that it has its own values, ideology, political standards and mode of development that distinguishes it from Western powerful states and because of this has experienced plenty of criticisms from them.[649] China sees itself as a major target of powerful Western political, military and media efforts to pursue neoliberal strategies of ideological world dominance. The strategy pursuing "peaceful" transitions from socialism to western democracy in communist countries was formulated during the Cold War by former US Secretary of State John Foster Dulles. After the collapse of the former communist regimes of Eastern Europe and the Soviet Union, Beijing became the major adversary of Western states in the soft war. The problem is that Beijing has its own agenda in which it rejects teachings from Western states. It characterizes its strategic intentions as mainly "inward-looking" while the United States are "outward-looking". Its spokesman states that the Chinese never meddle in the internal affairs of other countries or lecture others on how to handle their own business even though China has thousands upon thousands of

645 Yu Keping, "On Globalization and State Sovereignty" (论全球化与国家主权), Marxism and Reality (马克思主义与现实), No. 1, 2004, pp. 4–21.

646 Jiang Zeming, Speech at the 2000 Summit Conference, available at: http://www.cctv.com/news/special/zt1/qingnian/67.html.

647 Bates Gill and James Reilly, 2000, p. 41.

648 Chinese Diplomat: Implementing 'Responsibility to Protect' must not Contravene State Sovereignty, available at: http://news.xinhuanet.com/english/2009-07/25/content_11769124.htm.

649 Linda Jakobson, Innovation with Chinese Characteristics, High-Tech Research in China, London: Palgrave Macmillan, 2007, p. 18.

books with case studies based on China's experience on how to run a country.[650] It accuses the US of leading a "soft war" against the current Chinese political system and ideology. Western neo-liberalism is described by Chinese political commentators as a form of "postmodern imperialism", in which the objective is neither land, resources nor direct political control, but rather ideological dominance.[651] In recent years, China has become active in the international scene. Beijing explains those activities as being for "mutual benefit" and not for the "export of ideology and development mode, not to impose its own social system, not to attach political strings ... nor to seek privileges or a 'sphere of influence'".[652] Thirdly, China's internal instability and problems on the issues of Taiwan, Tibet, and Xingjiang also press Beijing into continuing its defensive stance on sovereignty, which means "strictly following the principle of sovereignty equality and non-intervention".[653] Fourthly, China always empathizes with developing states and sees itself as their representative. It is necessary for it to take a common stance on sovereignty to show its support. Fifthly, to counter-play "China's threat", Chinese leaders try to convince the world that China's peaceful rise benefits the world. Manifestly, "China needs to find its way to regional and global leadership without raising fears of hegemonic intentions".[654] The promise of respecting other's sovereignty and adhering to non-intervention is part of the guarantee to never engage in hegemony. In conclusion, on the one hand, China at present is seeking to comprehend the changing meanings and evolving practice of sovereignty in the age of globalization and on the other hand, it continues to adhere to non-intervention and respect for sovereignty.

4.3. Relative Limitations on Sovereignty

In fact, the shield of sovereignty has been perforated and the absolute line of sovereignty cannot strictly be kept at present by any state. China's conception of state sovereignty has undergone significant change in recent years, which has led it to embrace a notion of moderate rather than absolutist sovereignty.[655] Clearly, there are

---

650 Ambassador Li Baodong Delivers a Keynote Speech at the UN Women's International Forum, 2011/03/02, available at: http://www.china-un.org/eng/czthd/t794696.htm.

651 Zhang Caiguo, The Termination of Ideologies and the Nature of Neo-liberalism Ideology (意识形态终结论与新自由主义的意识形态本质), Tansuo, June 2006, pp. 186–188.

652 The address given at the 2010 China-Africa Economic Cooperation Seminar, available at: http://english.cri.cn/6909/2010/12/23/2741s611673.htm.

653 Nicholas Dynon, China's Ideological 'Soft War': Offense is the Best Defense, China Brief, Vol. 14, Iss. 4.

654 Ankit Panda, "Reflecting on China's Five Principles, 60 Years Later", The Diplomat, June 26, 2014, available at: http://thediplomat.com/2014/06/reflecting-on-chinas-five-principles-60-years-later/.

655 Xue Lei, China as a Permanent Member of the United Nations Security Council, April 2014, avaiable at: http://library.fes.de/pdf-files/iez/10740.pdf.

two discursive engagements with sovereignty in China. On one side, it is necessary for China to hold the traditional interpretation of sovereignty for its own sake. On the other, embracing globalization and accepting human rights as universal values could bring about China's vastly reduced sovereign authority. The extent and contents of limitations on sovereignty in China's perspective are extremely controversial. China's practice, public statements, and scholarly writing reveal a pragmatic orientation in the process of redefining sovereignty. First of all, China always stresses the limitations on external sovereignty. Moreover, Beijing cautiously endorses the concept of R2P and is willing to take responsibility to assist easing humanitarian crises and maintaining international peace. The fear that the UN becomes a 'supra-national government' always drives China to endorse with conditions. Host nation acquiescence and Security Council approval are two necessary preconditions for gaining Chinese support for initiating intervention.[656] However, China can also be very flexible during the process of decision-making. In fact, Beijing assents to interventions for humanitarian purpose without the consent of the host-state case by case. Therefore, China recognizes the limits on both internal sovereignty and external sovereignty. Even though there are a number of politicians, scholars and observers that misunderstand China's perception of sovereignty as an absolutist[657], China has definitely changed its perception of sovereignty to a restrictionist. Furthermore, China's perspective of sovereignty in restriction is much more conservative than that of European states. Despite that it agrees that symmetrically grave violation of human rights might be an international issue, it generally considers internal sovereignty out of international intervention, particularly territorial sovereignty as absolute with which no one can interfere. Indeed, China supports the idea that the limitation on sovereignty is mainly placed on external sovereignty to prevent hegemony. China's practice regarding restrictions of internal sovereignty is more characterized with pragmatism, which leaves Beijing flexible to employ sovereignty for national interests.

4.4. Human Rights Protection and Sovereignty

Beijing makes a clear recognition of the state's responsibility to its own people and to humanity, and admits that state sovereignty is conditional on the protection of universal human rights.[658] However, China retracts its support for intervention for the purpose of humanitarian reasons from time to time. Such a contradiction could be attributed to China's internal instability, the "Century Humiliation" China experienced, and the 'hypocrisy' of humanitarian intervention. China is a nation which remembers and learns from its history. The "Century Humiliation", witnessed when the state fell apart, sovereignty couldn't function, wars always came along and people were killed and suffered greatly. History taught China that human rights protection

656 Bates Gill and James Reilly, 2000, p. 44.
657 Pang Zhongying, 2006, pp. 17–22.
658 Yongjin Zhang, 2008, p. 114.

can be assured only by a strong sovereign state and foreign powers only cared about their profits and interests. Hence, China normally sees sovereignty prevailing over human rights when they are involved in conflict. Moreover, the humanitarian purpose is frequently invoked by powerful states as a façade with the actual intention of launching military interventions. It is worth noting that some states do not pay any attention to their reputations but most states value having a just cause for their actions. When states know for sure that their actions breach international law, they make hard efforts to find causes to justify them.[659] Both humanitarian intervention and RtoP can be perfect justifications for them. Admittedly, either humanitarian intervention or R2P cannot work without a coercive capacity which very much relies on the US, the only superpower in post-cold-war. In fact, UN-led or UN-approved operations with substantial military requirements only take place when Washington approves or at least acquiesces.[660] Actually, Washington's broad and loose application of humanitarian rhetoric to Afghanistan and Iraq ex post facto and wars involved with Washington on behalf of democracy suggests that RtoP or humanitarian intervention is nothing more than a smokescreen.[661] Unsurprisingly, China and other developing states maintain extreme caution when deciding on the development of RtoP and are sometimes even against humanitarian intervention. China's endorsement of R2P embodies the profound change of China's perception on sovereignty even while it refuses the humanitarian intervention. However, it still sees the R2P as a big chance to open a door to a general pattern of interventionism.[662] On the one hand, sovereignty equality and non-intervention shall continue to be value in international legal order. On the other hand, respect for human rights is an essential normative discourse in today's world with an international legitimacy.[663] Thus, China holds that R2P as a positive instrument may serve human freedom or the common good but as a negative instrument may serve for self-interests.

It is worth highlighting that China sees itself as a natural leader of the third world with common colonial history and therefore unwaveringly objects to humanitarian interventions or R2P for self-interest. It is important to note that Western penetration and domination of the world since the 19th century has profoundly influenced colonial countries' psychological and historical feelings about Western values, norms and standards. The antagonistic perspectives over state sovereignty between the West and developing countries also contribute to the latter's censorious attitudes towards the universal enforcement of Western norms, values and standards.[664] China as a leader of developing states has to adhere to sovereignty with its team and utilize

659 Thomas G. Weiss, The Sunset of Humanitarian Intervention? The Responsibility to Protect in a Unipolar Era, Security Dialogue, Vol. 35, 2004, p. 138.

660 Ibid, p. 141.

661 Ibid, p. 147.

662 Ibid, p. 143.

663 Yuchao Zhu, China and international 'human rights policy', China: An international journal, Vol. 9, Iss. 2 September 2011, p. 219.

664 Yuchao Zhu, 2011, pp. 217–245.

sovereignty against hegemonic behaviors. Meanwhile, the fact that China's position as a big power requires it to participate in international activities and pushes China into taking a more flexible interpretation on the sovereignty principle. In short, China's perspective on RtoP reflects the paradox that China is facing and therefore the inconsistency allows for a measure of flexibility and pragmatism.

Section 2. The Chinese Ancient Thoughts and Contemporary Chinese View of Sovereignty

An unavoidable fact is "that the structure of sovereignty, the identity of sovereignty, no less than the identity of an individual or people, is formed by its history, its origins in and engagement with the colonial encounter".[665] As Liang Qichao commented years ago, "The modern Egyptian, Arabs, or Greeks, can hardly claim that they are the true heirs of their respective civilizations, and we do not regard, the Italians as 'Romans', but there is no mistake about the Chinese". He said, "The Chinese are unique, for though we are by no means the only people possessing an ancient civilization, we are the only people who retain the essential features of that civilization."[666] It is unique that contemporary China continues not only as a state with almost the same size as the empire but also as a community where the Chinese have no doubt about their lasting identity of 'Chinese'. Both in theory and practice Chinese traditional thoughts have made an indelible mark on the governments, societies, educational practices, and family life in China. The Chinese think inclusively not exclusively, therefore, they absorb external experiences, thoughts, and theories into their culture. Certainly, when external thoughts or systems are once exploited by Chinese then they are normally marked with Chinese unique characteristics while they integrate into Chinese civilization. China's perspective on sovereignty reflects the full acceptance of the Westphalian order with Chinese traditional thoughts.

When man mentions China's traditional thoughts and Chinese civilization, Confucianism simply comes out without considering the main body of China's traditional thoughts. However, Confucianism was not the only major school in ancient China even though many writers assume that Confucianism is equal to Chinese traditional culture. The three schools of early Chinese thought have played a pivotal role to shape Chinese civilization. Confucianism, Daoism, and Legalism influence the Chinese variably according to circumstance. The Daoist pursuit is of a liberality and worship nature, which has blended into Chinese normal life for a long time; the Legalism emphasizes rule of law and brutal governance; the Confucianism requires benevolent and humane authority with moral strength and neo-Confucianism advocates

---

665 Antony Anghie, Imperialism, Sovereignty and the Making of International Law, Cambridge University Press, 2005, p. 132.

666 Xiaoqun Xu, Cosmopolitanism, Nationalism, and Individualism in Modern China: The Chenbao Fukan and the New Culture Era. 1918–1928, American Historical Review, 2015, Vol. 120, Iss. 4, pp. 1462–1464.

refraining oneself for the community. The three major philosophies disparate from each other and even contradict from one another but twist together to shape the character of the Chinese and the history of China. Likewise, Confucianism, Daoism and Legalism are also complementary and it is almost axiomatic to say that traditional Chinese are "Daoist in private, Confucian in public; and in some measure legalist, for people who entered government service also inevitably became partly Legalist".[667] The influence of Confucianism on China and the Chinese is rather exaggerated so that the substantial impact of Legalism and Daoism are overlooked. Such a view obscures the fact that the prevalent social and political doctrines of imperial times were a hybrid of elements from all three ancient ideological currents and, as time went on, elements from other currents as well.[668]

As Hegel said, "Every Philosophy is a philosophy of its own day ... and thus can only satisfaction for the interests belonging to its own particular time".[669] No doubt, Chinese ancient thoughts had its own moment. However, traditional Chinese thoughts, mainly composed of the Confucianism, Daoism and Legalism, are deeply rooted and permeated in Chinese blood and DNA over 2500 years and now are being modernized and revitalized. For instance, the theory of the "Great Unified State" is rooted deeply in China's perspective of sovereignty and can be decisive for Chinese foreign policy. Indeed, the influence of ancient philosophy can be tracked in the current Chinese perception of sovereignty as well. Nonetheless, it is worth emphasizing that the Tianxia world order is not included in the part of China's traditional thoughts which are still influential.

1. The Tianxia View is Outdated

Since China's world order was destroyed, China has been mainly a student and follower of western international order. "On balance, after 150 years of interactions, the Chinese have integrated outside and inside views sufficiently to begin to make contributions to a future international order."[670] Today, following China's rise, Beijing is seemly confident enough to redefine itself distinctively as a peaceful rising state. A number of core Chinese foreign policy elites have begun, for the first time in the history of the PRC, to give extended and public consideration within their written work to how the normative underpinnings of the international system might be reconstituted. During China's rise, China turned to support its traditional culture by reviving it strongly. Some Chinese scholars seemly work around the development of a 'Chinese international relations theory' by mixing up the western international relations with Chinese ancient thoughts. Recently, Zhao Tingyang suggests re-building

667 Charles O. Hucker, 1975, p. 70.

668 Ibid.

669 Georg Wilhelm Friedrich Hegel, Lectures on the History of Philosophy, translated by E.S. Halden, Oxford: Oxford University Press, 2009, p. 45.

670 Wang Gung Wu and Zheng Yongnian (editors), China and the New International Order, New York: Routledge, 2008, p. 30.

international politics in accordance with a revival of the Tianxia principles which once underscored politics within China's dynastic past. He recommends looking at some eliciting points in the all-under-heaven institutions and policies which are still worthy of consideration even today. Yan Xuetong also recommends using traditional Chinese thought to re-order a better international system than the current hegemonic system. Yan suggests that China should try to be a humane kingship country, a superstate grounded in high morals and ethics, to lead this world. He continues to suggest that China will be able to present such a kind of humane authority in the world by relying on moral power instead of material power of economic advantage or military strength. According to Xunzi's belief that a differentiated, a hierarchical norm would help prevent conflict between states and should bring about a world order more peaceful and secure than today.[671] Definitely, suggestions to revive China's ancient thoughts to re-shape a new international order are contrary to the principles of sovereignty and non-intervention. It is worth mentioning an analysis made by Kim decades ago,

> "[T]he Sinocentric world order was a concentric extension of the hierarchical principle which prevailed in the domestic social structure of the middle Kingdom ... It was not a system of international relations in the modern European sense, whose stability was maintained by the balance of power among more or less equal member states. It was instead a system of hierarchical harmony enforced by the preponderance of power and virtue anchored in China.[672] The principles of national independence, national sovereignty, and national equality, upon which modern international law are built, were meaningless for the Chinese; in fact, they were repugnant to their sense of a universal state and civilization".[673]

Certainly, the establishment of a Chinese school of international relations theory cannot be achieved simply by adding some Chinese ancient thoughts into western theories. Such an academic phenomenon has not made any difference in Chinese foreign policy but led certain countries to worry that a rising China might revive the old East-Asian tributary system.[674]

Actually, resurrection of the ancient Tianxian view could escalate the theory of 'China's threat' and increase neighboring states' anxieties. Even though the tributary system concerns more nominal hierarchy, sovereignty independence is also often about the face or dignity of a state. It does not matter whether the tributary system would bring peace or not. It matters that such a system will damage the peripheral states' dignity. Moreover, Beijing has sought to avoid any language that might feed into perceptions that China's military and economic rise is in any way threatening. Furthermore, Beijing consistently rejects the notion of "world law"

671 Yan Xuetong, 2011, p. 53.
672 Samuel S.Kim, 1979, p. 23.
673 Ibid., p. 23.
674 Yan Xuetong, 'Xun Zi's thoughts on international politics and their implications', The Chinese Journal of International Politics No. 1, 2008, p. 163.

and any form of supranational system.[675] Hence, the Chinese government stoutly denied the suggestion of reviving a Tianxia world order by reiterating the Five Principles of Peaceful Coexistence in foreign relations. Xi Jinping reiterates, "No one is superior or inferior to others... all countries, regardless of their size, strength or level of development, are equal members of the international community, and they are entitled to equal participation in international affairs. ... We should respect diversity of civilizations and promote exchanges, dialogue, peaceful and harmonious coexistence among different civilizations and nations."[676]

It is an explicit denouncement of the application of Chinese traditional view of Tianxia in contemporary international society. He comments that human history has proved that any attempt to establish a dominant civilization in the world is a delusion.[677] It is also a declaration that China will continue to stick to the sovereignty principle to counter the US and its allies.

2. The Great Unification Thought and One China Policy

As discussed in Chapter 4, the Chinese imperial from the Qin dynasty is widely accepted as the starting point of 'self-identity' of great unification. In the evolution of thousands of years, the thought of the "Great Unification" has evolved into the major ideology in Chinese society. This thought as an imagination in the pre-Qin dynasty came true in the Qin-Han dynasty. The former 'Tianxia'-Zhongguo was the territory effectively controlled by the emperors through one unitary centralized bureaucratic system. 'Zhongguo' gradually represented the "Great Unification", the identification of a nation that collided with state identification. Dong zongshu portrayed it as such, "Chun Qiu[678] valued 'the Great unification', as the principle among the sky and earth, and the common sense from the past to today".[679] In this thought, the central plain was always the heartland of Zhongguo of the legitimate central dynasties. During the forming and developing of the Great Unified State, its borders continued to expand and the idea remained and evolved both in theory and in practice. In the lengthy Chinese history, wars, conflicts and secessions happened from time to time, however, unification always followed the secessions. Just like the Chinese proverb says, "That which is long divided must unify; that which is long unified must divide". Consequently, since the Chinese imperial state first took shape in the Qin dynasty (221 B.C.), the landmass that makes up the heartland of the East Asian subcontinent has remained under the roof of the Great Unified State

675 Junwu Pan, 2013, p. 20.
676 Xi's speech at 'Five Principles of Peaceful Coexistence' anniversary, available at: http://www.china.org.cn/world/2014-07/07/content_32876905.htm.
677 Ibid.
678 Chun Qiu was known a works of Confucius.
679 Han Book, Dong Zongshu Zhuan.

which made the Chinese political system totally distinguishable from Europe.[680] It must be admitted that the Great Unification thought has been significantly influential on the identity of China as a nation and a state. The invisible coherence from it united all the Chinese in the same land. Today's China, as if the Europe of the Roman Empire and of Charlemagne had lasted until this day, is the only one of the ancient civilizations that has survived the test and scourge of time, and continued till this day in a reinvigorated form.[681] This phenomena is tightly connected to the traditional thought of the "great unification".

Due to historical reasons, from the day it was established the PRC government confronted the challenge from the ROC government, which was the former government, and the ROC had to relocate itself to Taiwan when it lost the Chinese Civil War. Unlike Germany or Korea which broke into two independent parts in the international community, China refuses to become two states.[682] China's 'One China' policy is embodied very clearly in the Shanghai communique of 1972: "The Government of the People's Republic of China is the sole legal government of China; Taiwan is a province of China which has long been returned to the motherland; the liberation of Taiwan is China's internal affair in which no other country has the right to interfere; and all U.S. forces and military installations must be withdrawn from Taiwan. The Chinese Government firmly opposes any activities which aim at the creation of "one China, one Taiwan", "one China, two governments", "two Chinas", an "independent Taiwan" or advocate that "the status of Taiwan remains to be determined". And The United States acknowledges that all Chinese on either side of the Taiwan Strait maintain there is but one China and that Taiwan is a part of China".[683]

The Chinese policy of 'One China' has been patently expressed in that document and has been carried out since. Any state that seeks diplomatic relations with the People's Republic of China ("PRC") must break official relations with the Republic of China ("ROC"), and vice versa. Hence, all the countries recognizing the ROC recognize it as the sole legitimate representative of all of China and not just the island of Taiwan and other islands but also with de jure sovereignty over all of China. The Taipei government considers 'One China' to mean the ROC, founded in 1912 and with de jure sovereignty over all of China. Later, the 1992 Consensus between the PRC and ROC employed the so-called 'One China principle' instead of the 'One China policy'. Under this principle, both governments agree that there is only one sovereign state encompassing both mainland China and Taiwan but disagree about which of the two governments is the legitimate government of China. Chen Shuibian, the leader of the ROC from 1996 to 2004, saw Taiwan as a country separate

680 Liang Qichao, Comparison of Chinese and European statecraft (论中国与欧洲国体异同), Nationality and Civil Morality-Liang Qichao selected works, Shanghai Far East Press, 1995, p. 21.

681 Ma Dazheng, 2002, pp..1–15.

682 The ROC has actual jurisdiction only over Taiwan, Penghu, Kinmen and Matsu.

683 Paras.11–12, Joint Communique of the USA and the People's Republic of China, 1972 Shanghai Communique.

from China, in opposition to the PRC's insistence that the 'One China principle' is a prerequisite for any negotiation. Currently this principle is still carried on by both sides of the Taiwan Strait. Apparently, it shows that the idea of the 'Great Unification' still heavily influences Chinese leaders and the common Chinese people. Fairbank, as the most prominent foreign scholar concerning Chinese history and politics, tried to elaborate why Chinese leaders felt so strongly about China's unification, commenting: "It cannot be expunged from the Chinese language or from the minds of the Chinese people. This is not only an idea, but a sentiment, a feeling habituated by millennia of conduct. It attaches the highest importance to Chinese civilization, which consists of all those people who live in a Chinese way ... and springs for a sense of culturalism, something a good deal stronger than a mere Western-style nationalism."[684]

He notes, "From inside looking out, it does seem that key Chinese leaders and thinkers take as their starting point the deep structure that gave shape to the civilization and state that came into being over 3,500 years ago." ... "The Son of Heaven was not merely a king or emperor but also the symbol of the system of values that made the Chinese what they were".[685]

In fact, the 'Great Unification' is one of those values. While all other ancient empires, such as the Roman Empire, ancient Egypt, ancient Persia, etc., disappeared in the past, it is a miracle that China has basically maintained its size today that it had in the empire. It is evident that the traditional idea of the 'Great Unification' is still deep in the Chinese conscience and is heavily attributed to such a phenomenon.

It is obvious that the idea of the 'Great Unification' conflicts with the independence movements of Tibet, Xingjiang and Taiwan. The sovereignty principle and non-intervention principle simply defend China against floods of condemnations of its responses to secession operations. The frequency with which Chinese spokesmen use sovereignty to defend their anti-secession action is simply countless. In such a context, sovereignty connotes that China has absolute rights in keeping the territory of China unified. China could not allow any secession and will try any peaceful measure (even military measures in an extreme situation)[686] to reunify the lost territories. In sum, it is not an exaggeration that territorial sovereignty always comes into the core issue of the national interest of China.

684 John King Fairbank, US and China, Harvard University Press, 1983, p. 463.

685 John King Fairbank, 1983, pp. 23–24.

686 Article eight of Anti-Secession Law articulates: In the event that the "Taiwan independence" secessionist forces should act under any name or by any means to cause the fact of Taiwan's secession from China, or that major incidents entailing Taiwan's secession from China should occur, or that possibilities for a peaceful reunification should be completely exhausted, the state shall employ non-peaceful means and other necessary measures to protect China's sovereignty and territorial integrity.

Chinese "reform and opening" policy has brought sweeping changes on the economic system without respective political reform[687] The Chinese Communist Party ("CCP") has consistently resisted democratic reforms in the last three decades while delivering impressive economic growth.[688] Beijing fears that the 'color revolutions' and Russian-style 'Big-Bang' might happen in China through ideological changing.[689] The CCP also worries that western constitutional democracy may undermine the current leadership and so-called "Chinese characteristics system of governance".[690] Beijing has sought to reinforce ideological influence against western political systems for years. Nonetheless, Beijing proposed the 'one state, two systems' policy which offers the territory 50 years of a "high degree of autonomy" in exchange for the reunification of Hong Kong and Macau. Generally speaking, the policy of 'one state, two systems' allows Hong Kong and Macau to keep the western political system and economical system almost untouched. The idea of reunification obviously overpowered the fear of loss the governance of China when territorial issues of Hong Long and Macau were at stake.[691]

3. "One state, Two Systems" and the Traditional Tributary System

Many foreigners could not understand China's insistence on the state's unconditional sovereignty over Hong Kong irrespective of the 'one country, two systems' arrangement, as well as its struggles for national reunification in regards to Taiwan.

This idea allows Chinese regions such as Hong Kong, Macau, and Taiwan to continue to have its own political system, legal, economic and financial affairs, including external relations with foreign countries. The Chinese government stations troops in Hong Kong to safeguard its national security, not to interfere in Hong Kong's internal affairs. Beijing even promised Taiwan that it could continue to maintain its

---

687 Deng Xiaoping said: "Why do people support us? Because over the last ten years our economy has been developing ... If the economy stagnated for five years or developed at only a slow rate – for example, at 4 or 5 percent, or even 2 or 3 percent - what effects would be produced? This would be not only an economic problem but also a political one." See Ezra F. Vogel, Deng Xiaoping and the Transformation of China, Harvard University Press, 2011.

688 Minxin Pei, China: Can Economic Growth Continue without Political Reform? In: Strategic Asia 2006–07: Trade, Interdependence, and Security"(ed. by Ashley J. Tellis and Michael Wills), Seattle: National Bureau of Asian Research, 2006, p. 304.

689 Peter R. Moody, Conservative Thought in Contemporary China, p. 130.

690 Ibid.

691 Gilbert Gornig, Hongkong, Von der britischen Kronkolonie zur chinesischen Sonderverwaltungszone, eine historische und rechtliche Betrachtung, Köln: Verlag Wissenschaft und Politik, 1998, S. 175.

own military force under 'one country, two systems'.[692] These regions have almost full jurisdiction over their lands except that they must keep the titles of China. Hong Kong and Macau are exempt from mainland laws, mainland political and economic systems, mainland education system, the use of simplified characters in publishing and Mandarin in public education and most broadcasting. Hong Kong continues to use the English common law and Macau continues using the Portuguese civil law system. The Chinese Supreme Court has no jurisdiction over Hong Kong and the National People's Congress has no legislative rights either. Chinese people and Chinese products cannot enter into Hong Kong's territory without going through particular processes and customs procedures. Such a high degree of autonomy makes China's sovereignty over these regions symbolic. Undoubtedly, it is an extreme compromise on China's sovereignty over Hong Kong and Macau.

For a long time, Beijing has fought and still fights against the so-called US-led 'soft war' which pursues to export the capitalism system into China to replace the socialism system. Nonetheless, the ideology security fear gives way to the traditional idea of the 'Great Unified State'. Interestingly, for the Chinese government and the Chinese people reunification is the top priority. It does not matter whether Hong Kong and Macau are profitable for Beijing or how much it costs Beijing to maintain the two regions. It does matter that the two regions are under the name of the Chinese sovereignty.

Such an arrangement is rather similar to the Chinese tributary system which only cared about hierarchy and had no intention of governing the tributary countries. As analyzed before, the tributary system was practically a defense system for China to maintain peace with peripheral states. It differed from modern imperialism or colonialism in that China merely claimed suzerainty over these states without the intention of exploiting their economic or other resources or intervening in internal affairs. The expectation of harmony was most easily maintained through a thin and distant official relationship by the tributary system.[693] Essentially, the Chinese tributary system required neighbors to be subordinate to China, symbolically paying their allegiance to China. Actually, China even gave in return to the tributary countries much more than what they had submitted to China which led some to comment that China bought tributary relations. The policy of 'one country, two systems' gives Hong Kong and Macau benefits without profit-pursuing. Like past tributary countries, the two zones maintain high autonomy and submit nothing to the Chinese central government which offers military defense.

On the one hand, the 'Great Unification' tradition makes China eager to reunify the lost territory; on the other hand, the tributary system allows the reunited territory to keep an extremely high level of autonomy, almost the same as that of a sovereign

---

692 One Country, Two Systems, June 22–23, 1984, http://www.china.org.cn/english/features/dengxiaoping/103372.htm.

693 Brantly Womack, Asymmetry and China's Tributary System, in: The Chinese Journal of International Politics, Vol. 5, 2012, p. 44.

state. When considering the traditional idea of the 'great unification' and the Chinese tributary system, one can easily understand why the Chinese accept the 'one country, two systems' and the creator of this system - Deng Xiaoping - therefore wins the Chinese's admiration.

4. Daoism and the Non-intervention Principle

Daoism maintains that everything exists by its own path or way and nothing can change its way. There is an adage reflecting Daoistic thoughts: 'Clean the snow in front of your house, never pay attention to the frost on the tiles of other people's house.' It suggests people managing their own business and never bothering to intervene others' life. Moreover, Daoism believes that everything has its own Dao (rule) and runs in its own Dao. Outside intervention could damage the Dao and so ruin the promising way of its intended development. Under the tributary arrangement, Imperial China needed the periphery countries to admit only symbolical Chinese leadership and did not concern itself with the internal affairs of the tributary countries. It is perfectly embodied in the Chinese non-intervention policy. Furthermore, ancient China has always been a self-sufficient country, self-reliance is a fine Chinese tradition. The Chinese believe that individual states must learn how to govern themselves, develop themselves by themselves because only they actually know what is the best way for them and only they have rights to choose their own way. After China's opening policy accomplished a rapid growth in economic development, Deng suggested African alliances, "do not follow Chinese model. You must find your own ways to develop."[694] When president Xi stated, "We should respect the right of a country to choose its own social system and model of development, and oppose the attempt to oust the legitimate government of a country through illegal means seeking self-interests or imposing one's own views",[695] he explicitly meant that every state should govern its own house and let other states worry about issues under their own roofs; otherwise the world would lose their own way and fall in chaos.

This Daoistic idea is deep in Chinese thoughts and consequently the Chinese cannot understand why Western powers try to intervene in China's own business all the time. Such confusion can be shown when Xi said, "Some foreigners with full stomachs and nothing better to do point fingers at us - but we don't export revolution, hunger or poverty, nor do we cause trouble for you." On the contrary, the Western politicians, activists, and writers have no idea why the Chinese refuse their help. Unsurprisingly, Lucian Pye, an experienced hand of China felt very frustrated stating, "China seems impelled to reject the helping hand and to act in ways that seem

---

694 Zhang Weiying, Deng Xiaoping in the Eyes of His Translator, available at: http://www.chinanews.com/gn/2014/08-21/6515237_3.shtml.

695 William Wan, While China's Territorial Disputes Drag on, Xi Jinping Tells Others to Seek Peace, in: The Washington Post, 2014/06/28.

perversely self-damaging in the eyes of those who believe they have that country's interests at heart."[696]

5. The other Ancient Thoughts that Influence Chinese Decision Making

In fact, legalism constructed the main frame of the Chinese bureaucrat system and legal system and had a significant impact on Chinese politics. Pragmatism, as the core tenet of Legalism, is everywhere in various aspects of contemporary China. Pragmatism means that foreign policy as well as the interpretation of sovereignty is driven by core national interests, which are identified as national security, reunification, sustaining growth, with its implications for securing resource and energy, and also means being willing to work within the realities of global power relationships. In the Chinese mind, wise and far-sighted statesmen are those who can 'adroitly guide action according to circumstances (yinshi lidao)'.[697] Under that influence, pragmatism is dominant in China's perception of sovereignty.

Moreover, all things in the traditional Chinese cosmos function in accordance with Dao which, in cosmological use, is the way and the process by which the cosmos operates. Since the Chinese conceive the Universe, seen and unseen, as a single integrated organism they are not inclined, as most Westerners are, to think in terms of contending, antagonistic polarities such as natural versus supernatural, life versus death, etc. It made Chinese thinking inclusive, not exclusive. Everything belongs in its appropriate form and role and on its appropriate plane in one undivided cosmic universe. Perhaps, it is the reason why the Chinese easily accommodate contradictions and it is unnecessary for them to differentiate between a 'true' God and 'false' God. As a result, unlike Westerners, they have not fought holy wars or gone on crusades. Even under the tributary system, Chinese did not like to interfere with others' internal issues because the Chinese believed that they had their own Dao. Such a thought can be easily found in modern China's non-intervention principle. Likewise, China also unremittingly insists on its own 'Dao' to develop and refuses to completely apply Western democracy.

Furthermore, the basic rule of 'mean' of Confucian, which pursues harmony by co-existing with heterogeneity, has contributed to the current policy of 'harmony society' which respects heterogeneity. Clearly, the 'Five Peaceful Co-exist Principles' also reflect the idea of peaceful 'co-exist of heterogeneities', the essence of rule of 'mean'. Additionally, Daoism's low profile has been carried on in China's foreign policy since the opening and reform policy began. Traditional China's thoughts can be found everywhere in both China's foreign policy and on its perspective of sovereignty. However, China's ancient thoughts are incredibly comprehensive so that

696 Lucian W. Pye, 1990 p. 56.
697 J. Wang 1998, 489–490.

it is no way for one to analyze the whole influence they have had and one can only see the tip of the iceberg.

Contemporary China is an amalgamation of heritage and modernity, continuity and change. It is doomed to be inherently unstable and infinitely complex.[698] Deng Xiaoping, who is described as the chief architect of China's reform, commented that the approach of China's model was "crossing a river by feeling the stones". Clearly, the ultimate objective has never been clear.[699] The current prime minister Li put forward "Reform as the biggest dividends".[700] Manifestly, continuous change is doomed. It implies plenty of stone-stepping. Chinese leaders may be responding to Western demands but it is doing so in its own way and at its own speed in whatever is necessary to propel China forward and integrate modern ideas for the best of its own national condition. They scrupulously try to make some changes in political and social levels step by step; meanwhile they attempt to avoid any possibility of repeating the play of secession which happened to the former Soviet Union. In order to do so, China knows for sure that it must stick to the sovereignty principle to exclude the outside interventions of Western powers.

Section 3. The Comparison between European and Chinese Perspectives on Sovereignty

Ironically, while the EU has moved away from the classical concept of sovereignty China, who was forced to accept the concept of sovereignty by European military force, has continued to hold the classic concept of sovereignty. There is no neutral ground when it comes to sovereignty.[701] Disagreements on interpretation of sovereignty of various states generally exist because of their different national concerns and different cultures, histories, religions, economic developments, political systems, and other factors. Despite the European countries sharing more values and having more similarity, the disparities of understanding of sovereignty from them are not small. While France believes that sovereignty cannot stop them from liberalizing human beings from tyrannies, Germany still considers that humanitarian intervention can only be carried on in the exceptional way since sovereignty is still the base of international law. However, no matter how big differences exist among European states, they still have a more common interpretation of it. This is proved by the fact that the great achievement of the integration of the EU as a unique organization gathers many sovereign rights under it. Their development on the concept of sovereignty will and does impact the views of other states. China, on the other hand,

698 Paul Evans, 2010, p. 54.

699 China's Reforms, The Second Long March, The Economist, Dec 11th 2008, available at: http://www.economist.com/node/12758848.

700 The Speech of Li Keqiang in Nov.22, 2012, available at: http://finance.people.com.cn/n/2012/1122/c1004-19667962.html.

701 Tanja Aalberts, 2012, p. 153.

as a latecomer to international society, was transformed into a steadfast supporter of sovereignty. It is obvious that Europe and China disagree on the concept of sovereignty. The Chinese government has maintained its insistence on the importance of sovereignty but 'often times China's adherence to the principle of sovereignty is simply misinterpreted in the west as a disregard of the development of international law, or worse still, considered an excuse to evade its international responsibility.'[702]

Under the broad and popular denominator of globalization, the development of the 'ever closer Union' in Europe has raised a debate about progress towards so-called "postmodern" statehood in the multilevel governance structure. Some may argue that the jurisdiction of territory seems to have been hollowed out and sovereignty has lost its meaning in this instance of statehood.[703] Indeed, the EU may collect partial sovereign rights from its sovereign states but the line between member states and the EU institutions is clear. The member states still have their own sovereignty but voluntarily and legally limit their sovereignty by transferring some sovereign rights to the EU institution, which emphasizes that the EU governance is not a governance above the state like a supra-state structure but a governance beyond the state more like governance with governments.[704] No doubt, the EU system does not connote a complete loss of sovereignty. To the contrary, multilevel governance continues to appoint sovereign states a key role in European politics.[705] It is particularly this notion of the mounting sharing of authority, among a variety of actors across different levels, which is characteristic of multilevel governance descriptions of the European Polity and which stands at right angles to both the notion of sovereignty as an individual and the absolute concept of *supremas potestas,* and its territorial grounding in the Westphalian archetype.[706] Multilevel governance cannot escape sovereignty.

As Dune, a British jurist, writes: "The society of states has no meaning independently from that rule [sovereignty and non-intervention]. Without sovereignty and non-intervention there is no society of states.[707]" "A state's right to sovereignty or independence is not a 'natural right'... it is a right enjoyed to the extent that it is recognized to exist by other states. So far from it being the case that the sovereignty of the states is something antithetical to international order, it is the foundation of the whole edifice."[708]

The German Constitutional Court also reached the same conclusion that the state is neither a myth nor an end in itself but the historically grown and globally

702 Xue Hanqing, 2007, p. 84.
703 Tanja Aalberts, 2012, p. 21.
704 Ibid., p. 24.
705 G. Marks, L. Hooghe, and K. Blank, European Integration and the State, EUI working paper RSC, 1995, No. 95/7.
706 Tanja E. Aalberts, 2012, p. 25.
707 Timm Dunne, The Social Construction of International Society', European Journal of International Relations, 1995, Vol. 1, Issue 3, p. 378.
708 Hedley Bull, The State's Positive Role in World Affairs', Daedalus, Vol. 108, Issue 4, 1979, pp. 111–123.

recognized form of organization of a viable political community.[709] The European Union was designed as an association of sovereign states (*Staatenverbund*) to which sovereign powers are transferred.[710]

Consequently, both China and European states still have a common sense of sovereignty. They all identify sovereignty as the bedrock of international law and international relations. Both of them agree that states keep being the main subject of international society. Hence, sovereignty is still indispensable. In spite of the consensus on existence of sovereignty, it must be admitted that the European states have a different perception of sovereignty from state to state even though China's scholars generally see Western states' interpretation on sovereignty as a whole. Here, it is not the purpose to analyze the different understandings of sovereignty among Germany, France, Britain or other European states but rather focus on the differences between China and European states as a whole.

1. The Different Views on the Relationship between Sovereignty and Human Rights

Europe wants to downplay the role of sovereignty and interpreted sovereignty as secondary to human rights while China adheres to the principle of sovereignty over human rights. Indeed, Europeans see human rights and democracy promotion as their destiny. They devote themselves to promoting human rights and democracy in the world where they think there is a lack of them. In order to do that, they have to undermine the role of sovereignty and let human rights prevail over sovereignty. As discussed before, China has plenty of reasons to maintain the priority of sovereignty over human rights. Its colonial experience, its domestic instability, its territorial integrity, its self-autonomy tradition, etc.; all of them drive China to stick to a traditional interpretation of sovereignty. However, as the international society is evolving, interpretation of sovereignty is evolving too. China has to move forward. Nonetheless, its policy on sovereignty is moving rather slowly and with caution. In practice, China accepts the idea that sovereignty might remit slightly to human rights in extreme circumstances. In that situation, China focuses on how the international society can stop a crisis while balancing its belief that the sovereignty of the target state could be respected. Therefore, the huge disagreements between Europe and China are on how to apply R2P. China emphasizes the value of sovereignty and the hazards of military intervention versus Europe that focuses on the potential pitfalls of a tepid international response in the face of state-sponsored violence.[711] China insists on the host states' consent as necessary for sending military forces.

709 Judgment of German Constitution Court in *Lisbon Treaty Case*, BVerfG, 2 BvE 2/08 from 30 June 2009, para. 224.

710 Judgment of *Lisbon Treaty Case*, para. 229.

711 Zhongying Pang, China's Non-intervention Question, Global Responsibility to Protect, Vol. 1, No. 2, 2009, p. 240.

Europe contends that the host states' consent should not be mandatory because it may be impossible to stop atrocities in time when the state is actually involved in the atrocities. China maintains that impartiality and objectivity shall be followed in the process of intervention to avoid reducing sovereignty; Europe argues that neutrality or impartiality may amount to letting the stronger or more ferocious party dictate the course of events or the political settlement and so cannot release people from suffering. China strongly opposes regime change as a legitimate way to protect human rights and condemns regime change as a serious violation of sovereignty. The European states argue that regime change can sometimes be the only way to protect human rights when the regime commits atrocities against its people.[712] Those disagreements manifested in the NATO intervention in Libya evidently bringing the R2P into a dilemma where the concept of R2P failed to apply in Syria.

2. The Fundamental Difference in Non-intervention

Sovereignty for China is a symbol of independence to exclude foreign-intervention but for Europe, who advocates interventionism, sovereignty is an excuse used to shield the government from accountability for violating human rights and the welfare of their people. Thus, China remains that restrictions on sovereignty shall concentrate on constraining external sovereignty from intervening in other's internal affair. Europe considers that internal sovereignty should be limited as much as external sovereignty. Even though China already endorses the R2P, its strategy still focuses on how to ensure states are allowed to play their roles and reduce the possibility that the R2P will impact sovereignty. Obviously, China safeguards sovereign independence and is suspicious of the intention of European states, while European states do as an interventionist and claim them for a noble purpose.

Moreover, Europe as an interventionist shows enthusiasm in promoting a democratic system in China. The fundamental disagreement between European states and China is that Europeans are truly convinced that liberal democracy and a market economy can ensure peace, economical flourishing and human rights; by contrast, China maintains that liberal democracy is not a panacea and that a one-size-fits-all model will not work.[713] The desire from the West to serve as China's teachers in the ways of the modern world encounters resistance from the Chinese government. Beijing argues that the Chinese are free to choose their own political and social systems, which only the Chinese will know what is best for its national condition. Indeed, China has a long way to go before its system and values are accepted as credible or inspiring by the Western countries. The fact that the western states see China's rising with skepticism and hostility pushes China to unwaveringly stick

712 M. Payandeh, The United Nations, Military Intervention and Regime Change in Libya, in: 52 VJIL 2012, p. 355, at 368.

713 Zhao Lei, Two Pillars of China's Global Peace Engagement Strategy: UN Peacekeeping and International Peacebuilding, International Peacekeeping, Vol. 8, Issue 3, 2011, p. 353.

to the principle of sovereignty and non-interference as one of its best weapons to defend the Chinese political system and human rights policies, etc. Furthermore, China, as an interest-driving doctrine believer, hardly trusts the Western 'goodness' and 'kindness'. It is foreseen for a rather long time that China will persistently maintain its stance on sovereignty and the non-intervention principle.

3. China and European in the Different Stage of Sovereignty

When sovereignty offered a shelter for a number of small states newly broken away from the Imperial Roman Empire in 1648, China was in an illusion to rule the world. When European powers conquered the world, China began to accept sovereignty and fought for its integrity and sovereignty. Relying on sovereignty, China initiated the Five Peaceful Co-exist Principles to build a consolidated sovereign state. At the same time, Europe was experiencing the movement of European integration to establish a regional polity pooling sovereign rights. Currently, adhering to the principles of mutual respect of sovereignty and non-intervention, China is writing its story of peaceful rising, while European is seeking further integration and global governance. China and the European states are not on the same page all the time, so far, and certainly Europe has kept taking the lead of the development of sovereignty. Now, China persists in sovereignty and independence taking precedence over normative principles and restraint of global governance, Europeans make an effort to reduce sovereignty's impeding effect on deeper regional integration and global governance. Manifestly, China is defending sovereignty while Europe wants sovereignty to give way to human rights, democracy, and global governance. Thus, Europe has to slow down to wait for other latecomers to catch up.

4. China's Equal Sovereignty vice versa EU's Supranationality

As a persistent objector of world law or a 'supranational system', China sticks to the sovereignty principle and non-intervention principle. In China's early perspective, "world law" implies or serves to justify a number of objectionable principles including the denial or deprecation of state sovereignty, supremacy of international law over domestic law, giving individuals the status of subjects of international law, legalization of collective intervention, compulsory jurisdiction of international tribunals, and the abolition or limitation of the immunity of foreign states[714] Recently, globalization, proliferation of international organizations, global governance and China's rise as a new emerging power has compelled China to abandon its rigid understanding of supranationalism and to embrace globalization and global governance with an attitude of anti-supranationalism. Even though Beijing has willingly transferred economical sovereign rights to the WTO, Chinese academic opinions argue that China still has the final words over those issues because it only transfers economic

714 Suzanne Ogden, 1974, p. 10; Zhou Gengsheng, International Law, Hongkong: The Commercial Press (H.K.) Ltd., 1976.

sovereign rights and not sovereignty. They stick to the supremacy of sovereignty, in other words, anti-supranationality. Therefore, Beijing tries to avoid the UN and other international organizations which are involved in turning into supranational institutions and so insists that the UN and others remain a state-based organization.[715]

The Europeans states established the EU as an intergovernmental organization with supranational characteristics. Ensuing the European integration, supranational governance through law making has evolved. The principles of sovereignty and supranationality co-apply in a "hybrid system". The European states generally create or help to create and accept supranationality of the European Court of Justice, the European Court of Human Rights and the International Criminal Court of Justice. Noticeably, Europe is deeply engaged in the promotion of supranationality in economic fields and others, from the EU to the world.

Conclusion

The traditional Chinese world order persisted over two millenniums until its final collapse at the turn of the twentieth century. However, the legacies of traditional China's thoughts did not disappear at the demise of the Chinese international system but still have substantial influence over China's foreign policies and perception of sovereignty. Moreover, China's interpretations and practices of sovereignty have been heavily connected to China's historical transformation from a central empire to a sovereign state.[716] In the early time of the PRC, the classical conception of sovereignty had absolute independence and was determinedly against hegemony. Due to sovereignty being a dynamic institution constantly reconstituted and reconstructed by practices among states, China's perception on sovereignty has experienced transformation as well. Chinese policies towards globalization, human rights, peacekeeping and humanitarian intervention have also shifted progressively, significantly softening its position on sovereignty and acknowledging more restrictions on sovereignty. Meanwhile, Beijing also sticks to guarding the sacrosanct nature of sovereignty. Consequently, contemporary Chinese discourse on sovereignty demonstrates that China has become increasingly ambivalent towards the Westphalian ideal of state sovereignty. Additionally, the paradox is deepened by China's dual-self-identification as a big power and as a leader of developing countries. As the only developing country among the P-5, China tends to counterbalance Western influence and to implement policies that benefit China's and non-Western countries' interests.[717] Specifically, the principle of sovereignty is enshrined by China as the crucial foundation. Variations

715 Bates Gill and James Reilly, 2000, p. 44.

716 Yongjin Zhang, Ambivalent Sovereignty: China and Re-imagining the Westphalian Ideal, in Re-envisioning Sovereignty: The End of Westphalia? (ed. by J., T., Sampford, C. & Thakur, R.), Vermont: Ashgate, 2008, p. 102.

717 Miwa Hirono and Marc Lanteigne, Introduction: China and UN Peacekeeping, International Peacekeeping, Vol. 18, Issue 3, 2011, pp. 243–256.

and contradictions in China's interpretations and practices of the sovereignty norm in international relations are understandable considering the specific historical context and social environment within which China interacts with other members of international society. Consequently, while Europe is downplaying the role of sovereignty, China recalcitrantly promotes sovereignty in a rather pragmatic way.

Chronological Outline of Chinese History[i]

ca. 2100–1600 BCE	Xia (Hsia) Dynasty
ca. 1600–1050 BCE	Shang Dynasty One of the Three Dynasties, or San Dai (Xia, Shang, and Zhou), thought to mark the beginning of Chinese civilization: characterized by its writing system, practice of divination, walled cities, bronze technology, and use of horse-drawn chariots.
ca. 1046–771 BCE	Western Zhou Dynasty (ca. 1046–771 BCE) A hierarchical political and social system with the Zhou royal house at its apex: power was bestowed upon aristocratic families as lords of their domains or principalities. Although often compared to European "feudalism" what actually gave the system cohesion was a hierarchical order of ancestral cults.
ca. 770–221 BCE	Eastern Zhou Dynasty (771–256 BCE), known as the Spring-and-Autumn period (ca. 770–475 BCE) and the Warring States (ca. 475–221 BCE) period. The feudalism eventually broke down into a competition for power between rival semi-autonomous states. It was during these tumultuous times that Confucius (551–479 BCE) lived.
221–206 BCE	Qin (Ch'in) Dynasty Created a unitary state by imposing a centralized administration and by standardizing the writing script, weights and measures. Known for its harsh methods of rule, including the suppression of dissenting thought.
206 BCE-220 CE	Han Dynasty: Western/Former Han (206 BCE-9 CE) and Eastern/Later Han (25–220 CE) Modified and consolidated the foundation of the imperial order. Confucianism was established as orthodoxy and open civil service examinations were introduced. Han power reached Korea and Vietnam. Records of Historian, which became the model for subsequent official histories, were completed.

220–589 CE	"Period of Disunity" or Six Dynasties Period The empire was fragmented. The North was dominated by invaders from the borderland and the steppes. The South was ruled by successive "Chinese" dynasties. Buddhism spread.
581–618 CE	Sui Dynasty China reunified.
618–906 CE	Tang Dynasty A time of cosmopolitanism and cultural flowering occurred. This period was the height of Buddhist influence in China until its repression around 845. Active territorial expansion until defeated by the Arabs at Talas in 751.
960–1279 CE	Song Dynasty: Northern Song (960–1127) and Southern Song (1127–1279) An era of significant economic and social changes: the monetization of the economy; growth in commerce and maritime trade; urban expansion and technological innovations. The examination system for bureaucratic recruitment of neo-Confucianism was to provide the intellectual underpinning for the political and social order of the late imperial period.
1279–1368	Yuan Dynasty Founded by the Mongols as part of their conquest of much of the world. Beijing was made the capital. Dramas, such as the famous *Story of the Western Wing*, flourished.
1368–1644	Ming Dynasty The first Ming emperor, Hongwu, laid the basis of an authoritarian political culture. Despite early expansion, it was an inward-looking state with an emphasis on its agrarian base. Gradual burgeoning of the commercial sector; important changes in the economy and social relations in the latter part of the dynasty; also a vibrant literary scene as represented by publication of the novel *Journey to the West.*

1644–1912	Qing Dynasty A Manzu dynasty. Continued the economic developments of the late Ming leading to prosperity but also complacency and a dramatic increase in population. Strains on the polity were intensified by a rapid incorporation of substantial new territories. Its authoritarian structure was subsequently unable to meet the military and cultural challenge of an expansive West.
1912–1949	Republic Period Weak central government following the collapse of the dynastic system in 1911–12; Western influence was shown through the promotion of "science" and "democracy" during the New Culture Movement. The attempt of the Nationalist government (est. 1928) to bring the entire country under its control was thwarted by both domestic revolts and the Japanese occupation (1937–45). The Nationalists fled to Taiwan after being defeated by the Communists.
1949-present	People's Republic of China

Reference

Aalberts, Tanja, Constructing Sovereignty between Political and Law, New York: Routledge, 2012.

Abe, Takeo (Japan), Chinese 'Tianxia' View- Analysis of Political Thoughts (中国人之天下观念——政治思想的试论), in Research on History of Yuan Dynasty (元代史之研究), Tokyo: Chuangweng Press (1972), as cited in Shinichiro Watanabe: Kingship of Ancient China and Tianxia Order (Translated by Xuchong), Beijing: Zhonghua Book Company, 2008.

Akzin, Benjamin, State and Nation, Hutchinson London, 1964.

Andornino, Giovanni, The Nature and Linkages of China's Tributary System under the Ming and Qing Dynasties, LSE Economic History Department, Global Economic History Network, Working Paper, available at: http://www.lse.ac.uk/collections/economicHistory/GEHN/ GEHNworkingPapers.htm.

Anghie, Antony, Imperialism, Sovereignty and the Making of International Law, Cambridge: Cambridge University Press, 2005.

Ayoob, Mohammed, Humanitarian Intervention and State Sovereignty, The International Journal of Human Rights, 2002, Vol. 6, No. 1, pp. 81–102.

Bálazs, Étienne, Political Theory and Administrative Reality in Traditional China, in: School of Oriental and African Studies, London, 1965.

Ban, Gu (AD 32–92), Hanshu (Chronicles of the Han Dynasty), Beijing: Zhonghua Book Company, 1962.

Barfield, Thomas J., The Perilous Frontier: Nomadic Empires and China. Cambridge and Oxford: Basil Blackwell, 1989.

Bartelson, Jens, A Genealogy of Sovereignty, Cambridge: Cambridge University Press, 1995.

Bellamy, Alex, and Williams, Paul, 'The New Politics of Protection? Cote d'Ivoire, Libya and the Responsibility to Protect', in: International Affairs, Vol. 87, Issue 4, 2011, pp. 825–850.

Bernstein, Richard, and Munro, Ross H., The Coming Conflict with America, in: Foreign Affairs, March/April 1997.

Berthrong, John, Human Rights and Responsibilities: A Confucian Perspective on the Universal Declaration of Human Rights" in Human Rights and Responsibilities in the World Religions (eds. Runzo, Martin and Sharma), Oxford: One world Publications, 2003.

Besson, Samantha, Sovereignty, International Law and Democracy, in: European Journal of International Law, Vol. 22, No. 2, 2011, pp. 373–387.

Betz, David J., Tim Stevens, Cyberal and the States, London: Rought, June 2014.

Bodde, Derk, and Morris, Clarence, Law in Imperial China, Philadelphia: University of Pennsylvania Press, 1967.

Bodin, Jean, Les six livres de la Republique ("Six Books Concerning Public Affairs"), Paris: Fayerd, 1986.

Bodin, Jean, On Sovereignty, Cambridge: Cambridge University Press, 1992.

Bottomore, Thomas, Political Sociology, Minneapolis, MN: University of Minnesota Press, 1993.

Bowden Brett, The Colonial Origins of International Law: European Expansion and the Classical Standard of Civilization, in: Journal of the History of International Law, Vol. 7, Issue 1, 2005, pp. 1–24.

Brown, Chris, Foreword of Politics without Sovereignty (ed. by Christopher J. Bickerton, Philip Cunliffe and Alexander Gourevitch), London, New York: University College London Press, 2007.

Bull, H., The Anarchical Society: A study of Order in World Politics', 2nd ed., London: Macmillan ([1977] 1995).

Buzan, Barry, and Little, Richard, International Systems in World History: Remaking the Study of International Relations, Oxford: Oxford University Press, 2000.

Cabestan Jean-Pierre, The Many Facets of Chinese Nationalism, in: China Perspectives, Vol. 59, May–June 2005.

Callahan, William A., National Insecurities: Humiliation, Salvation, and Chinese Nationalism, in: Alternatives, Vol. 29, 2004, pp. 199–218.

Carlson, Allen, More than Just Saying No: China's Evolving Approach to Sovereignty and Intervention Since Tiananmen, in: Alastair Johnston and Robert Ross (eds.) New Directions in the Study of China's Foreign Policy, Stanford: Stanford University Press, 2006.

Carlson, Allen, Moving Beyond Sovereignty? A Brief Consideration of Recent Changes in China's Approach to International Order and the Emergence of the Tianxia concept, in: Journal of Contemporary China, Vol. 20, Issue 68, 2011, pp. 89–102.

Cassel, Pär Kristoffer, Grounds of Judgment: Extraterritoriality and Imperial Power in Nineteenth-Century China and Japan, New York: Oxford University Press, 2012.

Casseses, Antonio, International Law, Oxford: Oxford University Press, 2005.

Ch'en, Liang, Lung-ch'uanw en-chi 龙川文集, The Commercial Press, 1936.

Chan, K. C., The Abrogation of British Extraterritoriality in China 1942–43: A Study of Anglo-American-Chinese Relations, in: Modern Asian Studies, Vol. 11, No. 2, 1977, pp. 257–291.

Chen, Tianhua, Shi Zi Hou (written in 1905), Qiushuo, Issue 4, 1983.

Chen, Zhimin, Nationalism, Internationalism and Chinese Foreign Policy, in: Journal of Contemporary China, Vol. 14, Issue 42, February 2005, pp. 35–53.

Chen, Zhishang, Rethinking on China's Human Rights Ideology, in: International Critical Thought, Vol. 1, No. 4, December 2011, pp. 408–415.

Cheng, Hongyi, Modern Rethinking Traditional Thoughts of Ancient Legalism (对古代法家思想传统的现代反思), The Study of Legal Modernization, 2002, pp. 83–108.

Cheng, Qiyun, Feud and Unification – on the Theories and History of Chinese Traditional Politic System (封建与大一统之间——关于中国传统政体的理论和史实), Academic Monthly, 2007, Vol. 2.

Chesneaux, Jean, Bastid, Marianne, and Bergere, Marie-Claire, China from the Opium Wars to the 1911 Revolution, Hassocks: Harvester Press, 1977.

Chin, Gregory, and Stubbs, Richard, China, Regional Institution-Building and the China-ASEAN Free Trade Area, in: Review of International Political Economy, Vol. 18, Issue 3, 2011, pp. 277–298.

Cohen, David, China and Non-intervention, the Diplomats, December 03, 2011, available at: http://thediplomat.com/2011/12/china-and-non-intervention/.

Cohen, Jerome Alan, China and Intervention: Theory and Practice, in: University of Pennsylvania Law Review, Vol. 121, 1973.

Cohen, Paul A., Discovering History in China: American Historical Writing on the Recent Chinese Past, New York: Columbia University Press, 1984.

Condon, Madison, China in Africa: What the Policy of Non-intervention Adds to the Western Development Dilemma, PRAXIS, in: The Fletcher Journal of Human Security, Vol. 27, 2012, pp. 5–25.

Confucius' Disciples, Analects (Lun Yu, ed. by Yang Bojun), Zhonghua Book Company, 1980.

Contessi, Nicola, 'Multilateralism, Intervention and Norm Contestation: China's Stance on Darfur in the UN Security Council', Security Dialogue, Vol. 41, Issue 3, 2010.

Copper, John F., Michael, Franz, and Wu, Yuan-li, Human Rights in Post-Mao China, Boulder: Westview Press, 1985.

Crawford, James, and Marks, Susan, The Global Democracy Deficit: An Essay on International Law and Its Limits, in: D. Archibugi et al. (eds), Re-Imagining Political Community: Studies in Cosmopolitan Democracy, Cambridge: Polity Press, 1998.

Crossley, Pamela Kyle, The Late Qing Empire in Global History, Education about Asia, Vol. 13, No. 2, Fall 2008.

Dakas, Dakas C. J., The Role of International Law in the Colonization of Africa: a Review in Light of Recent Calls for Re-conolization, 7 African Yearbook of International Law, 1999, pp. 85–118.

Dai, Bingguo, Stick to the Path of Peaceful Development, in: China Daily, 2010, pp. 12–13.

Dai, Sheng, Book of Rites (Liji, finished in Han dynasty), Cheng Hao's version, Shanghai: Guji Press, 1987.

Davis, Jonathan, From Ideology to Pragmatism: China's Position on Humanitarian Intervention in the Post-Cold War Era, in: Vanderbilt Journal of Transnational Law, Vol. 44, Issue 2, March, 2011, pp. 217–283.

De Barry, William Theodore, and Tu, Weiming (eds.), Confucianism and Human Rights, New York, NY: Columbia University Press, 1998.

De Barry, William Theodore, East Asian Civilizations: A Dialogue in Five Stages, Cambridge, Mass.: Harvard University Press, 1988.

Delbrück, Jost, Structural Changes in the International System and Its Legal Order: International Law in the Era of Globalization, in: Swiss Review of International and European Law, No. 1, 2001, pp. 13–17.

Delbrück, Jost, Prospects for a "World (Internal) Law"?: Legal Development in a Changing International System, in: Indiana Journal of Global Legal Studies, Vol. 9, Issue 2, 2002, pp. 401–431.

Deng, Xiaoping, Walking our own Path of Revolution and Construction (革命和建设都要走自己的路), the Speech in 26, Oct. 1984, in: Deng Xiaoping Selected Works, Vol. 3, Beijing: Remin Press, 1993.

Deng, Gang, The Foreign Staple Trade in China in the Pre-Modern Era, in: The International History Review, Vol. 19, No. 2 (1997), pp. 254–255.

Dillon, Dana, "Countering Beijing in the South China Sea," Hoover Institution Policy Review, June 1, 2011, available at: http://www.hoover.org/research/countering-beijing-south-china-sea.

Du, Gangjian, Two-way legal order and system of basic rights- new Benevolence perspective of Confucian Order (双向法治秩序与基本权利体系—儒家秩序观的新仁学思考), in: Studies of Law and Business, Issue 5, 1995.

Dull, Jack L., The Evolution of Government in China, in Heritage of China, (ed. by Paul S. Ropp.), 1990, Berkeley: University of California Press.

Dunne, Timm, The Social Construction of International Society', in: European Journal of International Relations, 1995, Vol. 1, Issue 3, pp. 367–389.

Dynon, Nicholas, China's Ideological 'Soft War': Offense is the Best Defense, China Brief Volume: 14 Issue 4.

Edwards, Randle, 'Ch'ing Legal Jurisdiction over Foreigners', in Jerome Alan Cohen, R. Randle Edwards and Fu-mei Chang Chen (eds.), Essays on China's Legal Tradition (Princeton University Press, Princeton, 1980), pp. 222–269.

Esherick, Joseph, Reform and Revolution in China: The 1911 Revolution in Hunan and Hubei, Berkeley: University of California Press, 1976.

Evans, Gareth, After Syria: the Future of the Responsibility to Protect, available at: http://www.gevans.org/speeches/speech545.html.

Evans, Paul, Human Security "in Extremis": East Asia Reactions to the Responsibility to Protect, in: Sorpong Peou (ed.) Human Security in East Asia: Challenges for Collaborative Action, London: Routledge, 2009, pp. 79–93.

Fairbank, John King, and Teng, S. Y., "On the Ch'ing Tributary System", Harvard Journal of Asiatic Studies, Vol. 6, No. 2 (June 1941), pp. 135–246.

Fairbank, John King, China a New History, Cambridge, Mass.: The Belknap Press of Harvard University Press, 1992.

Fairbank, John King, Reischauer, Edwin O., and Craig, Albert M., East Asia: Tradition and Transformation, Boston: Houghton Mifflin, 1973.

Fairbank, John King, The Chinese World Order. Traditional China's Foreign Relations, ed. Fairbank, Cambridge, Mass.: Harvard University Press, 1968.

Fairbank, John King, US and China, Cambridge, Mass.: Harvard University Press, 1983.

Fairbank, John King, A Preliminary Framework, in: The Chinese World Order, Cambridge, Mass.: Harvard University Press, 1968.

Fang, Qing (方卿), Autarchy and Order (专制与秩序), Doctor thesis of Fudan University, pp. 26–28.

Fang, Tie, 'A Study on the Thoughts of Borderland Administration in Ancient China'(论中国"守中治边"、"守在四夷"传统治边思想), in: Chen Shangsheng, ed., Theory, System and Policy of Traditional Chinese Foreign Relations, Jinan:. Shandong daxue chubanshe, 2007.

Fiore, Pasquale, and Borchard, Edwin M., International Law codified and its Legal Sanction or the Legal Organization of the Society of State [1890], New York: Baker, Voorhis and Company, 1918.

Fitzgerald, John, Awakening China Politics, Culture, and Class in the Nationalist Revolution, Marketing Flyer, 1995.

Flecker, Michael, A Ninth-Century AD Arab or Indian Shipwreck in Indonesia: First Evidence for Direct trade with China, in: World Archaeology 32, no. 3 (2001), p. 350.

Foot, Rosemary, The Responsibility to Protect (R2P) and its Evolution: Beijing's Influence on Norm Creation in Humanitarian Areas, in: St Antony's International Review, Volume 6, Number 2, February 2011.

Fravel, M. Taylor, China's Attitude Toward U.N. Peacekeeping Operations Since 1989, in: Asian Survey, Vol. 36, No. 11, November 1996, pp. 1102–1121.

Friedman, Edward, Chinese nationalism, Taiwan autonomy and the prospects of a larger war, in: Journal of Contemporary China, Vol. 6, No. 14, March 1997.

Fu, Yaozu, Guanyu jianshe zhongguo guoji guanxi lilun de jidian sikao (Some Thoughts about Building Chinese International Relations Theory), Waijiao pinglun (Foreign Affairs Review), No. 5, 2005.

Fung, Edmund S. K, The Military Dimension of the Chinese Revolution: The New Army and its Role in the Revolution of 1911, Vancouver: University of British Columbia Press, 1980.

Gao, Qi, History of Shibosi in Fujian Province (福建市舶提举司志), 1939 version.

Ge, Zhaoguang, "As scholar 'dwelling in China': on Reconstruction of Relative Chinese History, Beijing: Zhonghua Book Company, 2011.

Gill, Bates, and James Reilly, Sovereignty, Intervention and Peacekeeping: The View from Beijing, in: Survival, vol. 42, No. 3, Autumn 2000, pp. 41–59.

Gong, Gerrit W., The Standard of 'Civilisation' in International Society, Oxford: Clarendon, 1984.

Gornig, Gilbert, Hongkong. Von der britischen Kronkolonie zur chinesischen Sonderverwaltungszone. Eine historische und rechtliche Betrachtung, Köln: Verlag Wissenschaft und Politik 1998.

Granet, Marcel, Chinese Civilization, New York: Knopf, 1930.

Grewe, Wilhelm Georg, The Epoch of International Law, Berlin: de Gruyter, 2000.

Grie, Peter Hays, Jean-Pierre Cabestan, The Many Facets of Chinese Nationalism, in: China Perspectives, Vol. 59, May–June 2005.

Grimal, Henri, Decolonization: The British, French, Dutch and Belgian Empires, 1919–1963, translated by Stephan De Vos. Boulder, Colorado: Westview Press, 1978.

Guo, Feifei, The Evolution of the Central Plain Civilization in China, in: China & The World Cultural Exchange, Vol. 11, 2012.

Hackenesch, Christine, China and the EU's Engagement in Africa: Setting the Stage for Cooperation, Competition, or Conflict, German Development Institute Research Project, European Policy for Global Development, Discussion Paper 16/2009.

Hall, William Edward, Treatise on International Law. Oxford: The Clarendon Press, 1924.

Han, Fei (BC 280–233), Han Feizi (eds. Zhang Jue), Shanghai: Guji Press, 2004.

Harrison, James, Modern Chinese Nationalism, Hunter College of the City of New York: Research Institute on Modern Asia, 1969.

Harrison, Selig S., The Widening Gulf: Asian Nationalism and American Policy, New York: The Free Press, 1978.

He, Fangchuan, On the Order of Huan and Yi (华夷秩序论), in: Journal of Beijing University (Philosophy and Social Science edition), Vol. 6, 1998.

Hegel, Georg Wilhelm Friedrich, Lectures on the History of Philosophy, translated by E. S. Halden, Trubener Published 1892.

Held, David, The Changing Structure of International Law: Sovereignty Transformed? The Global Transformations Reader: an Introduction to the Globalization Debate (ed. by David Held and Anthony McGrew), Cambridge: Polity Press, 2003.

Hill, John E., Through the Jade Gate to Rome: A Study of the Silk Routes during the Later Han Dynasty, First to Second Centuries CE, North Charleston: BookSurge, 2009.

Hilpold, Peter, Intervening in the Name of Humanity: R2P and the Power of Ideas, Journal of Conflict & Security Law, Spring, 2012.

Hinsley, Francis Harry, Sovereignty, London: Penguin, 1986.

Hirono, Miwa, and Lanteigne, Marc, Introduction: China and UN Peacekeeping, International Peacekeeping, Vol. 18, Iss. 3, 2011, pp. 243–256.

Hobbes, Thomas, Leviathan: Or the Matter, Forme, and Power of a Common-Wealth Ecclesiastical and Civil (ed. by Ian Shapiro), New Haven: Yale University Press, 2010.

Hoeymissen, Sara Van, Regional Organizations in China's Security Strategy for Africa: The Sense of Supporting "African Solutions to African Problems", in: Journal of Current Chinese Affairs, Vol. 40, No. 4.

Holslag, Jonathan, China's Diplomatic Maneuvering on the Question of Darfur, Journal of Contemporary China, No. 1, January 2008, pp. 71–84.

Holsti, Kalevi, Taming the Sovereigns: Institutional Change in International Politics, Cambridge, Mass.: Cambridge University Press, 2004.

Huang, Chin-Hao, Principles and Praxis of China's Peacekeeping, in: International Peacekeeping, Vol. 18, Issue 3, 2011, pp. 257–270.

Hucker, Charles, China's Imperial Past: An Introduction to Chinese History and Culture, Stanford: Stanford University Press, 1975.

Hui, Victoria Tin-bor, Toward a Dynamic Theory of International Politics: Insights from Comparing Ancient China and Early Modern Europe, in: International Organization 58, Winter 2004, pp. 175–205.

Hui, Victoria Tin-bor, War and State Formation in Ancient China and Early Modern Europe, Cambridge, Mass.: Cambridge University Press, 2005.

Huntington, Samuel P., The Clash of Civilizations and the Remaking of World Order, New York: Simon & Schuster, 1996.

Jackson, Robert, Sovereignty in World Politics: a Glance at the Conceptual and Historical Landscape, in: Political Studies, Volume 47, Issue 3, 1999, pp. 431–456.

Jacques, Martin, When China Rules the World. The Rise of the Middle Kingdom and the End of the Western World, Allen Lane Penguin Books, 2009.

Jakobson, Linda, Innovation with Chinese Characteristics, High-Tech Research in China, Palgrave Macmillan, 2007.

Jennings, Robert, and Watts, Arthur (eds.), Oppenheim's International Law Vol. 1, London: Oxford University Press, 9th Edition, 2008.

Jennings, Robert, Sovereignty and International law, in: State, Sovereignty, and International Governance (ed. by Gerard Kreijen), London: Oxford University Press, 2002.

Jia, Jingyan, Hanren kao, in: Fei Xiaotong (ed.), Zhonghua minzu duoyuanyiti geju (Beijing: Zhongyang Minzu Xueyuan, 1989.

Jian, Buozan, The History of Pre-Qin (先秦史), Beijing: Beijing University Press, 1999.

Jiang, Yihua, On Chinese Nationalism in 20th Century, in: Nationalism and Chinese Modernization (Liu Qingfen ed.), Hongkong: Hongkong Chinese Press (1994).

Jianye Wang, What Drives China's Growing Role in Africa, IMF Working Paper, No. 07/211, August 2007.

Jin Yufu (金毓黻), The History of Song, Liao, Jing (宋辽金史), Beijing: The Commercial Press, Vol. 1, 1946.

Jin, Ling, The EU's New Approach to Global Governance, in: China International Studies, March/April 2013, pp. 90–108.

Jing, Men, Between Human Rights and Sovereignty – An Examination of EU–China Political Relations, in: European Law Journal, Vol. 17, No. 4, July 2011, pp. 534–550.

Jitsuzō, Kuwabara (桑原骘藏), Research on Trading Harbors in Tang and Song (Tang Song mao yi gang yan jiu (translated by Yang Lian), Beijing: The Commercial Press, 1935, p. 124.

Kang, David C., Hierarchy and Balancing in International Relations, in: International Security 28:3, 2003, pp. 165–180.

Kant, Immanuel, Eternal Peace, in: Philosophical Perspectives on Peace: An Anthology of Classical and Modern Sources (ed. by H. P. Kainz), Basinstoke: Macmillan, 1987.

Kant, Immanuel, Metaphysics of Morals, in Kant's Political Writings (ed. by H. Reiss), Cambridge, Mass.: Cambridge University Press, 1970.

Karl, Rebecca E., Staging the World: Chinese Nationalism at the Turn Twentieth Century, Durham: Duke University Press, 2002.

Kayaoğlu, Turan, Legal Imperialism: Sovereignty and Extraterritoriality in Japan, the Ottoman Empire, and China, Cambridge, Mass.: Cambridge University Press, 2010.

Kent, Ann, Between Freedom and Subsistence: China and Human Rights, Oxford: Oxford University Press, 1993.

Kent, Ann, China, the United Nations, and Human Rights, Philadelphia: University of Pennsylvania Press, 1999.

Keohane, Robert O., The Contingent Legitimacy of Multilateralism' in Multilateralism Under Challenge? Power, International Order, and Structural Change (Edward Newman, Ramesh Thakur, & John Tirman, eds.), Tokyo, United Nations University Press, 2006.

Kim, Samuel S., China, the United Nations, and World Order, New Jersey and Surrey: Princeton University Press, 1979.

Kim, Samuel, China's International Organization Behavior, in: Thomas Robinson and David Shambaugh (eds.), Chinese Foreign Policy: Theory and Practice, Oxford: Oxford University Press, 1995.

Kissinger, Henry, On China, New York: The Penguin Press, 2011.

Klabbers, Jan, Clinching the Concept of Sovereignty: Wimbledon Redux, in: 3 Austrian Review of International and European Law (1998), pp. 345–367.

Knapp, Keith, The Confucian Tradition in China, in Companion to Chinese Religions (ed. by Randall Nadeau), The Wiley Blackwell, 2012.

Kohen, Marcelo, The Principle of Non-Intervention 25 Years after the Nicaragua Judgment, in: Leiden Journal of International Law 2012, Vol. 25, pp. 157–164.

Koskeniemi, Martti, From Apology to Utopic: The Structure of International Legal Argument, Cambridge, Mass.: Cambridge University Press, [1989] 2005.

Krasner, Stephen, Sovereignty: Organized Hypocrisy, Princeton: Princeton University Press, 1999.

Kreijen, Gerard, The Transformation of Sovereignty an African Independence: No Shortcut to Statehood, in "State, Sovereignty, and International Governance (ed. by Gerard Kreijen), Oxford: Oxford University Press.

Lapper, Richard, China Deepens Links with South Africa, in: Financial Times, May 13, 2010.

Lauterpacht, Elihu, Sovereignty-Myth or Reality, in: Int'l. Aff., Vol. 73, 1997, pp. 137–145.

Lee, Steven, A Puzzle of Sovereignty: Sovereignty either is or is not?, in: California Western International Law Journal, 1997, Vol. 27, No. 2, pp. 241–263.

Levenson, Joseph R., Confucian China and its modern fate: A Trilogy, Berkeley and Los Angeles: University of California Press, 1968.

Levenson, Joseph R., Confucian China and its Modern Fate: The Problem of Intellectual Continuity, London: Reprinted by Routelege, 2005 (First printed in 1958).

Levy, Jack, War in the Modern Great Power System,1495–1975, Lexington: University Press of Kentucky, 1983.

Li Jingming, The Tang's Open up Policy and Oversea Trade (唐朝对外开放政策与海外贸易), in: Southeast Asian Affairs, Vol. 1, 1994.

Li, Anshan, On the Adjustments and Changes of China's Foreign Policy to Africa, in: West Asia and Africa, Issue 8, 2006.

Li, Anshan, China and Africa: Policy and Challenges, in: China Security Vol. 3, No. 3 Summer 2007.

Li, Jiasong (ed), Big Events in the History of Foreign Affairs of People's Republic of China Vol. 2, Beijing: World Affairs Press, 2001.

Li, Junru, Understanding Human Rights: An Issue in EU-China Relations, in: EU-China Observer, Issue 4, 2009, pp. 7–12.

Li, Tao (李焘), A Continuation of Zi Zhi Tong Jian (续资治通鉴长编), Vol. 58, Beijing: Zhonghua Book Company, 1980–1986, p. 1291.

Li, Yujie, The Identity of nationality and state: The Common Identity of Nationality and State of Huaxia Society (民族认同与国家认同一论华夏社会中民族、国家意识的同一性), in: Journal of Chongqing Normal University (the editions of philosophy and social science), 1999, vol. 2.

Liang, Qichao, Comparison of Chinese and European statecraft (论中国与欧洲国体异同) Nationality and Civil Morality-Liang Qichao selected works, Shanghai: Far East Press, 1995.

Liu Boji, Politics of Diplomatic Conventions and Alliances in the Spring and Autumn Period (春秋会盟政治), Taipei: Zhonghua Congshu, 1962.

Lin, Huixiang, Zhongguo Minzu Shi (History of ethnic nationalities in China). 2 vols., Beijing: Shangwu Yinshuguan, [1939] 1993.

Liu, James T. C., Yueh Fei (1103–41) and China's Heritage of Loyalty, in: The Journal of Asian Studies, Vol. 31, No. 2, Feb., 1972, pp. 291–297.

Liu, Liantai, 'Guoji renquan xianzhang yu woguo xianfa de xiangguan bijiao' (Comparison between the International Human Rights Charter and the Constitution of Our Country), 1999, No. 5, Zhonggong Zhejiang Shengwei Dangxiao Xuebao (Academic Journal of Chinese Communist Party School of Zhejiang Province).

Liu, Xiang (BC77-6), Stratagems, Shanghai: Guji Press, 1995.

Lu, Yi (ed.), Qiuji: Yige shijiexing de xuanze (Global Citizenship: A World-Wide Choice), Shanghai: Baijia chubanshe, 1989.

Lucia, Husenicová, The China Threat Theory Revisited, available at: https://www.academia.edu/3108370/The_China_Threat_Theory_Revisited_Chinese_Changing_Society_and_Future_Development.

Luo, Zhitian, The Pre-modern System of 'Wu Fu' and Ancient Chinese 'Tianxia' View (先秦的五服制与古代的天下中国观), in: Nationalism and Modern Chinese Thoughts (Luo Zhitian ed.), Taibei: Dongda Book Publishing Company, 1998.

Ma, Dazheng, Ancient China's Frontier Policies and Management (中国古代的边疆政策与边疆治理), Western Region Research, 2002, Vol. 4.

Maddison, Angus, The World Economy: A Millennial Perspective, Paris: Organization for Economic Co-operation and Development, 2006.

Mancall, Mark, The Persistence of Tradition in Chinese Foreign Policy, in: Annals of the American Academy of Political and Social Science 349 (1963).

Mao, Zedong, Tong Sulian zhuhua dashi youjin de tanhua (A conversation with the Soviet Ambassador to China, 22 July 1958), in: Mao Zedong Waijiao Wenxuan, Beijing: Central Party Literature Press, 1994.

Mao, Zedong, Zhongguo Gongchandang zai minzu zhanzheng zhong de diwei (The role of the Chinese communist party in the national war, 1938), in: Mao Zedong Xuanji, Vol. II, Abu Dhabi: Remin Press, 1991.

Marks, G., Hooghe L., and Blank, K., European Integration and the State, EUI working paper RSC (1995), No. 95/7.

Martin, William Alexander Parsons, Traces of International Law in Ancient China, in: International Review, 1874, pp. 63–77.

Massumi, Brian, First and Last Emperors: The Absolute State and the Body of the Despot, Autonomedia, December 1992.

Mencius' disciplines, Mencius (ed. by Xi Ran), Beijing: Renmin Wenxue Press, 2010.

Michael, Franz H., and Taylor, George E., The Far East in the Modern World (rev. ed.), New York, 1964.

Mirkine-Guétzevitch, B., L'Influence de la Révolution Française sur le Développement du Droit International sans l'Europe Orientale, in: Recueil des Cours, Vol. 22, Issue 2, 1928.

Morris, Christopher W., The Very Idea of Popular Sovereignty: "We the People Reconsideration", Social Philosophy and Policy, Vol. 17, Part 1, 2000, pp. 1–26.

Morris, Christopher W., An Essay on the Modern State, Cambridge.: Cambridge University Press, 2002.

Morse, Hosea Ballou, The International Relations of the Chinese Empire, Longmans, Green, and Co., vol. 1, 1910.

Muramatsu, Yuji, Some Themes in Chinese Rebel Ideologies, in: Arthur F. Wright (ed.), The Confucian Persuasion, Stanford: Stanford University Press, 1960.

Nagan, Winston, FRSA and Craig Hammer, The Hanging Character of Sovereignty in International Law and International Relations, in: 43 Colum. J. Transnat'l L. 141 (2004–2005).

Nanda, Ved P., The Protection of Human Rights Under International Law: Will the U.N. Human Rights Council and the Emerging New Norm "Responsibility To Protect" Make a Difference?, in: Denver Journal. International Law & Policy, Vol. 35, 2007, pp. 353–363.

Needham, Joseph, Encyclopedic Multivolume Science and Civilization in China, Cambridge: Cambridge University Press, 1954.

Needham, Joseph, The shorter science and civilization in China, Vol. 2. Abridged by Colin Ronan. Cambridge: Cambridge University Press, 1981.

Ogden, Suzanne, China and International Law: Implications for Foreign Policy, Pacific Affairs, Vol. 49, No. 1, Spring, 1976, pp. 28–48.

Ogden, Suzanne, Sovereignty and International Law: The Perspective of the People Republic of China, N.Y.U. Journal of International Law and Politics, Vol. 7, Iss.1, Spring 1974, pp. 1–32.

Ogden, Suzanne, Chinese Nationalism: The Precedence of Community and Identity over Individual Rights, Asian Perspective, Vol. 25, Iss. 4, 2001, pp. 157–185.

Onuma, Yasuaki, When Was the Law of International Society Born? – An Inquiry of the History of International Law from an Intercivilizational Perspective, in: Journal of the History of International Law, 2000, pp. 1–66.

Orend, Brian, Just War Theory and the Ethics of War and Peace, in: The Ashgate Research Companion to Ethics and International Relations (Patrick Hayden ed.), London: Routledge, 2009.

Ottaway, Marina, Soviet Marxism and African Socialism, in: Journal of Modern African Studies, Vol. 16, Issue 03, September 1978, pp. 477–487.

Pan, Junwu, Chinese Philosophy and International Law, in: Asian Journal of International Law, Vol. 1 (2), July 2011.

Pan, Junwu, Sovereignty Implication for China: Then and Now, in: Aspects of Sovereignty: Sino-Swedish Reflections (Per Sevastik ed.), Leiden: Martinus Nijhoff Publishers, 2013.

Pan, Junwu, Toward a New Framework for Peaceful Settlement of China's Territorial and Boundary Disputes, Leiden: Martinus Nijhoff Publishers, 2008.

Pang, Zhongying, China's Status and Role in the International System, in: Modern International Relations, No. 4, 2006, pp. 17–22.

Patrick, Stewart M., R2P in Crisis Following UN Syria Vote, available at: http://www.cfr.org/syria/r2p-crisis-following-un-syria-vote/p27303.

Patton, P., Deleuze and Political, London: Routledge, 2000.

Peerenboom, Randall, China Stands up: 100 Years of Humiliation, Sovereignty Concerns, and Resistance to Foreign Pressure on PRC Courts, in: Emory International Law Review, Vol. 24, 2010, pp. 653–670.

Pei, Minxin, China: Can Economic Growth Continue without Political Reform? In: Strategic Asia 2006–07, in Trade, Interdependence, and Security (ed. by Ashley J. Tellis and Michael Wills), Seattle: Published by National Bureau of Asian Research, 2006.

Pei, Monong, Introduction, in: Diplomatic Constellations in the Spring and Autumn and Warring States Periods, Chongqing: Chongqing Press Group, 1994, p. 1.

Pemberton, Jo-Anne, Sovereignty Interpretations, New York: Palgrave Macmillan, 2009.

Perdue, Peter C., The Tenacious Tributary System: Historical Perspectives on the Rise of China: Chinese Order, Great Harmony, and Tianxia, in: Journal of Contemporary China, Vol. 24, Issue 96, 2015.

Posor, Friederike Maria, Der Darfur-Konflikt und seine Auswirkungen auf die internationale Staatengemeinschaft: vor dem Hintergrund neuer völkerrechtlicher Rechtsfortbildung: Möglichkeiten und Grenzen der internationalen Friedenskonsolidierung, Frankfurt/Main: Peter Lang GmbH, Internationaler Verlag der Wissenschaften; 1 ed., July 26, 2013.

Pye, Lucian, China: Erratic State, Frustrated Society, in: Foreign Affairs, Vol. 69 Issue 4, Fall 1990.

Pye, Lucian, The Spirit of Chinese Politics: A Psychocultural Study of the Authority Crisis in Politica Development, Cambridge, Mass.: M.I.T. Press, 1968.

Reisman, W. Michael, Sovereignty and Human Rights in Contemporary International Law, in: The American Journal of International Law, Vol. 84, 1990.

Rossabi, Morris, China among Equals: The Middle Kingdom and its Neighbors 10th-14th Centuries, Berkeley: University of California Press, 1983.

Ruggie, John Gerard, Territoriality and Beyond: Problematizing Modernity in International Relations, in: International Organization, 1993, Vol. 47, Issue 1, pp. 139–174.

Ruggie, John Gerard, Continuity and Transformation in the World Polity: Towards a Neorealist Synthesis, World Politics, 1983, Vol. 35, Iss. 2, pp. 261–85.

Ruhlmann, Robert, Traditional Heroes in Chinese Popular Fiction in Arthur F. Wright (ed.), Confucianism and Chinese Civilization, Atheneum, New York, 1964.

Ruhlmann, Robert, Traditional Heroes in Chinese Popular Fiction, in: Arthur F. Wrighl (ed.), Confucianism and Chinese Civilization, New York: Atheneum, 1964.

Rummel, Rudolph Joseph, Human Rights, in: Protest, Power, and Change: An Encyclopedia of Nonviolence Action From Act-up to Women's Suffrage (William Vogele and Roger Powers, ed.), Hamden, CT: Garland Publishing, 1996.

Ruskola, Teemu, Colonialism Without Colonies: On Extraterritorial Jurisprudence of the U.S. Court for China, in: Law & Contemp. Probs, Vol. 71, 2008.

Russell, Bertrand, The Problem of China (originally published in 1904), Whitefish: Kessinger Publishing 2007.

Salrin, Melissa, A Family Beyond Blood: Race, Gender, and Colonialism in Action Sociale de la Femme, c. 1914–1940, Proceedings of the Western Society for French History, Vol. 33, 2005, pp. 379–391.

Sceats, Sonya, and Breslin, Shaun, China and the International Human Rights System, October 2012. Chatham House, available at: https://www.chathamhouse.org/sites/

files/ chathamhouse/public/Research/International%20Law/r1012_sceatsbreslin.pdf.

Schafer, Edward H., War Elephants in Ancient and Medieval China, in: Oriens, Vol. 10, Issue 2, 1957.

Schermers, Herry, Different Aspects of Sovereignty, in: State, Sovereignty, and International Governance (ed. by Gerard Kreijen), Oxford: Oxford University Press, 2002.

Schwartz, Benjamin, The Chinese Perception of the World Order, in: The Chinese World Order (ed. by Fairbank), New Haven: Harvard University Press, 1968.

Scott, David, China and the International System, 1840–1949: Power, Presence, and Perceptions in a Century of Humiliation, New York: SUNY Press, 2008.

Shatì, Boyd C., Nationalism: Myth and Reality, New York: Harvest, 1955.

Shen, Po, Analysis on Legalized transformation on Confucianism by Dong zhongshu (论董仲舒对儒学的法家化改造), in: Social science Journal of Southwest University of Nationalities, vol. 11, 2008.

Shi, Zhiyu and Zhang Dengji, The Epistemology of China's Rise and Its Narrative Derivatives (中国崛起的认识论及其叙事衍生), World Economics and Politics, No. 1, 2010, pp. 37–51.

Shi, Chih-yu and Yin, Jiwuy, Between Core National Interest and a Harmonious World: Reconciling Self-role Conceptions in Chinese Foreign Policy, in: The Chinese Journal of International Politics, Vol. 6, 2013.

Si, Maqian (BC 145- BC 90), Records of Historian (史记), Beijing: Zhonghua Book Company, 1959.

Smith, Richard J., Chinese Maps: Images of 'All Under Heaven', Oxford: Oxford University Press, 1996.

Snyder, Louis, Global Mini-Nationalisms: Autonomy or Independence, Westport Conn.: Greenwood Press 1982.

Sofer, Ken, China and the Collapse of its Noninterventionist Foreign Policy: Past Diplomatic Practices Collide with Rising Economic and Political Realities, Center for American Progress, 8 March 2012. Available at: https://www.americanprogress.org/wp-content/uploads/issues /2012/03/pdf/china_nonintervention.pdf.

Song, Lian, Yuzhongyuanjiao (谕中原檄), See "99 Replyes of Famous emperors" (Huang Jing and Yao Wenjuan ed.), Beijing: Hua Yi Publishing House (1992), pp. 333–334.

Sotloff, Steven, China's Libya Problem: China's Failure to Support the Rebels in Libya could Hurt its Investment Prospects there. Time for a Rethink?, in: The Diplomats, March 14, 2012.

Spcnce, Jonathan D., and Wills John E. Jr. (eds.), Varied manifestations of Chinese resistance to the Manchus are analyzed in 'From Ming to Ch'ing: Conquest

Region and Continuity in Seventeenth-Century China', New Haven: Yale University Press, 1979.

Stuart-Fox, Martin. A Short History of China and Southeast Asia: Tribute, Trade and Influence. Crows Nest: Allen & Unwin, 2003.

Stursberg, Peter, No Foreign Bones in China: Memoirs of Imperialism and its Ending, The University of Alberta Press, 2002.

Sun, Guangqi, History of Navigation in Ancient China, Beijing: Ocean Press; Bowman, John S. (2000), in: Columbia Chronologies of Asian History and Culture, New York: Columbia University Press, 1989.

Sun, Yun, Syria: What China Has Learned From its Libya Experience, in: Asia Pacific Bulletin, Number 152, February 27, 2012.

Sun, Zhongshan, On nationalism: lecture two (民族主义六讲之第二讲, 1924), in: Sun Zhongshan wenji, Vol. I, Beijing: Unity Press, 1997.

Suzuki, Chusei, China's Relations with Inner Asia, in: John King Fairbank, ed., The Chinese World Order, 1968.

Svensson, Marina, Debating Human Rights in China: A Conceptual and Political History, Lanham: Rowman & Littlefield Publishers, 2002.

Swaine, Michael D., Ashley J. Tellis, Interpreting China's Grand Strategy: Past, Present, and Future, Santa Monica: Rand 2000.

Tang, Wenfang, Benjamin Darr, Chinese Nationalism and its Political and Social Origins, in: Journal of Contemporary China, Vol. 21, No. 77, September, 2012.

Tao, Jing-shen, Two Sons of Heaven-Studies in Sung-Liao Relations, Tucson: The University of Arizona Press, 1988.

Teitt, Sarah, Assessing Polemics, Principles and Practices: China and the Responsibility to Protect, in: Global Responsibility to Protect1, No. 2, April 2009.

Teitt, Sarah, The Responsibility to Protect and China's Peacekeeping Policy, in: International Peacekeeping, Vol. 18, No. 3, 2011.

Temperley, Harlod William Vazeille, Life of Canning [1905], New York: Haskell House, 1968.

Thompson, Drew, Beijing's Participation in UN Peacekeeping Operation, in: China Brief Volume, Vol. 5, Issue 11, May 10, 2005.

Thomson, Janice, State Sovereignty in International Relations: Bridging the Gap between Theory and Empirical Research, in: International Studies Quarterly, Vol. 39, No. 2, June 1995.

Tillman, Hoyt Cleveland, Proto-Nationalism in Twelfth-Century China? The Case of Ch'en Liang, in: Harvard Journal of Asiatic Studies, Vol. 39, No. 2, Dec., 1979.

Townsend, James, Chinese Nationalism, in: The Australian Journal of Chinese Affairs, No. 27, January, 1992, pp. 97–130.

Tu, Weiming, The Confucian Tradition in Chinese History, in: Heritage of China: Contemporary Perspectives on Chinese Civilization, ed. Paul S. Ropp, Berkeley: University of California Press, 1990, pp. 112–137.

Tung, William L., China and the Foreign Powers, New York: Oceana Publications, 1970.

Tuo Tuo (脱脱), et al., The History of Jin (金史), Vol. 1, Issue 20 (边防二癸未甲申和战本末), Beijing: Zhonghua Book Company, 1975.

Tuo Tuo, et al. (脱脱、阿鲁图), The History of Song (宋史)), The Round of 154, the Legend of Fang Xingru (方信孺传), Beijing: Zhonghua Book Company, 1977.

Tutuianu, Simona, Towards Global Justice: Sovereignty in an Interdependent World, The Hague: T.M.C. Asser Press, 2012.

Uvin, Peter, and Biagiotti, Isabelle, Global Governance and the 'New' Political Conditionality, in: Global Governance, Vol. 1, No. 3, 1996, pp. 377–400.

Vogel, Ezra F., Deng Xiaoping and the Transformation of China. New Haven: Harvard University Press, 2011.

Wakcman, Frederic Jr., and Grant, Carolyn (eds), Conflict and Control in Late Imperial China, Berkeley: University of California Press, 1975.

Wan, William, While China's Territorial Disputes Drag on, Xi Jinping Tells Others to Seek Peace, in: The Washington Post, 2014/06/28.

Wang, Gungwu, Joining the Modern World: Inside and Outside China, Singapore: World Scientific Publishing Company, December 4, 2000.

Wang, Qing, Two Models of Traditional China's Foreign Relations – Analysis from the Perspectives of Interests Cognition and Systematic Structure. Dissertation Submitted to Tsinghua University.

Wang, Xiumei (ed.), The Book of Songs (also called Three Hundred Poems, the earliest general collection of ancient Chinese poems), Beijing: Zhonghua Book Company, 2015.

Wang, Yizhou, On Contemporary International Politics, Shanghai: Shanghai People Press, 1995, pp. 81–82.

Wang, Zaibang, International Situation 2008: Historic Transformations Highlight Urgent Need for Systemic Readjustments, in: Contemporary International Relations, Vol. 19, No. 2, March–April 2009.

Wang, Dong, The Discourse of Unequal Treaties in Modern China, in: Pacific Affairs, Vol. 76, No. 3, 2003.

Wang, GungWu and Zheng Yongnian (eds.), China and the New International Order, London: Routledge, 2008.

Wang, Hung-jen, Circumventing the Sovereign State? Intervention from Chinese Perspectives, Paper for 8th Pan-European Conference on International Relations:

One International Relations or Many? Multiple Worlds, Multiple Crises Warsaw, Poland, September 20, 2013.

Wang, Jianmei, Zuxi's Neo-Confucianism and Orthodox Theory in the early Yuan dynasty (朱熹理学与元初的正统论), in: Journal of Historiography, Vol. 2, 2006.

Wang, Mingming, All under Heaven (tianxia): Cosmological perspectives and Political Ontologies in Pre-modern China, in: Hau-Journal of Ethnographic Theory, 2 (1), 2012, pp. 26–31.

Wang, Wengxiu, Jing Lingnan Wang Guan Shiposhi Yuan Tubiao (进岭南王馆市舶使院图表), Quan Tang Wen (全唐文), Vol. 515.

Wang, Zhiqiang, A Review of J. K. Fairbank's On the Tributary System of the Qing Dynasty (西方朝贡制度研究的开拓与奠基之作–费正清《论清代的朝贡制度》评介), Journal of Haian Normal University (Social Sciences), Vol. 25, 2012, pp. 74–78.

Weiss, Thomas G., The Sunset of Humanitarian Intervention? The Responsibility to Protect in a Unipolar Era, in: Security Dialogue, Vol. 35, 2004.

Werner, Wouter, From Justus Hostis to Rogue State, International Journal for the Semiotics of Law, Vol. 3, 2004, pp. 74–92.

Wildhaber, Luzius, Sovereignty and International Law, in: R. S. J. Macdonald and D.M. Johnston (eds.), Structure and Process of International Law: Essays in Legal Philosophy Doctrine and Theory, The Hague: Martinus Nijhoff, 1983.

Wills, John E., Embassies and Illusions. Dutch and Portuguese Envoys to K'ang-hsi, 1666–1687, Cambridge, Mass.: Harvard University Asia Center 1984.

Womack, Brantly, Asymmetry and China's Tributary System, in: The Chinese Journal of International Politics, Vol. 5, 2012, pp. 37–54.

Wu Weiruo, Zhang Taiyan's Nationalism Historical Science. On Modern Thinkers: Nationalism, St. Petersburg, Fl.: Times Publishing Company, 1982.

Wu, Chengqiu, Sovereignty, Human Rights, and Responsibility: Changes in China's Response to International Humanitarian Crises, in: Journal of Chinese Political Science, Vol. 15, Issue 1, March 2010, pp. 71–97.

Wu, Guoguang, From Post-imperial to Late Communist Nationalism: Historical Change in Chinese Nationalism from May Fourth to the 1990s, in: Third World Quarterly, Vol. 29, No. 3, 2008.

Wu, Qimin, Notes: China Held a Top Diplomatic Envoys Meeting, President Hu Emphasized Promoting Economic and Political Power and Building Moral Image, in: People's Daily, July 20, 2009.

Xia, Yong, The Origin of Human Rights: the Historical Philosopy of Rights (人权概念起源: 权利的历史哲学), Beijing: Chinese University of Political Science and Law Press, 1992.

Xiao, Yong, Public Law, Vol. 1, Law Press, 1999.

Xin, Chunying, A Brief History of the Modern Human Rights Discourse in China, in: Human Rights Dialogue, Series 1, Number 3, Winter 1995.

Xing, Yitian, Tianxia as one Family, in: The Research on History of Qin and Han (秦汉史论稿), Taibei: Dongda Book Company, 1987.

Xu, Daoyuan, The Great Historical Sketch (历史大脉络), Guangxi: The Press of Guangxi Normal University, 2009.

Xu Jieling, A Study of the Diplomatic Relations in the Spring and Autumn Period (春秋邦交研究), Beijing: China Social Science Press, 2004.

Xu, Xiaoqun, Cosmopolitanism, Nationalism, and Individualism in Modern China: The Chenbao Fukan and the the New Culture Era. 1918–1928, Lanham: Lexington Books, 2014.

Xu, zhuoyun, Everlasting Land, the Breakthrough and Development of Chinese Historic Culture (万古江河：中国历史文化的转折与开展), Shanghai: Arts Press, 2006.

Xue Hanqing, Chinese Observations on International Law, in: Chinese Journal of International Law, Vol. 6, 2007, pp. 83–93.

Xue, Lei, China as a Permanent Member of the United Nations Security Council, April 2014, avaiable at: http://library.fes.de/pdf-files/iez/10740.pdf.

Xun, Kuang (BC 313–318), Xunzi, Shanghai: Guji Press, 2014.

Yan, Xuetong, Xun Zi's Thoughts on International Politics and their Implications', in: The Chinese Journal of International Politics. No. 1, 2008.

Yan, Xuetong, Ancient Chinese Thoughts, Modern Chinese Power (translated by Edmund Ryden), Princeton: Princeton University Press, 2011.

Yan, Xuetong, and Sun, Xuefeng, eds., Zhongguo jueqi ji qi zhanlve (The Rise of China and its Strategy), Beijing: Beijing University Press, 2005.

Yang, Kuan, A History of the Warring States Period (战国史), Shanghai: Shanghai Renmin Press; Sun Yurong, A study of international law in ancient China (古代中国国际法研究), Beijing: China Politics and Law University Press, 1999.

Yang, Jiemian, Peaceful Rise in Peaceful Coexistence: In Memory of 50th Anniversary of Fiver Principles of Peaceful Coexistence (论中国在和平共处中的和平崛起：纪念和平共处五项基本原则成立50周年), in: Journal of Study Mao and Deng, No. 6, 2004.

Yu, Keping, On Globalization and State Sovereignty (论全球化与国家主权), Marxism and Reality (马克思主义与现实), No. 1, 2004.

Yu, Keping, State Sovereignty in the Time of Globalization, Wenhuibao (Hongkong), 2004.11.4.

Yu, Yingshi, Chinese Modern Nationalists and Intellectual (中国现代的民族主义和知识分子), in: The supplement to United Daily News, 1st, May, 1975.

Zelic, Tomislav, The Paradox of Sovereignty in Modern German History Plays, Columbia University, 2009.

Zhang, Bincun, Analyzing the Navigation of "Zheng He" to West Ocean from the Economic Angle (从经济发展的角度看郑和下西洋), in: Chinese Economic History Research, Vol. 2, 2006.

Zhang, Caiguo, The Termination of Ideologies and the Nature of Neo-liberalism Ideology (意识形态终结论与新自由主义的意识形态本质), Tansuo, June 2006.

Zhang, Deguang, Struggle to Establish an Academic System of International Relation Order with Chinese Characteristics (努力构建中国特色的国际关系理论), Red Flag Manuscript, Vol. 18, 2008.

Zhang, Junqi, Three Points of the Legal Meanings of Transfer of Sovereignty, in: Modern Law Science, Vol. 27, No. 1, 2005, pp. 98–102.

Zhang, Ming, The Comparison between the Dangers of Reform and the New Policies of the Late Qing Dynasty (改革危局与清末新政比较), available at: http://history.news.163.com/09/0629/07/5CV6THC200013FLL.html.

Zhang, Qixian, 'Analysis on the Concepts of Zhongguo and Tainxia' (「中国」与「天下」概念探源), in: The Soochow Journal of Political Science, Vol. 27, 2009, pp. 169–256.

Zhang, Yongjin, China's Entry into International Society: Beyond the Standard of' Civilization, in: Review of International Studies 17, No. 1, 1991.

Zhang, Yongjin, Ambivalent Sovereignty: China and Re-imagining the Westphalian Ideal, in Re-envisioning Sovereignty: The End of Westphalia? (ed. by J., T., Sampford, C. & Thakur, R.), Vermont: Ashgate, 2008, pp. 101–115.

Zhao, Jianwen, Zhou Enlai's Thinking about Non-Interference Principle (周恩来关于互不干涉内政思想, Journal of Zhengzhou University, Vol. 31, No. 2, 1998.

Zhao, Lei, Two Pillars of China's Global Peace Engagement Strategy: UN Peacekeeping and International Peacebuilding, International Peacekeeping, Vol. 8, No. 3, 2011.

Zhao, Qichang ed., Ming document on Beijing (明实录北京史料) (the First Part), Beijing: Antique Literature Press, 1995.

Zhao, Shuisheng, 'A Stateled Nationalism: the Patriotic Education Campaign in post-Tiananmen China', in: Communist and Post-Communist Studies, Vol. 31, Issue 3, 1998.

Zhao, Shuisheng, Chinese Nationalism and its International Orientations, in: Political Science Quarterly, Vol. 115, Issue 1, 2000, pp. 1–33.

Zhao, Shuisheng, China's Pragmatic Nationalism: Is It Manageable?, in: The Washington Quarterly, Winter 2005–2006, Vol. 29, Issue 1, pp. 131–144.

Zheng, Bijian, China's Peaceful Rise to Great Power Status, in: Foreign Affairs, September 2005.

Zheng, Shiqu, Cultural Nationalism in Modern China, in; The Standing of Intertextual (Li Shitao ed.), Times Literature Press, 2000.

Zheng, Yongnian, Establishing China's International Rights of Discourse in Diplomatic Policies (确立中国外交政策的国际话语权), in: Public Diplomacy Quarterly, Spring 2010, pp. 11–15.

Zheng, Yongnian, The Relations between China and USA and the Future of International Order (中美关系和国际秩序的未来), Beijing: Beijing Forum 2013.

Zhou, Enlai, The Speech of Zhou Enlai in China and the Asian-African Conference (1955), in Selection of Zhou Enlai, Vol. 2, Beijing: Remin Press, 1984, pp. 60–62.

Zhou, Fangyin, Equilibrium Analysis of the Tributary System, in: The Chinese Journal of International Politics, Vol. 4, 2011, pp. 147–178.

Zhu, Yuchao, China and International 'Human Rights Policy', China: An international journal, Volume 9, Number 2 September 2011.

Zou, Rong, Revolutionary Army, Datong: Datong Book Press, 1903.

Zuo, Qiuming (BC 551-479), Chun Qiu Zuo Shi Zhuan (春秋左氏传, ed. by Shen Yucheng), Beijing: Zhonghua Book Company, 1981.

Zweig, David, "Resource Diplomacy" under Hegemony: The Sources of Sino-American Competition in the 21st Century, Los Angeles: Pacific Council on International Policy, April 2010.

The Speeches, Statements, Reports, and Other Documents:

Ambassador Li Baodong Speech in the UN Security Council Ministerial Conference in the Middle East, /2012/03/12, available at: http://www.china-un.org/eng/hyyfy/t913340.htm.

China Raises 6-point Statement for Resolving Syria Issue, March 4, 2012, available at: http://china.org.cn/world/2012-03/04/content_24797150.htm.

The Declaration on Principles of International Law concerning Friendly Relations and Co-operation among States in accordance with the Charter of the United Nations, 2625 (XXV).

Explanation of Vote by Ambassador Li Baodong after Adoption of Security Council Resolution on Libya', Permanent Mission of the People's Republic of China to the UN, 17 March 2011, available at: http://www.china-un.org/eng/hyyfy/t807544.htm.

Historic Documents Concerning Negotiations between Japan and China in Guang Xu of Qing Dynasty (清光绪朝中日交涉史料).

One Country, Two Systems, June 22–23, 1984, available at: http://www.china.org.cn/english/features/dengxiaoping/103372.htm

Questions For Readjustment, Submitted by China to the Peace Conference, Paris, 1919: 14–18, available at: http://archive.org/details/questionsforread00paririch.

Responsibility While Protecting: Elements for the Development and Promotion of a Concept, Presented to the Security Council on 9 November 2011 by Brazil's Permanent Representative to the UN, Maria Luiza Ribeiro Viotti, During the Council's Open Debate on the Protection of Civilians.

Security Council Votes to Set up UN Peacekeeping Force in Darfur, available at: http://www.un.org/apps/news/story.asp?NewsID=19685&Cr=Sudan&Cr1=Darfur#.VxswMDGUe6c

The Responsibility to Protect: Report of the International Commission on Intervention and State Sovereignty, ICISS. December 2001.

The Outcome Document of the 2005 United Nations World Summit (A/RES/60/1, para. 138–140).

The Secretary-General's 2009 Report (A/63/677) on Implementing the Responsibility to Protect. (A/RES/63/308).

The Secretary-General's 2010 Report: Early Warning, Assessment and the Responsibility to Protect. (A/64/864)

The Secretary-General's 2011 Report: "The Role of Regional and Sub-regional Arrangements in Implementing the Responsibility to Protect". (A/65/877-S2011/393)

The Secretary-General's 2012 Report: "The Responsibility to Protect: Timely and Decisive Response" (A/66/874-S/2012/578)

The Secretary General's 2013 Report: "Responsibility to Protect: State responsibility and Prevention" (A/67/929-S/2013/399).

The Secretary-General's 2014 Report: "Fulfilling our Collective Responsibility: International Assistance and the Responsibility to Protect" (A/68/947-S/2014/449).

The Secretary-General's 2015 Report: "A Vital and Enduring Commitment: Implementing the Responsibility to Protect" (A/69/981–S/2015/500).

The Summary of Chinese Deputy Foreign Minister Zhou Wenzhong in The New York Times, August 22, 2005.

Xi's speech at 'Five Principles of Peaceful Coexistence' Anniversary, 7 July 2014, available at: http://www.china.org.cn/world/2014-07/07/content_32876905.htm

Schriften zum internationalen und zum öffentlichen Recht

Herausgegeben von Gilbert Gornig

Band 1 Michael Waldstein: Das Asylgrundrecht im europäischen Kontext. Wege einer europäischen Harmonisierung des Asyl- und Flüchtlingsrechts. 1993.

Band 2 Axel Linneweber: Einführung in das US-amerikanische Verwaltungsrecht. Kompetenzen, Funktionen und Strukturen der „Agencies" im US-amerikanischen Verwaltungsrecht. 1994.

Band 3 Tai-Nam Chi: Das Herrschaftssystem Nordkoreas unter besonderer Berücksichtigung der Wiedervereinigungsproblematik. 1994.

Band 4 Jörg Rösing: Beamtenstatut und Europäische Gemeinschaften. Eine Untersuchung zu den gemeinschaftsrechtlichen Anforderungen an die Freizügigkeit der Arbeitnehmer im Bereich des öffentlichen Dienstes. 1994.

Band 5 Wolfgang Wegel: Presse und Rundfunk im Datenschutzrecht. Zur Regelung des journalistischen Umgangs mit personenbezogenen Daten. 1994.

Band 6 Sven Brandt: Eigentumsschutz in europäischen Völkerrechtsvereinbarungen. EMRK, Europäisches Gemeinschaftsrecht, KSZE – unter Berücksichtigung der historischen Entwicklung. 1995.

Band 7 Alejandro Alvarez: Die verfassunggebende Gewalt des Volkes unter besonderer Berücksichtigung des deutschen und chilenischen Grundgesetzes. 1995.

Band 8 Martin Thies: Zur Situation der gemeindlichen Selbstverwaltung im europäischen Einigungsprozeß. Unter besonderer Berücksichtigung der Vorschriften des EG-Vertrages über staatliche Beihilfen und der EG-Umweltpolitik. 1995.

Band 9 Rolf-Oliver Schwemer: Die Bindung des Gemeinschaftsgesetzgebers an die Grundfreiheiten. 1995.

Band 10 Holger Kremser: „Soft Law" der UNESCO und Grundgesetz. Dargestellt am Beispiel der Mediendeklaration. 1996.

Band 11 Michael Silagi: Staatsuntergang und Staatennachfolge: mit besonderer Berücksichtigung des Endes der DDR. 1996.

Band 12 Reinhard Franke: Der gerichtliche Vergleich im Verwaltungsprozeß. Auch ein Beitrag zum verwaltungsrechtlichen Vertrag. 1996.

Band 13 Christoph Eichhorn: Altlasten im Konkurs. 1996.

Band 14 Dietrich Ostertun: Gewohnheitsrecht in der Europäischen Union. Eine Untersuchung der normativen Geltung und der Funktion von Gewohnheitsrecht im Recht der Europäischen Union. 1996.

Band 15 Ulrike Pieper: Neutralität von Staaten. 1997.

Band 16 Harald Endemann: Kollektive Zwangsmaßnahmen zur Durchsetzung humanitärer Normen. Ein Beitrag zum Recht der humanitären Intervention. 1997.

Band 17 Jochen Anweiler: Die Auslegungsmethoden des Gerichtshofs der Europäischen Gemeinschaften. 1997.

Band 18 Henrik Ahlers: Grenzbereich zwischen Gefahrenabwehr und Strafverfolgung. 1998.

Band 19 Heinrich Hahn: Der italienische Verwaltungsakt im Lichte des Verwaltungsverfahrensgesetzes vom 7. August 1990 (Nr. 241/90). Eine rechtsvergleichende Darstellung. 1998.

Band 20 Christoph Deutsch: Elektromagnetische Strahlung und Öffentliches Recht. 1998.

Band 21 Cordula Fitzpatrick: Künstliche Inseln und Anlagen auf See. Der völkerrechtliche Rahmen für die Errichtung und den Betrieb künstlicher Inseln und Anlagen. 1998.

Band 22 Hans-Tjabert Conring: Korporative Religionsfreiheit in Europa. Eine rechtsvergleichende Betrachtung. Zugleich ein Beitrag zu Art. 9 EMRK. 1998.

Band 23 Jörg Karenfort: Die Hilfsorganisation im bewaffneten Konflikt. Rolle und Status unparteiischer humanitärer Organisationen im humanitären Völkerrecht. 1999.

Band 24 Matthias Schote: Die Rundfunkkompetenz des Bundes als Beispiel bundesstaatlicher Kulturkompetenz in der Bundesrepublik Deutschland. Eine Untersuchung unter besonderer Berücksichtigung natürlicher Kompetenzen und der neueren Entwicklung im Recht der Europäischen Union. 1999.

Band 25 Hermann Rothfuchs: Die traditionellen Personenverkehrsfreiheiten des EG-Vertrages und das Aufenthaltsrecht der Unionsbürger. Eine Gegenüberstellung der vertraglichen Gewährleistungen. 1999.

Band 26 Frank Alpert: Zur Beteiligung am Verwaltungsverfahren nach dem Verwaltungsverfahrensgesetz des Bundes. Die Beteiligtenstellung des § 13 Abs. 1 VwVfG. 1999.

Band 27 Matthias Reichart: Umweltschutz durch völkerrechtliches Strafrecht. 1999.

Band 28 Nikolas von Wrangell: Globalisierungstendenzen im internationalen Luftverkehr. Entwicklung der Regulierung und Liberalisierung unter Berücksichtigung strategischer Allianzen und des Code-Sharing. 1999.

Band 29 Marietta Hovehne: Ein demokratisches Verfahren für die Wahlen zum Europäischen Parlament. Legitimation gemeinschaftlicher Entscheidungsstrukturen im europäischen Integrationsprozeß. 1999.

Band 30 Nina Kaden: Der amerikanische Clean Air Act und das deutsche Luftreinhalterecht. Eine rechtsvergleichende Untersuchung. 1999.

Band 31 Brigitte Daum: Grenzverletzungen und Völkerrecht. Eine Untersuchung der Rechtsfolgen von Grenzverletzungen in der Staatenpraxis und Folgerungen für das Projekt der International Law Commission zur Kodifizierung des Rechts der Staatenverantwortlichkeit. 1999.

Band 32 Andreas Fürst: Die bildungspolitischen Kompetenzen der Europäischen Gemeinschaft. Umfang und Entwicklungsmöglichkeiten. 1999.

Band 33 Gilles Despeux: Die Anwendung des völkerrechtlichen Minderheitenrechts in Frankreich. 1999.

Band 34 Michael Reckhard: Die rechtlichen Rahmenbedingungen der Sanktionierung von Beitragsverweigerung im System der Vereinten Nationen. 1999.

Band 35 Carsten Pagels: Schutz- und förderpflichtrechtliche Aspekte der Religionsfreiheit. Zugleich ein Beitrag zur Auslegung eines speziellen Freiheitsrechts. 1999.

Band 36 Bernhard Mehner: Die grenzüberschreitende Wirkung direktempfangbaren Satellitenfernsehens aus völkerrechtlicher Sicht. 2000.

Band 37 Karl-Josef Ulmen: Pharmakologische Manipulationen (Doping) im Leistungssport der DDR. Eine juristische Untersuchung. 2000.

Band 38 Jochen Starke: Die verfassungsgerichtliche Normenkontrolle durch den Conseil constitutionnel. Zum Kompetenztitel des Art. 61 der französischen Verfassung. 2000.

Band 39 Marco Herzog: Rechtliche Probleme einer Inhaltsbeschränkung im Internet. 2000.

Band 40 Gilles Despeux: Droit de la délimitation maritime. Commentaire de quelques décisions plutoniennes. 2000.

Band 41 Christina Hackel: Der Untergang des Landes Braunschweig und der Anspruch auf Restitution nach der Wiedervereinigung Deutschlands. 2000.

Band 42 Peter Aertker: Europäisches Zulassungsrecht für Industrieanlagen. Die Richtlinie über die integrierte Vermeidung und Verminderung der Umweltverschmutzung und ihre Auswirkungen auf das Anlagenzulassungsrecht der Bundesrepublik Deutschland. 2000.

Band 43 Karsten Bertram: Die Gesetzgebung zur Neuregelung des Grundeigentums in der ersten Phase der Französischen Revolution (bis 1793) und deren Bedeutung für die deutsche Eigentumsdogmatik der Gegenwart. 2000.

Band 44 Ulrike Hartmann: Die Entwicklung im internationalen Umwelthaftungsrecht unter besonderer Berücksichtigung von erga omnes-Normen. 2000.

Band 45 Thomas Jesch: Die Wirtschaftsverfassung der Sonderverwaltungsregion Hongkong. Eine Darstellung vor dem Hintergrund der Wiedereingliederung in die Souveränität der Volksrepublik China. 2001.

Band 46 Sven Gottschalkson: Der Ausschluß des Zivilrechtsweges bei Eigentumsverlusten an Immobilien in der ehemaligen DDR. 2002.

Band 47 Gilbert Hanno Gornig/Gilles Despeux: Seeabgrenzungsrecht in der Ostsee. Eine Darstellung des völkerrechtlichen Seeabgrenzungsrechts unter besonderer Berücksichtigung der Praxis der Ostseestaaten. 2002.

Band 48 Andreas Zühlsdorff: Rechtsverordnungsersetzende Verträge unter besonderer Berücksichtigung des Umweltrechts. 2003.

Band 49 Katja Schmitz: Durchgriffswirkung von Maßnahmen der UN und ihrer Sonderorganisationen unter besonderer Berücksichtigung von Resolutionen des UN-Sicherheitsrates – Die Entwicklung supranationaler Strukturen. 2003.

Band 50 Stefanie Rothenberger: Die angemessene Nutzung gemeinschaftlicher Ressourcen am Beispiel von Flüssen und speziellen Ökosystemen. Eine vergleichende Betrachtung zum modernen Verständnis eines klassischen völkerrechtlichen Nutzungsprinzips. 2003.

Band 51 Christoph von Burgsdorff: Die Umsetzung der EG-Datenschutzrichtlinie im nicht-öffentlichen Bereich. Möglichkeit einer zukunftsorientierten Konzeption des Datenschutzes in der Privatwirtschaft unter besonderer Berücksichtigung des BDSG. 2003.

Band 52 Frank Reinhardt: Powerline. Verfassungs-, verwaltungs- und telekommunikationsrechtliche Probleme. 2003.

Band 53 Chie Sato: Immunität Internationaler Organisationen. 2004.

Band 54 Johannes Thoma: EU-Recht und Schranken hoheitlicher Staatstätigkeit. 2004.

Band 55 Wolf Peterhoff: Rechtsansprüche enteigneter Volksgruppen und ihre Durchsetzbarkeit. 2004.

Band 56 Do-Hyub Kim: Das deutsche parlamentarische Regierungssystem als mögliches Modell für Korea. 2004.

Band 57 Alexander Koberg: Die Exilregierung im Völkerrecht. Eine Untersuchung ihrer rechtlichen Klassifikation. 2005.

Band 58 Nils Christian Carstensen: Das Verhältnis des Seerechtsübereinkommens der Vereinten Nationen von 1982 zu fischereirechtlichen Übereinkommen und deren Streitbeilegungsvorschriften. 2005.

Band 59 Oliver Franz: Osttimor und das Recht auf Selbstbestimmung. Eine Untersuchung zur Anwendung des Selbstbestimmungsrechts der Völker am Beispiel Osttimors. 2005.

Band 60 Michael Kadgien: Das Habsburgergesetz. 2005.

Band 61 Felix Wolf: Terrorversicherungen und europäisches Wettbewerbsrecht. Verschiedene Modelle staatlicher Beteiligung an einer Terrorversicherung für Wirtschaftsbetriebe und ihre Vereinbarkeit mit dem europäischen Wettbewerbsrecht. 2005.

Band 62 Heiko Bertelmann: Die Europäisierung des Staatshaftungsrechts. Eine Untersuchung zum Einfluss des Europäischen Gemeinschaftsrechts auf das deutsche Staatshaftungsrecht unter besonderer Berücksichtigung der Haftung für judikatives Unrecht. 2005.

Band 63 Cedric Christian Meyer: Konkretisierung unbestimmter Rechtsbegriffe im deutschen und französischen Anlagenzulassungsrecht. 2005.

Band 64 Philippe Gréciano: Die Gerichtsbarkeit der Europäischen Gemeinschaften. Rechtsprechung und Rechtssprache Europas aus französischer Perspektive. Mit einem Vorwort von Theodor Öhlinger. 2007.

Band 65 Anne-Louise Schümer: Die Stellung des Ministerpräsidenten in den Bundesländern im Vergleich. 2006.

Band 66 Helen Ghebrewebet: Identifying Units of Statehood and Determining International Boundaries. A Revised Look at the Doctrine of Uti Possidetis and the Principle of Self-Determination. 2006.

Band 67 Arne Hertel: Beihilfen an kleine und mittlere Unternehmen. 2006.

Band 68 Markus Günther: Europol. Rechtsschutzmöglichkeiten und deren Vereinbarkeit mit nationalen und internationalen Anforderungen. 2006.

Band 69 Christian Wicker: The Concepts of Proportionality and State Crimes in International Law. An Analysis of the Scope of Proportionality in the Right of Self-Defence and in the Regime of International Countermeasures and an Evaluation of the Concept of State Crimes. 2006.

Band 70 Hauke Stöwsand: Zyperns Beitritt zur Europäischen Union. Vom Antrag auf Mitgliedschaft bis zum Protokoll der Beitrittsakte. 2007.

Band 71 Natalie Rowohl: Weltbank und Internationaler Währungsfonds: Ihre Mandate und deren Abgrenzung. Stand und Reformvorschläge. 2007.

Band 72 Ru-Huei Liu: Europäisierung des deutschen Umweltrechts. 2008.

Band 73 Katja Lange: Der Status der Aufständischen im modernen humanitären Völkerrecht. 2007.

Band 74 Tarik El-Shabassy: Die Durchsetzung finanzieller Sanktionen der Europäischen Gemeinschaften gegen ihre Mitgliedstaaten. 2008.

Band 75 Karsten Seifert: Das interamerikanische System zum Schutz der Menschenrechte und seine Reformierung. 2008.

Band 76 Nora Graaff: Staatenverantwortlichkeit. Vom „völkerrechtlichen Verbrechen" zur „schwerwiegenden Verletzung einer zwingenden Völkerrechtsnorm" anhand der ILC-Kodifikationsarbeit. 2008.

Band 77 Aldona Szczeponek: Die Umsetzung des Völkerrechts und des europäischen Gemeinschaftsrechts in Polen. Unter Berücksichtigung verfassungsrechtlicher Lösungen anderer europäischer Staaten. 2008.

Band 78 Christian Friedrich Fonk: Europäische Luftqualitätsziele und nationale Erfüllungsverantwortung. 2009.

Band 79 Christina Prinzhorn: Der Grundsatz des öffentlichen Zugangs zu amtlichen Dokumenten aus der Perspektive des internationalen Rechts. Materiell-rechtliche Vorgaben durch das internationale Recht für Informationszugangsrechte in den nationalen Rechtsordnungen Europas. 2009.

Band 80 Steffen Eicker: Der Deutsch-Herero-Krieg und das Völkerrecht. Die völkerrechtliche Haftung der Bundesrepublik Deutschland für das Vorgehen des Deutschen Reiches gegen die Herero in Deutsch-Südwestafrika im Jahre 1904 und ihre Durchsetzung vor einem nationalen Gericht. 2009.

Band 81 Niels Beisinghoff: Corporations and Human Rights. An Analysis of ATCA Litigation against Corporations. 2009.

Band 82 Gesine Wolf-Zimper: Zielgerichtete Sanktionen des Sicherheitsrates der Vereinten Nationen und effektiver Rechtsschutz. 2009.

Band 83 David Bergius: Die offene Frage des Privateigentums der Vertriebenen im deutsch-polnischen Verhältnis. 2009.

Band 84 Axel Rolf Schneider: Petitionen zum Europäischen Parlament mit Berücksichtigung des Bürgerbeauftragten. 2009.

Band 85 Tobias Nord: Rechtsnachfolge bei zwischenstaatlichen Organisationen. 2010.

Band 86 Marcel Bongard: Emissionshandel und effektiver Rechtsschutz: Ein unvereinbarer Gegensatz? Eine Untersuchung zu den Auswirkungen marktwirtschaftlicher Umweltschutzinstrumente auf den Individualrechtsschutz am Beispiel des Emissionshandelssystems. 2010.

Band 87 Armin Huhn: Amtshaftung im bewaffneten Auslandseinsatz. Anwendbarkeit und Leistungsfähigkeit des Amtshaftungsrechts bei Verletzung des ius in bello. 2010.

Band 88 Johannes Mosters: Ethische Beschaffung. Sekundärzwecke im Zeitalter der Globalisierung. 2010.

Band 89 Thomas Herntrich: Thüringen. Von den thüringischen Kleinstaaten nach Zerfall des Alten Reiches bis zum Freistaat Thüringen. Eine völkerrechtliche und verfassungsrechtliche Betrachtung. 2010.

Band 90 Marcelo Antonio Villagrán Abarzúa: Verfassungsrechtliche Grundlagen der Gemeindeverwaltung in Chile. Auch ein Beitrag zur Dezentralisierung und Dekonzentration. 2010.

Band 91 Manfred Hechtl: Die offensive Defensive: Das Recht der präventiven Selbstverteidigung? Lösungsansätze für (scheinbare) Bedrohungen durch einzelne Staaten und internationale Terrornetzwerke. 2011.

Band 92 Christian Grüner: Quantität und Qualität der europäischen Rechtsetzung. 2011.

Band 93 Anna Keller: Der neue Rechtsrahmen für den öffentlichen Rundfunk in Frankreich. 2011.

Band 94 Jörn Eschment: Musterprozesse vor dem Europäischen Gerichtshof für Menschenrechte. Probleme und Perspektiven des Piloturteilsverfahrens. 2011.

Band 95 Marija Dietrich: Staatliches Souveränitätsverständnis im Wandel der gesellschaftspolitischen Strukturen. Eine Perspektive der Europäischen Union nach Inkrafttreten des Vertrags von Lissabon. 2011.

Band 96 Philipp Austermann: Die Anrechnungsbestimmungen im Abgeordnetenrecht des Bundes und der Länder. Eine verfassungsrechtliche und verfassungspolitische Untersuchung unter besonderer Berücksichtigung des Abgeordnetenstatus. 2011.

Band 97 Gilbert Gornig (Hrsg.): Krisengebiete der Welt. Völkerrechtliche und politische Aspekte. 2011.

Band 98 Jörg Brackmann: Genehmigung, Anmeldung und Anzeige gentechnischer Arbeiten und Anlagen. Nach den µnderungen des Gentechnikrechts 2002, 2005 und 2008. 2011.

Band 99 Giuseppe de Vergottini/Valeria Piergigli (eds.): Topographical Names and Protection of Linguistic Minorities. 2011.

Band 100 Nevzat Kirkagac: Verdachtsausweisungen im deutschen Rechtsstaat. 2011.

Band 101 Karlheinz Rode: Verfassungsidentität und Ewigkeitsgarantie. Anmerkungen zu einem Mythos der Deutschen Staatsrechtslehre. 2012.

Band 102 Markus Kühnl: Enteignung und Mediation. Ansätze mediativer Konfliktlösung hinsichtlich einer Enteignung zur Realisierung planfeststellungsbedürftiger Großvorhaben. 2012.

Band 103 Max Fischer: Das System konsistenter Entgeltregulierung im deutschen Telekommunikationsrecht. 2012.

Band 104 Jennifer Satish: Nationale Handlungsspielräume beim Anbau von gentechnisch veränderten Organismen (GVO). Europa- und welthandelsrechtliche Implikationen. 2012.

Band 105 Eva Marie Lischka: Völkerrechtliches und nationales Schifffahrtsrecht. 2013.

Band 106 Friederike Maria Posor: Der Darfur-Konflikt und seine Auswirkungen auf die internationale Staatengemeinschaft. Vor dem Hintergrund neuer völkerrechtlicher Rechtsfortbildung. Möglichkeiten und Grenzen der internationalen Friedenskonsolidierung. 2013.

Band 107 Kai Georg Krenz: Rechtliche Probleme des internationalen Kulturgüterschutzes. Durchsetzung, Harmonisierungsbestrebungen und Restitutionen von Kulturgütern. 2013.

Band 108 Jörg Sommer: Das Recht der Kriegsgefangenen in modernen bewaffneten Konflikten. 2013.

Band 109 Henning Hildebrandt: Die Rechtsproblematik multipler Regulierungsstrukturen in der Doping-Bekämpfung. Zur Notwendigkeit und Möglichkeit einer globalen öffentlich-rechtlichen Kontrolle sozialmächtiger Sportverbände. 2013.

Band 110 Isabelle Reutzel: Das Weltraumrecht in Europa. Eine Analyse der nationalen Regelungen zur Raumfahrt. 2014.

Band 111 Lì Lǐ: Potenzial und Grenzen der Missbrauchskontrollregelung in der Europäischen Union und in der Volksrepublik China. Eine rechtsvergleichende Analyse am Beispiel der Kampfpreisstrategien. 2014.

Band 112 Adrianna Agata Michel: Polens Staatlichkeit in sieben Jahrhunderten. Eine völkerrechtliche Analyse zur Staatensukzession. 2015.

Band 113 René Ghouse: Langzeitverantwortlichkeit im parlamentarischen Gesetzgebungsverfahren. Ausgewählte Reformbemühungen zum Schutz nachrückender Generationen auf dem Prüfstand. 2016.

Band 114 Jan Ulrich Heinemann: Die Entwicklung der Außenkompetenzen der Europäischen Union im Vergleich der Rechtslagen vor und nach dem Reformvertrag von Lissabon. Unter besonderer Berücksichtigung der impliziten Außenkompetenzen. 2016.

Band 115 Christian Ehlenz: Zum Verhältnis von Recht und Ökonomik beim Behinderungsmissbrauch gemäß Art. 102 AEUV. Die Zwangslizenzierung von Immaterialgüterrechten als Paradigma des More Economic Approach. 2016.

www.peterlang.com

www.ingramcontent.com/pod-product-compliance
Ingram Content Group UK Ltd.
Pitfield, Milton Keynes, MK11 3LW, UK
UKHW051133020425
1725IPUK00004B/5

9 783631 719282